Manuel Kretzer, Ludger Hovestadt (Eds.)

ΛLIVE
Advancements in Adaptive Architecture

Birkhäuser
Basel

"What are you, my colleague architects and engineers doing? How do you use your super power given to you by the universe? Why do you remain routine draftsmen, cocktail sippers, coffee gulpers, and making routine love? Wake up, there's a new world to be created within our world."

Frederick J. Kiesler, 2001.

0	Foreword Carole Collet	8
1	Preface Ludger Hovestadt	10
2	Introduction Manuel Kretzer	16
3	Bioinspiration Philip Beesley / Claudia Pasquero / Marco Poletto / Achim Menges / Steffen Reichert / Oliver David Krieg / Areti Markopoulou / Alex Haw	24
4	Materiability Ludger Hovestadt / Manuel Kretzer / Martina Decker / Nicola Burggraf / Aurélie Mossé / John Sarik	60
5	Intelligence Kas Oosterhuis / Stefan Dulman / Jose Sanchez / Jason Bruges / Tomasz Jaskiewicz	112
6	Outlook Branko Kolarevic	148
7	Postscript Vera Bühlmann	158

a   Conversation . Bioinspiration   54

b   Conversation . Materiability   98

c   Conversation . Intelligence   140

images	164
biographies	208
credits	212
index	214
imprint + acknowledgments	218

Carole Collet

/ Reader in Textile Futures, Central Saint Martins UAL, London.
/ Curator, 'Alive, New Design Frontiers', Espace Fondation EDF, Paris, April–September 2013.

Foreword

¶ What is life? Answering this question has remained a struggle to this day, and still feeds a prolific array of scientific perspectives, theories, and arguments. More than sixty years ago, DNA, the structure of life, made a groundbreaking entry into the twentieth century and revolutionized the field of molecular biology. Forty years later, the human genome was decoded, the so-called program of life. Today we can take a cell apart and identify each of its components. Yet there is no agreed consensus on what defines life, nor how it began. Is life a set of chemicals, a process, a dynamic system?

¶ With recent advances in synthetic biology, we can also reconfigure living organisms to create new man-made, engineered, "synthetic" species—species of a kind that have never existed on the planet before, but that can be designed and "fabricated" for a specified purpose. The "industry of living organisms" is born. And with it comes a profound need to question how we orchestrate the living with the nonliving. How do we define our relationships to a programmable synthetic nature? How do we rethink architecture as a dynamic self-aware living system? Can we surpass nature, yet build with the same biological tools?

¶ This is why this book is more pertinent than ever. In a context where the very concept of "nature" is challenged not only in its philosophical dimension, but in the core of its biological materiality, we need to reconsider the interrelations between architecture and nature. We are facing many a paradigm shift in the decades to come, and this book unravels compelling innovative and forward-thinking design narratives that will be strategic to the emergence of a new kind of architecture. One that correlates living with nonliving, passive with dynamic, sustainable with self-adaptive. If we want to progress toward a more resilient humankind, converging on models of life as found in nature can lead to an architecture that is inherently part of our ecosystems, an architecture that both enriches the human experience and contributes to nurturing our planet.

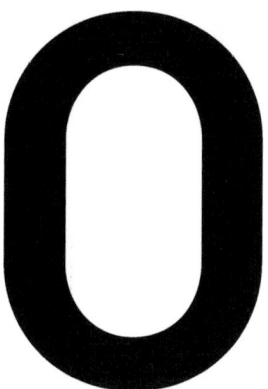

And it is time we commit to such a future.

¶ The book is structured around three key paradigms that interlace theoretical and critical thinking with the documentation of architectural research in practice. *Bioinspiration* invites us to delve into the invisible materiality of the nano–world, whereby the control of matter becomes a means to create a new ordered intelligence for interactive smart interfaces. *Materiability* interrogates principles of biomimicry and biotechnologies for extraordinary architecture. And finally *Intelligence* brings up notions of system thinking and swarm intelligence.

¶ This book engages with the starting point of an emerging new design field, where the symbiosis of physics, biology, computing, and design promises the redefinition of what we call architecture today.

Ludger Hovestadt
/ Professor for Computer Aided Architectural Design, Swiss Federal Institute of Technology, Zurich.
/ Inventor of digitalSTROM® chip and Founder of several Spin–off Companies.

Preface

WELCOME *Alive: Advancements in Adaptive Architecture* emerged from an eponymous symposium held at the Chair for Computer Aided Architectural Design (CAAD), ETH Zurich, in July 2013. The one–day event addressed the inseparable interrelations between architecture, nature, and humanity and invited a number of leading international practitioners and researchers to present their views and approaches towards creating a future, alive architecture focusing on adaptivity and technological evolution. The present book draws upon the same idea and can be seen as a summary and extension of the symposium, featuring articles of speakers at the conference and additional invited authors.

As the hosts of the conference and editors of the book we would like to briefly introduce ourselves. Our field is Computer Aided Architectural Design, and in truth, this name has long ceased to be appropriate. We started out in computer graphics, then moved into artificial intelligence, then virtual reality, and in 2000, we set out in a new direction, which one might possibly best term "back to reality."

After our initial research into architectural modeling with information technology, our focus became the development of an architectonics that is impossible without computing. Or, to put this in slightly more acute terms: an architectonics, which lies beyond known possibilities and beyond a real or imagined "optimum." We want to very clearly highlight this impossibility of working beyond optimization and beyond possibilities outside the realm of computing.

You can optimize an engine or a machine, and bring it to the limits of its potential. With a computer this is impossible, because a computer is not a machine and so the rules that apply to machines do not apply to computers. It's a bit like the fable of the hare and the tortoise: no matter how fast the hare runs, the tortoise, with its tiny, slow legs, will always get there first.

So we've started to understand ourselves as scouts for applications of information technology in architecture. And we're using the term "application" here not just within but also outside the bounds of a machinist vocabulary that encompasses systems and processes.

Time and again we make seemingly obvious observations, which then turn out to be baffling after all: applications, for example, cannot be used up, they can't be consumed. And they are not scarce. Which means that political concepts, concerned with labor, production and the fair distribution of wealth and resources, have no meaning when dealing with applications in information technology. Which is why, incidentally, we don't agree with the sociological analysis, for example, of a Manuel Castells, who coined the term "information society."

So our research centers on the statement: "computers are not machines." Up until 2010, we were involved with, and founded, a number of company start-ups, but by then, this new plateau had, for us scouts, been explored and in 2009 we summarized our many enquiries in a book entitled *Beyond the Grid*.

Today, the computer is omnipresent. In some respects, our efforts, and those of our many colleagues who, as architects, were fascinated by information technology, have been more than successful. But in a disquieting way, we also realize today that while in architecture the tools have changed, the thinking really hasn't. Architects today—all the talk notwithstanding—still use computers as machines. And in this respect, we haven't succeeded at all.

There is no way we can overstate this: computers are not machines. Again and again: *computers are not machines*! But it falls on deaf ears. And this is why, for the last five years, we have taken a step back. We have left the sphere of "possible applications" in our discipline behind, and are now concentrating— and we don't mind if we announce this in a somewhat bold and provocative fashion—on architectural thinking in the information age. And this is what we would like to touch upon here, because this new thinking concerns itself with the concept of the *alive* and thus, to invoke Michel Serres, with our contract with nature. It therefore concerns itself also with the substance of this book.

INTOXICATED Today we are all intoxicated by the speed of computers as machines. A gargantuan feast and bacchanalia. And, of course, also invited to this party are the prophets of doom, who but nibble at the fringes and hardly enjoy their reticent sip of wine. But what can we actually achieve at an orgy of wild dance, loud music and tables laden with temptations? Things that used to take months today take hours; tomorrow, they will only take minutes. Yet rarely is it about anything other than performance: bigger, faster, better. Hardly ever is it about more subtlety, more refinement, more differentiation.

Today, you can "build" a whole city, in every minute detail, on your laptop. Put hundreds of square miles to some use, as if they were nothing. Move mountains, at the click of a mouse. Design a skyscraper, in just a few days. Twisted, conjoined, interlaced, with a touch of greenery on top for decoration? No problem. Problems no longer exist: there are no more problems with computers as machines. Computers analyze the problems and the same computers then synthesize the corresponding solutions. One great big and very loud cybernetic feedback loop. And fine–tuning is not going to slow us down either: computers analyze and synthesize in the blink of an eye. Not a problem at all. Problems are gone. And there's no point trying to stand up to this performance in an attempt to decelerate the loop. Anyone doing so will immediately be analyzed as a problem and soon a solution will be synthesized which brings any resistance back in harmony with the system. The computers simply acknowledge the attempt at deceleration and, fed by the new input, spin even faster.

Looking around today, is there anyone who can show us a way out of this loop? Hadid is certainly an accelerator; Zumthor, by contrast a decelerator. How about Derrida, Luhmann, Latour? Only Koolhaas seems to at least affirm us in our dilemma. But even his concepts of a "generic city," for example, or "junkspace," don't really show us a way forward and out of the dead end we're in. We're stuck in the trap that is our idea of the computer as a machine.

We want to pose the question what would happen if we were going to do all the planning for the whole world with computers as machines, optimizing them, adjusting and fine–tuning them? Let's be generous and give ourselves a whole year for the process. The answer is very simple: the year after there would be no more architecture. So for us architects, this can't be the way. Which is why we are saying: computers aren't machines. The world is not a machine.

The moment we take this position, we are confronted with the machine–orientated, fighting language of our opponents: *World Systems Analysis* by Immanuel Wallerstein (2004), for example. The world as a machine. And also the slogans of traditional cybernetics: "the medium is the message." What is there left to say, if technology is supposed to demarcate the horizon of language? And an architect delivers the *Operating Manual for Spaceship Earth*.

Today, we are witnessing an escalating systemization under the umbrella term "world climate": if your carbon footprint is moderate, you are good for the system, if your carbon footprint is large, you are bad for the system. Buckminster Fuller himself would not have been able to dream up a better, more powerful, more performance–defined lever for steering the world, and with all the best intentions too. This is what we would call the performance mindset of the decelerators.

We seem surprised and genuinely agitated when we hear the disclosures of Edward Snowden. But of course there is a dark side too to the cybernetic loops on the part of the accelerators, and they attain the same levels of "performance" as those of the climate campaigners.

Let's have another look at the tools that both camps use, decelerators and accelerators: parameters and grammars, corresponding forms and structures. Nothing else. "Is there anything else?" we hear people ask, astonished. That's how deeply we are set in our dilemma. Many people sense that things can't go on like this, and that is probably why today we come across so many dystopias and so much sarcasm in every type of discussion, not just around architecture and cities.

BEYOND THE MACHINE

We do not believe that it is possible to do justice to today's architecture with Euclidean or analytical geometry any longer. There is—justifiably—a lot of talk about non–Euclidean geometry or "manifolds" with regard to Bernhard Riemann. But we immediately visualize this new geometry on our screens and that means we immediately fall back on our instrumental and analytical interpretation patterns. It's a bit like taking a picture of a Palladio villa and then claiming: this is the Palladio villa. Of course, you can take a picture of anything and you can do a visual analysis of anything. But the manifold, the aliveness, the actual villa by Palladio: that's not what you get. All you get is a copy, a picture, an imagination, perhaps.

Let's have a look, then, at the pixels on our screens and the colors and pictures that they serve to conjure. Yes, the material pixel has a color, a shape, a size, and is electronically connected: part of a generic infrastructure. But the colors of this electric interplay are of a different nature. If we tried to arrest them, keep them, after the electricity has been turned off, they would disappear: dead. Grey shimmering pixels in a naked microscopic physics. A smartphone without electricity or applications is uninteresting: a block of material weighing less than 200 grams. Like a book, whose language suddenly can no longer be understood. But the moment we power our pixels with electricity, we can read the language again: the world regains its color. Or take quantum physics. It describes its phenomena as a flickering image made up of amplitudes of spatially dispersed probabilities and in doing so establishes a horizon of all possible imaginations of cause and effect, as well as of a directional time arrow.[1]

As soon as we want to get to the matter of things, as soon as we try to fix time and space, these probabilities collapse onto a concrete particle. Dead like a fascinating beetle that we catch, pin down with a needle, and then label, secure inside its glass case. Dead, and therefore capable of being analyzed. If it were to fly off, we would have to catch it before we were able to analyze it. So the beetle is alive and well before being

---

1   See also the very compelling introduction to quantum electrodynamics by Richard Feynman.

analyzed, yet its flight and its aliveness are both part of being a beetle, so they have to be part of the analysis. But there can't be an analysis as long as it's alive and well and flying about. Then again, once it's dead, there can't be any analysis either, because it's no longer a beetle that expresses its beetleness by flying around and being alive: it's a dead beetle carcass pricked on the tip of a needle. First the flying about and being alive, then the analysis. The analysis is specific, the flying is pre–specific. Of course, we could also analyze the flying, but in doing so, instead of fixing the beetle, we would be fixing the beetle's flight, and so even the flight would be dead, not just the beetle: it would amount to the same.

What the example shows us is that there obviously is existence and there is such a thing as a geometry of the alive of everything before it is dead, a machine, fixed and generic. This is why we are thinking, with our computers, in terms of a new politics, a new economics and a new architecture: to learn how to cultivate the generic, the machine.

NEW ARCHITECTURE

A situation where we find ourselves standing before the familiar and the known, tasked with negotiating a new compact is not, in itself, anything new. Our culture has been through many situations like this before.

Let's attempt to briefly—all too briefly, and all too coarsely, perhaps—sketch this out:

1. The Ancient Greeks left behind the mythical cosmos of the Egyptians and, with their phonetic alphabet and their geometry, first established a spatial order and subsequently also, with their logic, cultivated the sophist chaos.

2. With modernity, we left behind the medieval cosmos of space and established, with imperialism and the Renaissance, a powerful geometric order of time, and subsequently also, with the new logic of the Baroque, cultivated the vulgar chaos.

3. And a bit more than a century ago, we effectively left behind, by means of electricity and quantum physics, the temporal cosmos of modernity and started to measure our world anew with a geometry of values and of the alive. This is what today we call globalization.

And so today, here we stand once again, looking at the limits of this globalization, talking sophist nonsense and staring at each other in need of a new order and a new logic. New contracts with a new partner. Once again, as many times before, it's about the whole, not the sum of the parts.

To describe our situation today, let's take a look at the deliberations of philosopher Michel Serres. With his concept of the contract with nature, he can give us a hint: the bomb, the network, the satellite, for him they are world objects. While man–made, they embody, for him, an objective power. Objective power is something we experience as immediate, and we are ourselves powerless when facing it. The tragedy for us human beings is that we created world objects because we carefully copied and, with the best of intentions, quite literally internalized nature. And about a hundred years ago we started to realize, by looking at ourselves, that not only does nature not really care about us, she is also fickle.

Serres maintains that our culture knows no other way of dealing with objective power than to domesticate it by means of contracts. Contracts are entered into by active subjects, against the background of universal rights, in order to allocate certain rights and duties to passive objects, in other words, so as to turn them into legal, active subjects themselves. Contracts are small partnerships, dealing with legal subjects, because they don't know what big thing may come along tomorrow. Even our objects and technologies are therefore understood, by Serres, as contracts for the domestication of an objective power.

And so here we are again, in a dead end street, just like the one described above: the cultural means we employ to domesticate objective power have themselves turned into objective power. And Serres' answer to this is not: "pull back," nor is it "full steam ahead," but instead it is this: we not only have to give ourselves human rights, as we have painstakingly been doing ever since modernity, we have to treat *all* natural and cultural objects as legal subjects. Serres calls this a contract with nature. Those whom previously we've described as decelerators will complain that these legal subjects will have to do as they're told and thus lose their liberty. At the same time, the accelerators will complain that they can do whatever they like and thus have too much liberty. But what we really get are identities that step out of the dead–end confrontations we're stuck in and thus are able to move freely about in partnership with technology and nature on a new plateau.

And what about architecture? These considerations would suggest that we can view the architecture of the 20th century, with Bauhaus, international style, and post–modernism (whichever way we want to label and allocate these phases) as a temporal architectonics, which therefore stands in symmetry with the spatial architectonics of the Renaissance and the mythical architectonics of Greek antiquity. Therefore, we can also describe the 20th century as a renaissance of symbolism.

All these phases expand onto a new plateau and demand, once they have measured the boundaries of their world, for a new self–projection, and that is a new logic. If we follow these symmetries then that means that—being able so clearly to detect the boundaries of globalization—in architecture we can expect a new Baroque of symbolism: a digital Baroque of symbolism, expressed as a contract with nature. This is precisely what today we would expect from a new architecture. Welcome!

Manuel Kretzer

/ Initiator of the materiability research network, Chair for CAAD, ETH Zurich.
/ Co-Founder and Partner of Responsive Design Studio, Zurich, Cologne.

Introduction

Among the most crucial aspects architects have to consider when designing spatially is the relationship between architecture and nature, built form and living system, anthropogenic construction and organic evolution. This applies equally to strategies of environmental responsibility, geological or meteorological impacts, anticipatory human behavior, transient occupation, or cultural, social, and demographic variety.

But despite the fact that everything that is generally engaged with architecture—all that surrounds it, that pervades, senses, and occupies it—is of living origin, built spaces are still far from exhibiting *vital* phenomena; although we obviously keep trying.

The 1960s and early '70s were particularly vibrant times, with architects strongly investigating concepts that led to more responsive, interactive, adaptive, and eventually alive environments. This generation of designers was deeply influenced by the broad availability of new materials, especially advancements in plastics and composites, and the sudden open access to information and technologies through such novelties like the *Whole Earth Catalog*, which provided education and unrestricted "access to tools." On top of prevailing technological optimism, artists and architects during those times were affected by critical social and political events, like the anti–Vietnam War movement, the Woodstock festival, and the widespread use of mind–amplifying drugs. These factors led to architectural exploration that wanted to break from established paradigms and, through their provocation and radicalism, to not only question the current system of dogmatic stereotypes but, moreover, to encourage new thinking and experimentation based on self–expression and individualism.

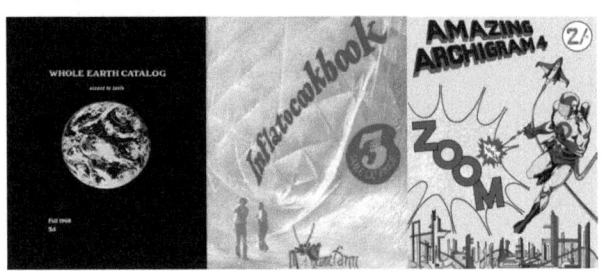

Figs. 1–3: Covers of decisive magazines published during the 1960s. From left to right: Whole Earth Catalog (1968), Inflatocookbook (1971), Amazing Archigram 4 (1964).

This includes the grand visions of Ron Herron and his fellow members of Archigram with the Walking City

Spaces of Adaptivity: Thoughts on the Relationship of Life and Architecture

(1964) and the Plugin City (1964), Yona Friedman's Ville Spatiale (1960), Constant Nieuwenhuys's New Babylon (1959–74), and Superstudio's Continuous Monument (1969), as well as less urban–scale experiments such as Archigram's Living Pod (1966), Haus Rucker Co.'s Oasis No. 7 (1972), and Coop Himmelb(l)au's Villa Rosa (1968). Even entirely temporary interventions like Coop Himmelb(l)au's Softspace and Hardspace (1970), E.A.T.'s Fog Sculpture at the Expo '70 in Osaka, Ant Farm's Inflatables (1971), and subsequently their *Inflatocookbook* (1971), continue to remain inspiring and groundbreaking.

With equally substantial ideas, Cedric Price was particularly devoted to advances in computer science and cybernetics. Intellectually related to Yona Friedman and Constant Nieuwenhuys, he believed that architecture was a service that should enable its users to reconfigure it in relation to their individual needs and criteria. As a consequence, he worked closely with cyberneticists like Gordon Pask and John Frazer, and was one of the first to conceptualize real adaptive environments that could physically move and respond to changing programmatic and environmental conditions (Frazer 1995, pp. 20–21).

Not least because of him, the '60s is readily referred to as the genuine beginning of "adaptive architecture," and some might argue that not much has happened since then. Contemporary architectural design is still overly founded in a functionalist belief in rigidity, solidity, and longevity, and ruled by norms and guidelines assuming a standardized people performing standard actions and exhibiting standard interests.

Fig.4: Le Corbusier's (1887–1965) Modulor, here visualised on the facade of the Cité Radieuse, located in Marseille, France, is an anthropometric scale system based on the golden ratio and the height of a man with his arm raised.

Yet in the current era of accelerating technological change, economic and political globalization, ethnic diversity, multimedial connectivity, techno–social systems, and younger generations who strive for independence, self–expression, and the celebration of their individuality and diversity, it is more than ever questionable whether such torpid architectural polemics are still adequate. Architecture today faces very new challenges on all levels, in research, practice, and education, and should by no means get stuck in retrogressive ideologies.

With the world population having doubled in the last fifty years and predicted to reach 9.6 billion by the end of 2050,[1] and an increase in global life expectancy from fifty–two years of age in 1962 to about seventy–one today (and likely seventy–six in 2050),[2] a consequent increase and densification of built volume is not only an observation but a mere necessity—especially since 70 percent of all people are believed to relocate to cities and urban areas by the middle of this century.[3] With such developments in sight, immediate questions arise: How will cities evolve and what will happen to the countryside? What will everyone eat, and how much, particularly since two thirds of the global population are expected to be obese by 2030?[4] At the same time, at least in Europe, birth rates are decreasing, which will lead to a significant decline in population. How will the infrastructure and economy be maintained? Who will take care of the elderly, and what kind of pressures and responsibilities will the young have to bear?

---

1 UN News Centre (2013) "World Population Projected to Reach 9.6 billion by 2050 – UN Report." June 13, 2013. http://www.un.org/apps/news/story.asp?NewsID=45165#.Ue0wn2QmIqI. Accessed: July 22, 2013.

2 Central Intelligence Agency "Country Comparison: Life Expectancy at Birth." The World Factbook. https://www.cia.gov/library/publications/the–world–factbook/rankorder/2102rank.html. Accessed: July 22, 2013.

3 CBS News (2008) "U.N.: World Population Increasingly Urban." February 26, 2008. http://www.cbsnews.com/news/un–world–population–increasingly–urban. Accessed: March 20, 2014.

4 Airbus "The Future: The Concept Plane; Smart Tech Zone." http://www.airbus.com/innovation/future–by–airbus/concept–planes/the–airbus–concept–cabin/smart–tech–zone. Accessed: July 22, 2013.

The author and futurist Ray Kurzweil argues that the rate of change in a large number of systems, including technological ones, increases exponentially. He predicts that by 2045 continuous evolution in computing capacity will lead to a technological singularity "representing a profound and disruptive transformation in human capability," essentially allowing mankind to overcome the biological limitations of the mortal body and brain, to reach a state of *transhumanism*, the next step of human evolution (Kurzweil 2005, p. 56). The gerontologist Aubrey de Grey explores the capabilities of regenerative medicine to slow down and eventually prevent age–related physical and cognitive decline. In his opinion, the fundamental knowledge required to design effective anti–aging drugs is already existent, yet has to be promoted accurately to create therapies that current and future generations can benefit from (de Grey and Rae 2008). A very similar approach is pursued by geneticist J. Craig Venter, who became known for creating the very first synthetically created life form in 2010 (Sample 2010). With Robert Hariri and Peter Diamandis, he cofounded Human Longevity Inc., a company that aims to build the largest human DNA sequencing project to date, processing up to forty thousand genomes annually, and assisting scientists in developing treatments for age–related diseases (Pollack 2014). Natasha Vita–More builds upon the concept of biological longevity and describes "substrate–autonomous persons," people who will be able to form identities in various substrates, more related to a certain environment than a specific body. "Depending on the platform, the substrate–autonomous person would upload and download into a form or shape (body) that conforms to the environment. So, for a biospheric environment, the person would use a biological body, for the Metaverse, a person would use an avatar, and for virtual reality, the person would use a digital form" (Dvorsky 2014).

Undoubtedly these prospects sound exciting and definitely make for great publicity, especially when large companies like Google or Apple are funding the research (Woolatson 2013). Yet, it remains unclear who would be profiting from such power, and how it could be used morally and ethically; certainly not all ten billion people on the planet could live forever while continuing to grow and propagate.

In the cyberpunk noir novel *Altered Carbon*, Richard K. Morgan describes a dystopian future in which every human is implanted at birth with a cortical stack—a digitized, cloud–connected mind. Personalities are thus stored online and, if required, downloaded into new bodies called "sleeves." However, the general public can only afford resleeving once or twice, and when they do so they have to live through the full and arduous process of aging before being able to acquire a new body. Only a few very wealthy individuals, so–called Meths, can acquire genetically bred and sensually and physically enhanced replacement sleeves on a regular basis, and thus remain unaltered ad infinitum. This leads to a strangely perverted cultural system where the gap of social inequality is not only an economic discrepancy, but the meaning and ultimately the value of (a person's) life is challenged at its utmost foundation (Morgan 2003).

While all this is set in a deeply disturbing, yet highly entertaining, fictional universe, the envisioned social instability is not so far–fetched, and according to a recent NASA–funded study, next to the over–exploitation of natural resources, it is the major cause of inevitable societal collapse (Motesharrei et al. 2014). It is also interesting to realize that the underlying excitement with such visions and prophecies bears apparent similarities to widespread and well–known mythologies, and seems to stem from a collective, deeply rooted human desire to extend one's life eternally—hence from the inevitable fear of transience, decay, and death. This anxiety, which in the present time is most obviously epitomized in an almost sick apotheosis of juvenility, a Botox–bleared aestheticization of the human body, and a plethora of narcissistic hand–held self–portrayal, is consequently projected onto every aspect of the human environment. Moreover, striving to continuously possess the latest technological appliances and at the same time superficially avoiding the indication of deterioration at all means, especially considering the appearance of architectural buildings, seems to stand in direct contrast to the inherent principles of life and nature, where growth and decay are closely interrelated and utterly dependent on each other.

Fig. 5: The desire for immortality, reincarnation, or rejuvenation, as depicted in the Fountain of Youth by Lucas Cranach the Elder, is a common theme in ancient tales and myths.

Returning to the initial statement, what then is the role and relationship between architecture, nature, and life? Since it most likely isn't '42',[5] how does then the natural, the dynamic, evolving and vivid, merge with the artificial, the static, solid, anthropogenic, and man–made, and what is humanity's role, as mediator between the two but also as part of both?

Frank Lloyd Wright (1867–1959) saw the connection in what he called "organic architecture." He promoted the harmony between human environments and the natural world through an architecture where essentially every element of the building was sought to relate to the other, reflecting the symbiotic ordering systems of nature (Laseau and Tice 1992, p. 4).

---

5   42 is the "answer to the ultimate question of life, the universe, and everything" from the supercomputer *Deep Thought* in Douglas Adam's *The Hitchhiker's Guide to the Galaxy*.

Fig. 6: Frank Lloyd Wright's Laura Gale House, in Oak Park, Chicago, is considering architecture as being part of a larger whole.

R. Buckminster Fuller (1895–1983) related to the environment more literally. He thought that if humans were part of nature, all of humans' creations must consequently be natural as well. In that sense he was closely looking at the environment and was trying to understand some of its principles in order to use them as design guidelines. From these observations he developed lightweight, dynamic, and flexible shelter systems, but also concepts for so-called biospheres, autonomous ecosystems, and microclimates, which were eventually supposed to span over whole cities to control and reduce energy consumption (Fuller 1960).

Fig. 7: The Montreal Biosphère (1967), Montreal, is a geodesic dome designed by Buckminster Fuller for the World Fair Expo 67. It originally featured a system of retractable shading screens that were computationally adjusted toward the direction of the sun to control the temperature inside the pavilion.

Today the architectural analogy to nature happens predominantly on a formal level. So-called biomimetic principles, processes that can be observed in or among living organisms, are adapted and implemented for form-finding methods and simulations. Many popular algorithms are concerning self-organization, a process where a larger order emerges from local interactions between multiple elements of a previously random structure. In nature it can be observed in a variety of physical, chemical, biological, social, or cognitive systems, and is often visually explained in the swarming behavior of birds or fish. Other principles include the imitation of natural growth through L-systems or cellular automata, the simulation of reaction-diffusion mechanisms, which emulate the amalgamation of chemical substances, or the reproduction of biological evolution, simulated with the help of genetic and evolutionary algorithms.

Fig. 8: In their study Digital Grotesque, the German architects Michael Hansmeyer and Benjamin Dillenburger use algorithmic processes to create intricate, uncanny computational forms and geometries.

On a structural or material level the interaction is, however, rather limited (Gruber 2011, p. 190). Questions concerning temporality and decay, or concepts dealing with performance, feedback, and progression, are generally not explored. Moreover there is a lack of proposals addressing changing occupational demands, the varying needs of simultaneously existing generations, different cultures or even genders, and in that respect architectural visions and ideas that can respond and dynamically adapt to these issues.

The following collection of essays challenges these questions in a critical way, embracing the unknown, and cultivating the architectural discipline toward an integrated, cooperative, and cross–disciplinary practice that responds to natural evolution through more than formally adapting it. *Alive: Advancements in Adaptive Architecture* brings together a group of internationally renowned and well–established researchers and practitioners who share a common curiosity, who investigate novel interrelations between space, nature, and humanity, and who dare to go beyond the classical definitions of architecture in a speculative and experimental way.

The essays are organized into three complementary chapters, each of them concluding with a conversation between some of the authors, which took place at the Alive 2013 symposium.[6]

BIOINSPIRATION highlights a sensitive observation of biological processes and their transfer into novel design methodologies for the creation of innovative architectural explorations. The chapter is introduced with an essay entitled *Quasiperiodic Near–Living Systems: Paradigms for Form–Language* by professor Philip Beesley, University of Waterloo, in which he argues for an architecture that, in contrast to the reductionist language of modernism, wants to diffuse and engage through a maximum possible resonance with its surroundings. Claudia Pasquero and Marco Poletto, founders of ecoLogicStudio in London,

contribute *Ecology beyond Nature* and exemplify a new significance of the term "ecology" that goes beyond its obvious biological meaning and rather describes a mutually affecting relationship between humankind, technology, and nature. Professor Achim Menges, Steffen Reichert, and Oliver David Krieg from the Institute for Computational Design, University of Stuttgart, present *Meteorosensitive Architectures*, discussing structures that build upon biological principles and the inherent and energy–autonomous responsive properties of organic materials as alternatives to complex techno–mechanical kinetics. The essay *In[form]ation: Digital Matter, Intelligent Construction, and Cities*, by Areti Markopoulou, director of the masters program at the Institute of Advanced Architecture of Catalonia, Barcelona, calls for the development of new forms of technology–enhanced habitation that interact and evolve with their surroundings rather than aestheticize formal *bio–inspired* aspirations within urban contexts. In his article *Building Nature: On Sex and Ducks, Chicken and Shit, Architecture and Apples*, Alex Haw, head of atmos studio in London, critically investigates the role of nature, architecture, urbanism, and life, and represents his personal approach and understanding in the recent work of his office.

MATERIABILITY addresses the potential to control and design matter at a nano– or micro–scale and construct materials that are dynamic, active, and responsive to environmental conditions. Professor Ludger Hovestadt from the Chair for CAAD, ETH Zurich, opens the section with *Domesticating a World of Printed Physics*, which encourages a new way of abstract thinking enabled through an abundance of information technology and liberated from the predominant paradigms concerning scarcities and sustainability. I follow with an article entitled *Beyond Performance*, describing the potential of smart materials in the architectural profession and particular didactic methodologies I developed as the founder of the materiability research network at the Chair for CAAD, to cultivate a better understanding of their properties. The essay *Adapting Matter*, by

---

6 See alive2013.wordpress.com/.

Martina Decker, assistant professor at the New Jersey Institute of Technology, builds upon the topic by emphasizing the crucial importance of interdisciplinary collaboration and development. Aurélie Mossé, who is a researcher at the Center for Information Technology and Architecture at the Royal Danish Academy of Fine Arts, contributes *Smart Materials: Designing a Timescape of Interconnectivity for More Resilient Practices of Inhabitation*, which describes her approach toward appropriating smart materials in an architectural context. The Stuttgart–based designer Nicola Burggraf speaks in her paper *Bioluminescence: Toward Design with Living Light* about the use of light–emitting organisms as novel ways of illumination. The chapter is concluded by *The Unconventional Electronics Approach to the Internet of Things* by John Sarik, electrical engineer at Xenex, who describes the potential of smart, autonomous object networks and the thrilling experience of developing real world applications.

INTERACTION elaborates on concepts concerning interaction and adaptation that exceed pure control and automation mechanisms but attempt to change, learn, and evolve dynamically. Kas Oosterhuis, professor at Hyperbody, TU Delft, introduces the chapter with *Caught in the Act*, an essay that focuses on the power of swarm behavior and intelligence to describe the (social) interrelations between devices, buildings, and people. Stefan Dulman is cofounder of Hive Systems, and emphasizes in his article *Spatial Computing in Interactive Architecture* the need for new concepts to control adaptive environments based on distributed intelligence and networked objects. *Polyomino: The Missing Topology Mechanic*, by Jose Sanchez, assistant professor at the University of Southern California, points out counter–paradigms to robotic fabrication and precision control, based on playful exploration and iterative learning processes. Jason Bruges, founder of the London–based Jason Bruges Studio, describes in the article *Architecture and Audience* his practical experience and approach in developing interactive projects for a variety of clients, scenarios, audiences, and locations. And finally, Tomasz Jaskiewicz, assistant professor of Interactive Design Prototyping at TU Delft, writes in *Approaching Distributed Architectural Ecosystems* about alive spaces without a centralized control unit and the possibilities that lie within self–sustaining, evolving systems.

The chapters conclude with an outlook by Branko Kolarevic, professor and chair in integrated design at the University of Calgary, entitled *Adaptive Architecture: Low–Tech, High–Tech, or Both?* reflecting on the potential and development of adaptive architecture and the role evolving and changing technologies and materials have played throughout its history.

In the postscript, Vera Bühlmann, head of the theory lab for applied virtuality at the Chair for CAAD, ETH Zurich, describes a certain neo–Babylonian confusion considering the current use of, and attitude toward, matter and suggests focusing on the symbolic level of mathematics as a commonly understandable denominator.

The collection of articles is intended to reflect a critical contemporary involvement with the topic, but even more importantly, aims to motivate and inspire. As Albert Einstein wrote in 1931 (p. 97):

> *"Imagination is more important than knowledge. For knowledge is limited, whereas imagination embraces the entire world, stimulating progress, giving birth to evolution".*

references

- De Grey, Aubrey, and Michael Rae (2008) Ending Aging: The Rejuvenation Breakthroughs That Could Reverse Human Aging in Our Lifetime. New York: St. Martin's Press.
- Dvorsky, George (2014) "20 Crucial Terms Every 21st Century Futurist Should Know." io9. March 17, 2014. http://io9.com/20-crucial-terms-every-21st-century-futurist-should-kno-1545499202. Accessed: March 17, 2014.
- Einstein, Albert (1931) Cosmic Religion: With Other Opinions and Aphorisms. New York: Covici–Friede.
- Fuller, R. Buckminster, The Case for a Domed City, 1960, Eco Redux: Design Remedies for a Dying Planet, http://www.ecoredux.com/archive_project03_01.html (accessed: July 22, 2013).
- Frazer, John (1995) An Evolutionary Architecture. London: Architectural Association Publications.
- Gruber, Petra (2011) Biomimetics in Architecture: Architecture of Life and Buildings. Vienna: Springer.
- Kurzweil, Ray (2005) The Singularity Is Near: When Humans Transcend Biology. New York: Viking.
- Laseau, Paul, and James Tice (1992) Frank Lloyd Wright: Between Principle and Form. New York: Van Nostrand Reinhold.
- Morgan, Richard K. (2003) Altered Carbon. New York: Ballantine Books.
- Motesharrei, Safa, Jorge Rivas, and Eugenia Kalnay. (2014) "Human Nature and Dynamics (HANDY): Modeling Inequality and Use of Resources in the Collapse or Sustainability of Societies." March 18, 2014.
- Pollack, Andrew (2014) "A Genetic Entrepreneur Sets His Sights on Ageing and Death." New York Times. March 4, 2014. http://www.nytimes.com/2014/03/05/business/in-pursuit-of-longevity-a-plan-to-harness-dna-sequencing.html?_r=2. Accessed March 17, 2014.
- Sample, Ian (2010) "Craig Venter Creates Synthetic Life Form." Guardian. May 20, 2010. http://www.theguardian.com/science/2010/may/20/craig-venter-synthetic-life-form. Accessed: March 20, 2014.

Bioinspiration

"Nature isn't classical, dammit, and if you want to make a simulation of nature, you'd better make it quantum mechanical, and by golly it's a wonderful problem, because it doesn't look so easy."

Richard Feynman, 1982.

Philip Beesley 26
Quasiperiodic Near–Living Systems : Paradigms for Form–Language

Claudia Pasquero, Marco Poletto 34
Ecology Beyond Nature

Achim Menges, Steffen Reichert, Oliver David Krieg 39
Meteorosensitive Architectures

Areti Markopoulou 43
In[form]ations : Digital Matter on Buildings and Cities

Alex Haw 49
Building Nature : On Sex and Ducks, Chicken and Shit,
Architecture and Apples

Conversation 54

Quasiperiodic Near–Living Systems: Paradigms for Form–Language

Philip Beesley
/ Director Philip Beesley Architect Inc. (PBAI), Toronto.
/ Professor at Architecture School, University of Waterloo, Cambridge.

<small>tradition</small>

For 2,500 years, Western artists and designers have been speaking about emulating life. The imagery and forms that tradition has quite consistently followed show hope for inanimate forms of craft and art coming alive. Yet at the same time, the speech and evocations of visual art and architecture have often treated that term—life—as governed by a boundary that sharply separates it from human craft. The symbolism that evokes life has, with only rare exceptions, distinguished human artifice from the viable organisms of nature. The discipline of architecture seems to have been especially emphatic in maintaining this divide. Architecture has consistently been conceived as a counter–form to nature, staying deliberately distinct from the living world and preferring instead the role of a stripped stage that supports the living world by means of clear restraint.[1] Perhaps this kind of separation has a moral imperative, avoiding trespass. Indeed, if we think about the atrocities of the past century, then there would be a very good reason to make a clean, empty place where we could be free, where a clear sanctuary could support nuanced interactions that could start to rebuild humanity between us.

<small>humanity</small>

Yet the distinct progress of science and technology in recent decades invites a change to this strategy of restraint. The achievement of comprehensive information within the Human Genome Project, the parallel achievement of potent learning functions in computational controls, and the increasing fluency of designers in programming physical materials and projecting complex ecological system modeling can all conspire to demonstrate that living systems no longer need to be maintained as a sacrament separate from human intervention. The ability to see our traces and to understand the dimensions of our impact forms an ethical key to this change. With that sensitivity it becomes possible to speak about full–blooded fertile involvement for designers. The shift offers a symmetrical opposite to the kind of deliberately empty, existentialist freedom that has defined generations of preceding architecture.

---

1 This follows a general argument among a wide and sometimes polemical range of literature in George Baird's *The Space of Appearance* (2003). Baird evinces a deep suspicion of organicism within this volume.

Emerging from the distancing functions of reverence into a new phase of highly involved stewardship, living systems can now occupy the space of architectural design.

living system

I want to describe a particular kind of form language rooted within our intimate bodies. I will try to articulate the sensing of traces of subtle phenomena that pursue emplacement and are measured by intense mutual relationships of exchange with surrounding environments. The qualities that I will describe are characterized by stuttering oscillation. They use the paradigm of dissipative structures and diffusion as a fundament that guides their design and their forms. These qualities will be used to describe architectural projects that I will claim have living qualities. Personal involvement moves, in turn, into boundaries that oscillate between hard facts and hopeful fictions exploring the future.

exchange

In this discussion I will make comments about emplacement in pursuit of a fundamental relationship with the environment rooted in diffusive form. I will describe subtle phenomena that evoke expanded physiologies, embodying the forms of diffusion. Building from these qualities, projects will be described that approach living qualities. I argue for a particular kind of form language. This morphology stands distinctly against the prevailing modern preference for stripped, minimal stages offering freedom. The language I argue for instead pursues culpable involvement. A quasiperiodic metabolism is evoked by this series of projects. Rather than polarizing a working method that moves in rigid sequence from its highest levels down to its details, or conversely from its details upward to its most general aspects, I will argue for oscillations where the deeply folded and involved cycles of emerging systems, in which things stutter and convulse, can produce vitality.

environment

metabolism

The surface of the world is no longer stable. In poignant contrast to the architectural tradition framed by *firmitas*, today's environment seems distant from the stable hold of natural cycles. Instead of the eternity of nature, we are surrounded by convulsive turbulence. What kind of design methods might contribute to such instability? It would be tempting to follow optimums within natural form finding that are exemplified by the space of a raindrop. If Plato were teaching today's designers, he might say that the elegant reductions of primary geometry provide keys to architecture by using the minimum possible envelope and the maximum possible territory enclosing an interior territory. Yet the reductive form language that guides such efficiency is a kind of machine for resisting interaction as well. There can be no less surface for interaction than that of a sphere. The reductive form languages of spheres and crystals achieve maximum possible territory and maximum possible inertia by minimizing their exposure to their surroundings. Such a form can be effective in a cold climate that requires retention of energy. It can also be effective if you want to destroy as much as possible with the embodied energy of ballistics. However, cooling requires the opposite. The opposite of a

interaction

spherical raindrop appears in the form of snowflakes. Snowflakes epitomize dissipation—the operation harvests the internal heat by optimizing release through an efflorescence of exchange. Such a form offers a strategy for a diffusive architecture in which surfaces are devoted to the maximum possible intensity and resonance with their surroundings.

<small>boundary</small>

This terminology has common ground with Western religious imagery. Neri di Bicci's beautiful fifteenth–century Italian painting of a mandorla offers a maternal vesica form that wraps around a divine figure and makes a tangible architectural space of an expanded physiology. Such a vision implies multiple boundaries lying around each human figure. Fra Angelico's Madonna and Child, painted in the preceding century, offers a model for architecture conceived as a field, a great vale that mediates between outside and inside. Such a condition is nearly coterminous with the human skin of its painted subjects. Roiling and glittering in a kind of inner rapture, its procedurally generated geometry gathers from the surrounding exterior of a garden outside and resonates in that imagery. A carnation blushes and speaks in the iconography of the blood of the Son. Strewn flowers speak of harvesting a fertility from the external soil. Below the figures is a cloud of fluxing, gaseous matters peaking of genesis, a lovely mediating soil–like matrix. The layered anatomy evoked by Di Bicci and the vivid enclosing fields painted by Fra Angelico offer conceptual models for the design of architecture. The forms of these paintings suggest that architecture can be conceived as an active filter.

<small>filter</small>

The form languages pursued in this discussion can contribute to a lexicon, a system for design. In such a pursuit, there might be a lurking assumption that we are searching for a universal system, transcendent and revolutionary. We have had the devastating experience of fascism in this last century, making a quest for comprehensive order seem forever stained. Yet the hunt for language remains, working to share and engender. This search for fertile, generative language can be informed by theories of growth in the parallel discipline of human psychology. A traditional sequence of growing from infancy might follow the mid–twentieth–century American psychologist Abraham Maslow's ladder of self-actualization. Maslow's series of developmental stages follows a sequence of growth. As a very young person, you lose things and you learn to cope with having lost things; you get hurt a bit and you learn the consequences of hurt; you cope with that and then you take responsibility; you move into agency and increasing freedom, able to handle separation and opposition. In such a sequence a goal is set up that moves distinctly from a diffuse, turbulent beginning into the destination of a clear, isolated, and bounded whole. Artists use similar terms when they speak about relationships in their visual compositions: they often speak of "figures" and "grounds," and it seems that clear, bounded figures are almost always pursued as goals, emerging out of dark and uncertain grounds.

<small>language</small>

<small>freedom</small>

Donald W. Winnicott theorized the emergence of the infant psyche at the same time as Maslow, but his way of seeing our environment seems distinct from Maslow's prevailing views of growth and development. Similar to Maslow, Winnicott looked closely at the conditions that would allow someone to turn into a thinking, functioning, happy being, but he looked especially at the states that came before a person knows they are a person and before they know their name. He used his most vivid language for womb development and stages of early infancy, evoking states in which an emerging person is bound up as an intermediate, amphibian being. He described consciousness coming in stuttering and gently condensing apparitions, amid bodies that were quite literally interwoven. Even more interestingly, he talks about objects and physical things as having a key relationship with living bodies and with emerging consciousness. Winnicott describes "transitional objects"—blankets, stuffed animals, favorite objects that you would constantly carry as a child. In those early times such things can be said to be coterminous with your body and with your mind. I do, dimly, remember my own "blanky"—perhaps I was almost fused with it when I was a tiny boy. Winnicott says some extraordinary things about trying to deliberately extend and delay the growth out of such an ambiguous state.

infancy

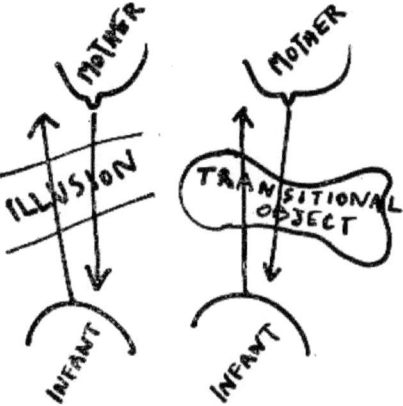

Fig. 1. Donald Winnicott's hand drawings illustrate the mediating role that transitional objects can play for the emerging consciousness of an infant.

Speaking to an infant's care when holding a blanky, he describes the need for a delicacy of operations quite different from the kinds of manipulation that we might assume are needed to achieve clear identity. Rather than something being cut, pulled, and firmed up, this approach encourages quite slow and gentle condensation, allowing self–determined forms to crystallize out of a continuum. Far from a responsible, willful use of tools and manipulation of objects, he evokes a continuum that seems to offer delicious, delirious potential. In such a sensitive state there is a sense of being connected still.

identity

From objects, Winnicott goes on to conceive of "transitional fields," suggesting that cultural expressions could function in similar ways to objects handled by a preconscious infant, and implying in turn that public identity can emerge in ways that seem directly analogous to the emergence of individual consciousness.[2]

consciousness

---

2   "I am here staking a claim for an intermediate state between a baby's inability and growing ability to recognize and accept reality. I am therefore studying the substance of illusion, that which

Winnicott (1953, p. 94) says:

> *The transitional objects and transitional phenomena belong to the realm of illusion which is at the basis of initiation of experience. This early stage in development is made possible by the mother's special capacity for making adaptation to the needs of her infant, thus allowing the infant the illusion that what the infant creates really exists. [...] The task of reality–acceptance is never completed, that no human being is free from the strain of relating inner and outer reality, and that relief from this strain is provided by an intermediate area of experience which is not challenged (arts, religion, etc.). This intermediate area is in direct continuity with the play area of the small child who is "lost" in play.*

Illusions become *prima materia* in such an exchange. It seems that Winnicott has confidence in the continuity of the world. He offers a potent response to the lingering question of how words and language might contribute to the generation of collective experience.

_{thermodynamics}

_{energy}

We can look carefully and see the traces that we make. In my own work, I have started to work with thermodynamics, seeking tangible exchange for the reality of an expanded physiology. Layers of exchange wrap around each of us. You can see the translucency of the heat as it propagates out through the polymer tines of the digitally fabricated frond in the image presented here / fig.01 p.164 /. As the subject being photographed in that image, I ask if I am pushing that heat–energy outward or whether the surrounding milieu of vapors is pulling energy out of me. Perhaps both of those states intermingle. If we look at the cycle, heat exchanges reveal themselves at first as obvious: I emit heat, the world receives my energy. The imagery presented here is aided by increased precision in which notch filters are tuned in order to reveal a flux of carbon dioxide in the air as it carries a thermal plume into this frond. We can see it propagate and then bleed into the mass and be pulled into the middle. However, certainty in a one–way flow fades when the

#01

---

is allowed to the infant, and which in adult life is inherent in art and religion, and yet becomes the hallmark of madness when an adult puts too powerful a claim on the credulity of others, forcing them to acknowledge a sharing of illusion that is not their own. We can share a respect for illusory experience, and if we wish we may collect together and form a group on the basis of the similarity of our illusory experience. [...] In infancy this intermediate area is necessary for the initiation of a relationship between the child and the world, and is made possible by good enough mothering at the early critical phase. Essential to all this is continuity (in time) of the external emotional environment and of particular elements in the physical environment such as the transitional object or objects. The transitional phenomena are allowable to the infant because of the parents' intuitive recognition of the strain inherent in objective perception, and we do not challenge the infant in regard to subjectivity or objectivity just here where there is the transitional object. Should an adult make claims on us for our acceptance of the objectivity of his subjective phenomena we discern or diagnose madness. If, however, the adult can manage to enjoy the personal intermediate area without making claims, then we can acknowledge our own corresponding intermediate areas, and are pleased to find overlapping, that is to say common experience between members of a group in art or religion or philosophy" (Winnicott 1953).

later stages of this sequence of images appear / fig.02 p.164 /. In the final images of the cycle, we can see that the temperature of the tines of the frond nearest my face recorded in dark tones show levels that are distinctly lower than when the cycle began. The ambient environment is not only receiving my action, but is also actively pulling heat from me. The surrounding air has pulled that energy outward, perhaps literally ingesting part of me.

The hardened boundaries exemplified by Plato's world of spheres and reductive forms might be replaced by form languages that pursue intense involvement and exchange. I make footprints in the world, but not as an individual figure leaving things about for them to dissolve into nothing. Rather, there's an active sense of the environment recoiling in multiple cycles. This implies a mutual kind of relationship. In turn, it suggests a craft of designing with materials conceived as filters that can expand our influence and expand the influence of the world on us, in an oscillating register: catching, harvesting, pulling, and pushing. While personal boundaries can readily be found as functions of central systems—brain, spine, and heart define cores that we know well—parallel to those cores lie bundles of ganglia in our elbows or in our sternum and pineal. Neural matter is riddled throughout our bodies, making a great shambling kind of network. Much of our consciousness is bound up in loops and reflexes that happen at the outer edges of cognition. Such a model working internally could be expanded outward. In such a layered space, we could build up a deeply layered, deeply fissured set of relationships in which there are multiple sensitive boundaries. We might be able to build up a sense of fertility reconstructing a kind of a soil and ground. We could measure values within that constructed ground by measuring resonance.

The projects that my collaborators and I have been making pursue the construction of a synthetic new kind of soil / fig.03 p.165 /. These projects have moved through several stages. Structures tend to be lightweight and ephemeral. One stage has concentrated on geometry and on periodic structures, looking at the kind of resilience that comes from textile matrices, in turn moving toward quasiperiodic systems in which things shift and multiply and effloresce, producing resonance. A further stage of development has involved construction of diffusive metabolisms in which protocell chemistries can start to set up exchanges and material flux, raising the possibility of renewing skins of material. Weaving those together, active agents within this work lead to questions that ask what geometries define our own personal worlds.

Hylozoic Ground, installed within the Canadian Pavilion at the 2010 Architecture Biennale in Venice, was organized by a hyperbolic waffle structure that could be pulled and pushed into continuous double–curved shell surfaces. The structural scaffold was clothed with layers of mechanisms. Kinetic components were grouped together, making tribal organizations of multiple clusters that would speak to each other and listen. In turn, these clusters would be organized in larger tribes that *aggregation*

spoke in quasi–national ways. Ripples of reaction and counter–reaction flow in this exchange. The behavior is only partially predictable, but it is by no means random. It is the result of a tissue–like aggregation of multiple gestures. The hyperbolic scaffold is a resilient network made of tetrahedral structures, clothed with hanging filters that pass gentle convective plumes of ear and filter the environment. Electroacoustic "cricket" fields of polymer are shown in images accompanying this text / fig.04 p.166 /. Each one of the elements is powered by a miniature shape–memory alloy actuator. In concert, the mechanisms ripple out and resonate. They chirp as you come close, stimulated by touch. Protocell fields of glass flasks cycle water from the Venice canals and contribute cleaning and refreshment. These do not achieve high, efficient functions; instead, they offer a sketch of possibility.

#04

communication

Recent work expands into larger fields in which plumes of breathing vessels hover above and vibrations ripple through the entire field. Multiple vibrations shiver through it, activated by direct–current miniature motors fitted with offset weights that create oscillating motion. Tribal communications move out into rippling fields. Protocell environments start to work as a kind of a soil. Inside the flasks are slowly evolving reactions. Saturation is built up in layers using custom glasswork that create suspended fluid reticulums. A copper compound blooms out under osmotic "pumping" through an aqueous solution of potassium ferric cyanide, making walnut–like reticulated structures. Intensely multiplied small elements work together, chained through vessels imparting a blooming fertility. Humidity and scent are exuded. Small glands are wrapped around with traps. The elements with their humidity and with their scent gather and trap and start to harvest themselves. The sensation is of being bathed, but also of being eaten / fig.05 p.167 /.

#05

perception

Our work pursues tribal beginnings for public emplacement. Large membranes made tangible rooms for gathering in a recent installation for Toronto's 2011 Luminato festival at Allen Lambert Galleria in Brookfield Place. The hanging layers of the sculpture were programmed for slightly convulsive breathing motions, working to amplify the large flows of public movement that occurred each day. Overhead, a whispering field of stories was cued by arrays of proximity sensors. A breathing field around that employed approximately one hundred bladders, breathing and harvesting in response to people standing below. Such installations tend to be organized along two axes that work in parallel. Working laterally, the spaces are framed to support collective experience, the realm of the public common. Along with the mediation of who we are together, a vertical axis is used that frames personal physiology, encouraging perception of a fundament below and aerial dimensions reaching far above. This expanded emplacement reaches beyond social boundaries toward multiple dimensions / fig.06 p.167 /.

#06

intimacy

A change in recent work is a collaboration with fashion, which is starting to contribute to the sense of an expanded physiology in literal ways. Iris van Herpen's studio offers a radical intimacy where the skin is only one boundary among many.

Using simple fissured forms configured like leaky heart valves, hovering leaf–like layers slightly push and pump in the gentlest of ways. They encourage plumes of air to rise around you in a three–dimensional lace made of silicon and impact–resistant acrylic. They make a live performance as they harvest your own energy and ripple around you. Layers immediately outside human bodies are organized in octaves of potential exploration, moving into turbulence. Musculature could be considered a mask, and an active fire–like metabolism can be sensed radiating through human skin. A corollary can be seen in a building composed of multiple layers. Traces are pulling at you. You become aware of the impact of your own tread in the world.

skin

In summary, this work has been guided by opposing Plato's idea of a sphere, of the kind of skin that might claim to be efficient, that might claim to be responsible by reducing consumption and yet, somehow, that speaks much more potently of mortality than of a kind of fertility. Spheres can speak of violence, and of a claim. Instead of the optimal, reductive forms of raindrops, I've suggested that snowflakes offer a potent form language that could guide emerging architecture. New projects from my studio are deeply layered and are founded in intimacy and touch. These works invite practice where we can see our traces. We can start to design in a way that can pull and harvest and resonate. Oscillating combinations of bottom–up and top–down design methods guide this work. The diffusive, dissipative form language described here offers a strategy for constructing fertile, near–living architecture.

mortality

references

+ Winnicott, Donald Woods (1953) "Transitional Objects and Transitional Phenomena: A Study of the First Not–Me Possession." International Journal of Psycho–Analysis 34, pp. 89–97.

Ecology beyond Nature

Claudia Pasquero, Marco Poletto
/ Co–Founders and Directors of ecoLogicStudio, London.
/ Unit Masters, Graduate School in Urban Design, Bartlett School of Architecture, UCL London.

PREAMBLE So we shall start with a cow. Like one of the many we can see from the window seat of our train to Zurich, on our way to ETH. Swiss cows are undoubtedly part of a landscape that has become a symbol of greenness and ecology; beyond Switzerland, we can argue, grazing cows are indeed associated with a form of picturesque landscape of preindustrial farming and life in symbiosis with nature and such. This dominant image associated with the cow, however, contrasts enormously with the reality of cow breeding and the industry dedicated to the production of milk and meat. This became apparent in Milan during a research project we conducted on the Milanese metropolitan network of urban farms dedicated to the production of milk derivates. The life and death of the cow appears streamlined and optimized toward production: the metabolism of the animal is accelerated to its limits in order to achieve a maximum ratio of production to occupation of the land. Insemination, delivery, milking, feeding, resting, and slathering define the daily rhythm, accordingly to exact and rigid schedules in the form of an assembly line.

However, one of the discoveries we made was that in order to further increase production, some farmers were adopting new technological solutions; among them, the recent acquisition of robots, to enable the milking process triggered our curiosity. The cow is equipped with a microchip and communicates in real time with the milking robot as well as a computer. The computer monitors the cow's metabolism and the robot responds to the cow's desire to be milked. During milking the computer analyzes the composition of the milk, determining the pressure that the robot must exercise on the cow's mammary gland at any given moment, thus preventing excessive stress on the organs. Also the general health of the cow is monitored, preventing infections and other health–related problems. The cow can visit the robot when it wants and for as long as it feels like. It turns out that this form of cybernetic milking is more productive than the traditional manual technique or the more recent mechanical one. But we can also imagine that the cybernetic framework involving robot, computer, environment, farmer, and cow could lead to the coevolution of production patterns that optimize the system by making it more robust, resilient, and economically effective. Optimization becomes more of a nonlinear dynamic process leading to multiple states of equilibrium that may switch depending on season, climate, surrounding landscape, and so on.

ECOLOGY BEYOND NATURE With this preamble we wish to exemplify a new significance for the term "ecology" that may find more relevance in our contemporary digital, interconnected, real–time, and rapidly urbanizing society. This significance extends beyond the realm of the natural and the biological to encompass the mechanical, the digital, and the biotechnological.

From this perspective Mother Nature disappears; she no longer exists. Any so-called natural or biological organism, any system or landscape is indeed contaminated, influenced by some kind of dynamic relationship with a human, technological, or biotechnological entity. Even the most remote ecosystems of the biosphere today are indirectly influenced by some kind of human–induced or man–made system. Even an unexplored sand dune in the middle of the largest desert on earth is contaminated by atmospheric particles containing traces of civilization, as well as being regularly observed and scanned by high–definition satellite sensors, where the act of measuring in itself constitutes an alteration of the measured or observed system. Both the nature of the observed and that of the observing system are transformed through this relationship.

biosphere

Within this conceptual framework, common definitions such as "ecological urbanism" and "sustainable architecture" may as a consequence be reframed to encompass all those technological systems as well as material and immaterial infrastructures that define contemporary urbanity. By refusing to accept the illusory and anachronistic picturesque image of the green city or architecture camouflaged in nature, we open the possibility to radicalize the idea of an adaptive, evolving bio-city where it is impossible to distinguish the biological from the biotechnological, the natural from the synthetic. We can then focus on a more evolved participatory framework for architecture and urbanism, one where biological, mechanical, electronic, chemical, human, and digital systems communicate and coevolve; where material life and optimized behaviors emerge out of this interaction and conversation.

biotechnological

We are convinced that this non–anthropocentric point of view reflects our contemporary world much more than the traditional idea of nature as the ethical plane of reference, from which we came and to which we must return, to evaluate our future actions. Let's face it: we are in the *Anthropocene*, a new and uncharted territory where Mother Nature no longer exists. As a consequence, the intellectual framework of biomimicry and the specifics of biomimetic design can be revisited as biocybernetics or biohacking. That is to say, yes, beautiful design solutions have evolved in nature to solve critical problems and we shall look at these as inspiration; however, it is not about us humans copying them to design a new breed of man-made technologies but rather us humans understanding the dynamic mechanisms underpinning such problem–solving machines of "nature" to hack them, to connect directly to them in order to establish immediate relationships between observed natural systems and observing man–made ones, or vice versa.

biohacking

THE METAFOLLY FOR THE METROPOLITAN LANDSCAPE

"Mere purposive rationality unaided by such phenomena as art, religion, dream, and the like, is necessarily pathogenic and destructive of life."
Gregory Bateson, *Steps Towards an Ecology of Mind*

One of ecoLogicStudio's most courageous excursions in this conceptual realm is the project titled *METAfolly*, a pod–like pavilion produced for the FRAC collection, based in Orléans, and first exhibited to the public for the 9th ArchiLab exhibition in September 2013. The *METAfolly* is a sonic architecture, a spatial mechanism that aims to establish a playful dialogue with the visitor based on a real–time meta–conversation. The project was first conceived as a response to Slavoj Žižek's call for the synthesis of a "new terrifying form of abstract materialism," confronting the artificiality of the contemporary urban landscape with the production of a new form of hyper–artificiality. It later became apparent that the project's main ambition is in offering refuge and consolation to the crowd of post–ecologists who, like us, have stopped searching for a new arcadia and are determined to develop a shanty version of it in the "city." Within this paradigm, aesthetic codes are redefined; the idealizations of classical ecologists are substituted by the abstractions of digital post–ecologists. In the *METAfolly*, algorithmic protocols define the assemblage of new hybrid material systems composed of postconsumer recycled plastic, cheap Chinese piezoelectric disks, and bio–inspired chameleonic nano–flakes / fig.07 p.168 /. Such an improbable assemblage is pushed to the limit and engineered to reveal a new Eden, a new aesthetic, spatial, and behavioral milieu, a new urban eco–language / fig.08 p.168 /.

This concept is reflected in the manufacturing method of the *METAfolly*. Since trashing is necessary in our society, which far exceeds the conventional notion of wasting, urban trash now encompasses a multilayered assemblage of products, landscapes, media content, attitudes, and lifestyles. We should begin to accept this condition; perhaps we shall take trash seriously, with mathematical rigor, digital precision, and crafting care. This ambition drove the prototyping of the *METAfolly*. It is meticulously manufactured by manipulating multiple forms of trash: from the machining of recycled plastic panels to the hacking of cheap gadgets and the systematic deployment of "mathematics prêt–à–porter."

In terms of fabrication and material technologies, such an attitude leads to a process that can be defined as a form of "slow prototyping." In fact, on the one hand, we custom–prototype few specific components of the project, while on the other, we reuse, recycle, and hack existing trash technologies (like Chinese greeting–card kits) to become an integral part of our new prototype. Rather than investing in the manufacturing of "new" components, we did work on the development of a dedicated "know–how," a protocol for the gathering of recycled bits and the detailing of their assemblage. By defining a system of transformations of found objects and manufacturing connections between recycled parts we finally "knit together" the pavilion / fig.09 p.169 /.

What a *folie*, some might say! In fact the pavilion engages the tradition of the architectural folly with the same playful attitude, where architecture becomes a device to establish a new relationship with the natural. Think of grottos, for instance, with their artificial stalactites and rocks typically sited in man–made parks and accessed by boats floating within artificial lakes. Real lights and sound reflections played a crucial role in amplifying the intimacy for the visitors and stimulating the perception of a new nature. A sonic swarm animates the *METAfolly*: a field of digitally materialized sensitivity agitates a proliferation of three hundred piezo–buzzers analogically modulated in four different tones. Programmed to operate like a swarm of crickets, they react to the speed of visitors' movements around the folly, developing ripples of sound that bounce back and forth until dissolution, synchronization, or complete interference. The convoluted geometry causes the emergence of unique sonic niches to be decoded by human ears inside the folly. An architecture that operates like a swarm, or in the swarm, able to convert a multitude of simple instructions into an emergent meta–language of forms, movements, and effects. An architecture that's *alive* / fig.10 p.170 /.

HORTUS: CYBER–GARDENING THE BIOSPHERE

> *"If we look at the earth as a territory devoted to life, it would appear as an enclosed space, delimited by the boundaries of living systems (the biosphere). In other words, it would appear as a garden (the etymology of the word garden comes from the German Garten, the etymological root for which is enclosed or bounded space)."*
> Gilles Clement, *Il giardiniere planetario*, 2008; translation by Marco Poletto

Clement's definition of the biosphere as a garden reinforces our conception of the biosphere as no longer natural to us, but a system that has coevolved with a multitude of man–made and other biotechnological systems. At the same time, we are making a step in radicalizing our understanding of the notion of the garden outside of its picturesque image (see urban parks and gardens). Moreover, since there is no garden without gardening—i.e., reality is contained within experience—the practice of gardening claims a pivotal role in the development of sustainable practices of coevolution of our civilization with the biosphere. The practice of gardening here has acquired a whole new meaning outside the boundaries of the craft of tending gardens; it is a more abstract meaning, a new definition that embraces the architect and any human being involved in the project of architecture and urbanism. We become all gardeners tending our "biosphere."
As Clement points out in his beautiful description of the "moving garden," the gardener operates through a process of intensification of difference; his only chance to reconcile his desire for beautification and the natural expressivity of

living processes resides in movement (intended in its biological and physical sense). The formalization of the garden becomes for Clement a process of formalized transmission of biological messages or, in our terms, of algorithmic coding; for the gardener, algorithms are machines for breeding biodiversity. Differences in slope, insulation, soil moisture, and so on, are registered and then exploited by the "gardening algorithm" to promote the growth of different arboreal species; also the growth, being itself a variable and partially unpredictable process, needs to be read, assessed and then considered in the formulation of future actions, or in the future lines of the gardening code. The garden grows and beautification progresses in loops, each step generating more difference and local complexity that can be in turn recognized and bred. The management of this generative process is what makes the garden a potentially beautiful and healthy organism. From this conceptual framework the notion of cyber–gardening emerges, which for us represents a radical rereading of the notion of sustainability in the field of architectural and urban design.

In the *HORTUS* project, one of ecoLogicStudio's cyber–gardens, created for the Architectural Association's public program and installed in the Front Members room in January 2012 and then further developed for the "Alive" exhibition in Paris in the form of *HORTUS.Paris* in April 2013, the notion of urban self–sufficiency is challenged through a new gardening prototype designed to stimulate the emergence of novel material practices and related spatial narratives; the proto–garden hosts micro– and macro–algal organisms and is fitted with ambient light, sensing technologies, and a custom–designed virtual interface / fig.11 p.171 /. *HORTUS* proposes an experimental and hands–on engagement with the notion of self–sufficiency, questioning its applicability in the planning of large landscapes and the retro–fitting of rural as well as postindustrial territories (as exemplified in the Algae Farm project developed by ecoLogicStudio for the Swedish region of Osterlen).

Flows of energy (light radiation), matter (biomass, CO_2), and information (images, Tweets, stats) are triggered during the four–week–long growing loop, inducing multiple mechanisms of self–regulation and evolving novel forms of self–organization. Visitors are invited to engage daily with *HORTUS*, imagining new protocols of cyber–gardening to breed the urban biological diversity found in the lakes and ponds of London or Paris. As algal organisms require CO_2 to grow, visitors are invited to contribute by activating an air–pumping system inside the photo–bioreactors as well as adjust their nutrient content. Oxygen is released as a result, feeding the algae growth until percolation onto a filtering surface, *HORTUS*'s harvesting terrain. Data flow daily through *HORTUS*, feeding its emergent virtual garden, accessible via smartphone. Its virtual plots are nurtured by the flow of Tweets posted by each visitor, locally and remotely. A form of collective intelligence may evolve, enriching the direct material experience of the visitor–turned–urban–cyber–gardener.

Meteorosensitive Architectures

Achim Menges[1], Steffen Reichert[2], Oliver David Krieg[3]
/ [1] Director, [2] Research Associate, [3] Doctoral Researcher.
/ Institute for Computational Design, University of Stuttgart.

"It is a question of surrendering to the wood, then following where it leads by connecting operations to a materiality, instead of imposing a form upon a matter."

Gilles Deleuze and Félix Guattari

Responsive architecture is typically conceived as a technical function enabled by myriad sensing, actuating, and regulating devices. Mechanical and electronic equipment is employed to receive, process, and translate a stimulus into a response. In contrast to this superimposition of high–tech equipment on otherwise inert material, in nature a fundamentally different, no–tech strategy can be observed: in various biological systems the responsive capacity is quite literally ingrained in the material itself. The two projects presented here explore similar design strategies of physically programming a responsive material system that computes form in exchange with the environment, requiring neither extraneous mechanical or electronic controls, nor the supply of energy, to do so.

EMBEDDED RESPONSIVENESS Nature has evolved a great variety of dynamic systems interacting with climatic influences. For architecture, one particularly interesting way is the moisture–driven movement that can be observed in spruce cones. Unlike other plant movements that are produced by active cell–pressure changes, this movement takes place through a passive response to humidity changes. Therefore, it does not require any sensory system or motor function. The movement is independent from any metabolic function and hence it does not consume any energy. Here, the responsive capacity is intrinsic to the material's hygroscopic behavior and its own anisotropic characteristics. Anisotropy denotes the directional dependence of a material's characteristics. Hygroscopicity refers to a substance's ability to take in moisture from the atmosphere when dry and yield moisture to the atmosphere when wet, thereby maintaining a moisture content in equilibrium with the surrounding relative humidity.

Both projects presented here build on multiple years of design research investigating the biomimetic principles offered by the spruce cone to develop responsive architectural systems. The research enables the use of wood, one of the oldest and most common construction materials, as a climate–responsive, natural composite. Wood's anisotropic dimensional behavior was exploited in the development of a humidity–responsive veneer–composite element based on simple quarter–cut maple veneer. In the process of adsorption and desorption of moisture triggered by ambient humidity changes, the distance between the microfibrils in the wood cell tissue changes, resulting in a significant anisotropic change in dimension. Through a precise morphological articulation, this dimensional change can be employed to trigger the shape change of a responsive element.

The developed material can be physically programmed to compute different shapes in response to changes in relative humidity. In the *HygroScope* project the elements change from open to closed due to increasing relative humidity, while the *HygroSkin* project was calibrated in the inverted manner; closing with increasing relative humidity. The veneer–composite element instrumentalizes the material's responsive capacity in one surprisingly simple component that is at the same time embedded sensor, no–energy motor, and integrated regulating element. The reversibility and reliability of this movement has been tested and verified in a large number of long–term tests, both in controlled laboratory conditions and in outdoor applications.

human body

The human body is very sensitive to temperature fluctuations. Even small changes are actively recognized—for example, when moving between spaces with slightly different air temperature. In contrast to this, changes in the humidity level are hardly ever consciously perceived, except for extreme situations. In this way, both projects presented below are not merely architectural systems that respond to climatic changes with variable degrees of sheltering and ventilation. They also perform as visual devices enabling the experience of subtle climate dynamics that usually escape our perception.

HYGROSCOPE – METEOROSENSITIVE MORPHOLOGY

The project *HygroScope – Meteorosensitive Morphology* / fig.12 p.173 / was commissioned by the Centre Pompidou in Paris for its permanent collection and was first shown in the exhibition Multiversités Créatives. The meteorosensitive morphology floats in a fully transparent glass case. Within this case the climate corresponds to the relative humidity changes in Paris. In this way, the case functions less as a separation from the interior space of the Centre Pompidou, arguably one of the most stable climate zones in the world, but rather provides a virtual connection to the outside weather conditions. Thus, the variations in humidity levels that

environment

are an intrinsic characteristic of our environment but are hardly ever consciously perceived are translated into a visual experience by the system's silent movement. A mere increase in relative humidity triggers the system to open / fig.13 p.173 // fig.14 p.173 /. Although there really are only simple composite elements, the system embodies the capacity to sense, actuate, and respond.

HYGROSKIN – METEOROSENSITIVE PAVILION The project HygroSkin – Meteorosensitive Pavilion / fig.15 p.175 / was commissioned by the FRAC Centre Orléans for its permanent collection and was first shown in the exhibition ArchiLab 2013: Naturalizing Architecture.

The pavilion explores the tension between an archetypical architectural volume, the box, and a deep, undulating skin imbedding clusters of intricate climate-responsive apertures. The traveling pavilion's modular envelope, which is at the same time a load-bearing structure and meteorosensitive skin, is computationally derived from the elastic bending behavior of thin plywood sheets. The material's ability to form elastically bent conical surfaces is used in combination with a seven-axis robotic manufacturing process to construct twenty-eight geometrically differentiated components, housing 1,100 humidity-responsive apertures. Developable surfaces can be bent into their geometry using initially planar sheets of plywood. Here, the cone geometry is of special interest as it increases structural stability compared to a flat sheet. At the same time, the principle of employing conical geometries to a global structure opens up the possibility to generate differentiated modules that all have a common base geometry.

The project taps into several years of design research on robotic prefabrication, component-based construction, and elastically self-forming structures. For this pavilion a computational design process was developed based on the elastic behavior of thin planar plywood sheets. Each component consists of a double-layered skin, which initially self-forms as conical surfaces that are subsequently joined to produce a sandwich-panel by vacuum pressing. Final form definition on the modular panels, to specify tolerance levels, is achieved through robotic trimming. The robotic fabrication process is based on interactive simulation of the robot kinematics and automated machine code generation. In order to minimize fabrication tolerances the module geometry is first surveyed with the robotic arm before being processed by trimming the edges with a circular saw and milling the foam core. The structural capacity of the elastically bent skin surfaces allows for a lightweight, easily transportable yet robust system. Within the deep concave surface of each robotically fabricated module a weather-responsive aperture is placed. Materially programming the humidity-responsive behavior of these apertures opens up the possibility for a strikingly simple yet truly ecologically embedded architecture in constant feedback and interaction with its surrounding environment / fig.16 p.175 // fig.17 p.175 /. The apertures respond to relative humidity changes within a range from 30 to 90 percent, which equals the humidity range from sunny to rainy weather in a moderate climate. In direct feedback with the local microclimate the pavilion constantly adjusts its degree of openness and porosity, modulating the light transmission and visual permeability of the envelope. The responsive wood-composite skin adjusts the porosity of the pavilion in direct response to changes in ambient relative humidity. The hygroscopic actuation of the surface provides for a unique convergence of environmental and spatial experience; the perception of the delicate, locally varied, and ever–changing environmental dynamics is intensified through the subtle and silent movement of the meteorosensitive architectural skin.

CONCLUSION Both projects presented above are based on the same hygroscopically actuated system. While they respond in different ways – the HygroScope opening and the HygroSkin closing when relative humidity increases – each movement remains in a direct relation with the stimulus: once the system is defined the shape change will always be the same for a given amount of moisture content. Despite this linear dependency between cause and effect the experience of the system is perceived as complex. As relative humidity is also a function of temperature, and as the decisive relative humidity level of the interface layer between air volume and element is affected by both ambient air temperature and heat radiation, the system's response is often counterintuitive. In addition, we are not accustomed to predicting a particular relative humidity level in the same way that we anticipate, for example, temperature changes. Thus, the system's state often remains unexpected, leading to a perceived complexity of behavior and triggering a keen interest in unraveling the ecology in which it is embedded.

In[form]ations: Digital Matter on Buildings and Cities

Areti Markopoulou
/ Director of Masters Program and R+D Department, IAAC, Barcelona.
/ Initiator and Partner of Fab Lab Athens.

We are currently facing a paradigm change in the field of architecture. Information–era technologies and their impact on architecture are developing at a drastic pace, and their relationship calls for new or adapted concepts where physical space seamlessly intertwines with digital content, and where the language of electronic connections ties in with that of physical connections. We are consequently moving toward a different form of "habitat," where architecture is not merely inhabited, but becomes technologically integrated, interactive, and evolutionary.

habitat

If computers were once the size of buildings, buildings are now becoming computers, both performative (on I/O communication protocols) and programmable (at a material–molecule nanoscale) or even operational, thanks to self–learning genetic algorithms. If the public space we inhabit today was basically constructed at the start of the Industrial Revolution, the information society is now bringing to bear new principles and technologies with which to rethink the functioning and structure of the streets, avenues, squares, and infrastructure of the city.

Industrial Revolution

Architecture and information and communications technology (ICT) open up a series of possibilities and new projects on different architectural scales—from a nanoscale of matter to buildings and cities, from bits to geography. The Institute for Advanced Architecture of Catalonia's (IAAC) Digital Matter and Intelligent Construction research agenda focuses on the development of new design ideas and bottom–up processes where importance is placed not on the final aesthetics but rather on data and information that prepare the ground for the birth of efficient, responsive, and informed architecture of cities and buildings.

Digital Matter

DIGITAL MATTER AND BUILDINGS / fig.18 p.176 // fig.19 p.176 / In the early twentieth century, "dwelling" was conceptualized as a "machine for living" (Le Corbusier), a reference to a new way of understanding the construction of inhabitable spaces that characterized the machine age. Today, a century later, we face the challenge of constructing intelligent and sustainable prototypes; living organisms that interact and interchange resources with their environment, following the principles of ecology or biology rather than those of mere construction, and which

organism

function as entirely self-sufficient and responsive nodes with the potential to use and produce resources.

Digital Matter in Buildings tackles questions regarding material intelligence. The extended use of smart materials such as shape-memory materials—piezoelectric, thermoelectric, or biomaterials, able to adjust their properties in different environmental conditions—allow buildings to be programmed at a nanoscale, and open up a series of applications on an industrial or architectural scale. Furthermore, new composite materials that present preset combinations of mechanical multi-functional properties of non-homogeneous materials in shape and composition across a wide scale bring forth the exploration of a shift in design culture, taking us to a new level of material awareness. Material intelligence in combination with artificial and computational intelligence, simulations, sensors, and actuators, as well as with biomimetic innovations, provide revolutionary ideas on growth, adaptability, repair, sensitivity, replication, and energy savings in architecture. Should we continue constructing rigid and fixed structures? Or can buildings begin to think?

The work at IAAC within the agenda on smart and self-sufficient buildings is motivated by the hypothesis that form follows energy (information). The work in progress includes the full-scale construction of buildings, such as the *Fab Lab House* and the *Endesa Pavilion*, two parametrically designed houses in which form follows the data of the solar path of the area and the final form is digitally calculated by an optimization software, so that the buildings can collect the maximum amount of solar energy throughout the year / fig.20 p.177 // fig.21 p.177 /. The *Fab Lab House* has been entirely digitally fabricated by a group of researchers and students and is able to generate twice as much energy as it needs through flexible solar cells adjusted to the optimum form of the building.

This brings us to a second path of material intelligence, that of digital fabrication. In design, architecture, and many other disciplines, Computer Numerical Control (CNC) fabrication equipment has given designers unprecedented means for executing formally challenging projects directly from computers. Digital fabrication gives us the potential and the ability to design and fabricate building components with varied properties of density, translucency, elasticity, and much more. However, until now, digital fabrication tools have been used by designers to materialize their design by accessing materials as a library of consistent and physically homogeneous properties. Neri Oxman (2010) writes:

> "Functionally graded digital fabrication is a novel design approach offering the potential to program physical matter. [...] It expands the potential of prototyping, since the varying of properties allows for optimization of material properties relative to their structural and functional performance, and for formal expressions directly and materially informed by environmental stimuli."

The IAAC research on digital manufacturing in construction includes antigravity 3–D printing manufacturing processes through robotic arms and polymer mixes for new automatized and databased construction systems / fig.22 p.177 // fig.23 p.178 /. This innovative additive manufacturing method allows objects to be formed on any given working surface independently of its inclination and smoothness, without the need of support structures. It's a method that would allow making three–dimensional laminae or curves instead of two–dimensional ones, as occurs in conventional additive manufacturing methods.

manufacturing

Other fabrication techniques include the creation of composite materials (silicone and wood) to provide a basic panel system for designers and architects who can assemble or even redesign it according to their needs. Conforming to the density and location of the cuts, different angles of deformation can be approached / fig.24 p.178 /. The silicone in this research takes over two functions. On the one hand, it is part of the air/water system, and on the other it connects the panels to each other to create a larger component–based surface. In other words, structure, system, and joint are made out of the same material.

Finally, the IAAC's work on the combination of digital manufacturing techniques with smart–material manipulation explores how digital fabrication goes beyond assigning material properties to rigid construction components. A 3–D printer is used to deposit different densities of multicolored conductive gel on a window panel. Dots of CMY color expand when they receive an electrical impulse, creating a new kind of window that mimics the camouflage capabilities of an octopus's skin by changing color in response to an electrical impulse / fig.25 p.178 /.

3–D printer

As pilot projects, these allow us to explore how material, artificial, and computational intelligence generate new and efficient design and manufacturing processes for intelligent building constructions.

INTELLIGENT CITIES / fig.26 p.179 / Advances in building–design technologies and construction cannot be separated from their effects on an urban scale. Each action on the territory implies a manipulation of multiple environmental forces connected to numerous information flows and networks, such as energy, transport, logistics, and information, generating new inhabitable and responsive nodes with the potential to use and produce resources. Territorial and urban strategies and building operations must therefore be coordinated processes that extend architectural knowledge to new forms of management and planning, in which a multi–scalar thinking also entails an understanding of shifting dynamics, energy and information transmission, and continuous adaptation.

energy

> "The city is a connective network among human beings and their activities. This is what led to urbanization in the first place: individuals clustered so that communication distances would shrink to a minimum, while the number of connective nodes increased."
>
> Nikos Salingaros, 2010

megacities

We are currently facing a new phase of urbanization with a real need for major innovation in urban design, technologies, and services. The next forty years will see an unprecedented transformation in the global urban landscape. In the next three decades the number of people living in cities will soar from 3.6 billion to 6.3 billion and by 2025 there will be thirty-seven megacities, each with a population of more than ten million (Navigant Research 2013). Information and communication technologies will be deeply embedded in the fabric of both old and new cities and will change the way we think of city operations and how we live and work in these environments. After all, urban environments have always stood in close relationship to the technologies of production, transport, and communications. The IAAC research in the "intelligent cities" field is based on the hypothesis that the application of ICT in spatial planning can be conceptualized as a new type of

infrastructure

infrastructure for the transport of invisible—though measurable—data that allow cities to perform as organisms and become behavioral.

Projects such as *City Protocol* and *Smart Public Space* are research agendas initiated by IAAC in the effort to understand the ICT implementation in urban environments and how cities could be responsive to environmental or social data and user needs.[1] Why do streets continue to route traffic in the same direction over time? How do people interact with public space? What happens when the Internet of

Internet of Cities

Things becomes the Internet of Cities?

The projects focus on monitoring technologies, such as sensor devices that collect data, and on using applications and visualization tools to process this data. Urban applications and real-time visualizations contribute to raising awareness and allow communities and users to adopt their behavior or define their actions based on efficiency factors.

Cities are able to filter water (the kidney system), manage ventilation and air quality (the lung system), locate and balance traffic levels (the visual system), process waste in order to produce biofuel (the digestive system), to create real-time-data urban-farming irrigation systems, to blur the lines of the current highways and pavements with responsive tile systems.

---

1   City Protocol was initiated by IAAC in 2011 and currently led by the Barcelona city council. It is a nonprofit corporation formed by cities, commercial and nonprofit organizations, universities, and research institutions whose role is to develop the City Protocol – i.e., a system's approach to rationalize and document city transformation. See http://www.cityprotocol.org/.

Citizens, on the other hand, are able to visualize their neighborhood data, participate in public–space distribution, access urban interfaces and open data platforms, calculate the shortest routes to their destination, be aware of their energy–consumption impact on their urban block, and finally be part of an urban evolution based on self–organization rules related to local parameters and social or emotional factors of citizens when occupying space.

self–organization

Far beyond sensors and monitoring systems, the new type of emerging city is not just an increasingly important system of virtual spaces interconnected by the information superhighway (Mitchell 1996). Future urban planning and urban management calls for connection with concepts such as open innovation or new citizen–based services and the necessary processes and tools for how cities, surrounding regions, and rural areas can evolve toward sustainable open and user–driven innovation ecosystems to boost future Internet–enabled services of public interest and citizen participation.

open innovation

The great challenge for a new urban metabolism lies in the city's capacity to interact, to give and receive information among interconnected nodes with different scales and natures: infrastructure, buildings, elements of the public space, environmental conditions, flows, and so on. This anticipates fundamental concepts related to the importance of proposing symbiotic systems of organization based on real–time data that can be further articulated into responsive systems and metabolic organizations, where small decisions can have a large impact on an urban scale.

data

We are moving, thus, toward a different form of "habitats," where we don't just inhabit our architecture but we integrate, interact, and evolve with it. Internet of Cities, buildings whose form and matter follow data, and materials responding to environmental conditions and digital content are part of an architecture that is not just mimicking the living but is roaring into life.

It is necessary to generate knowledge with a complex, multilayered reading of realities that have traditionally been thought of as separate, such as energy manipulation, nature, urban mobility, dwelling, systems of production and fabrication, and the development of software and information networks. This opens up the possibility of generating new architectural prototypes based on principles of different disciplines and capable of engaging with complex and adaptive environments. No doubt: If there were ever a time to go deeper into the architectural metabolism of our "habitats" through new multidisciplinary and technological models, this is certainly it.

knowledge

references

+ Mitchell, William J. (1996) City of Bits: Space, Place and the Infobahn. Cambridge, MA: MIT Press.
+ Navigant Research. (2013) "Smart Cities: Infrastructure, Information, and Communications Technologies for Energy, Transportation, Buildings, and Government: City and Supplier Profiles, Market Analysis, and Forecasts." Available from: http://www.navigantresearch.com/research/smart–cities.
+ Oxman, Neri (2010) "Methods and Apparatus for Variable Property Rapid Prototyping," Google Patents.
+ Salingaros, Nikos (2010) Introduction Article, "Networked City:, IAAC GSS.

Building Nature:
On Sex and Ducks, Chicken and Shit, Architecture and Apples

Alex Haw
/ Artist, Architect, Lecturer, and Writer.
/ Director of atmos, design practice, London.

LONGING FOR LIFE
I wonder about this architectural fascination with life.
Life is our subject, client, and purpose; we build for living people.
But is life our building material? Can we engineer life?
Are our buildings truly alive?

ARCHITECTURE V. NATURE
Architects tussle with nature.

If nature were hospitable, we'd be out of business.[1]
We need rain to sell shelter. We need nature to build against.   shelter

But we also need it to build *with*. Tons of it. Buildings are great heaps of relocated nature—whether freshly chopped green oak or age–old stone, mined metals or minced minerals.

Sometimes this gives the impression that our buildings are indeed alive. Timbers creak and groan; stone roofs contract and expand; foundations settle, like old animals slumping with age.

If buildings have always been made *from* local nature, they have also always looked *to* it—feeding on its wider warmth and nutrients, and orienting to its vectors—   warmth
even its astral ones.

Our cities once followed the course of rivers, feeding on their energy, as we now feed on theirs. We go to a city because we seek opportunity, the birth of possibility,   opportunity
and the presence of others; "life." Architecture is the building block of that life we seek. Its spaces are the cells that tooth and tile together to form the tissues of our complex urban organs.

---

1   If humans were more hospitable, we'd also need less architecture to keep us from ourselves.

URBAN LIFE + URBAN NATURE Cities are our new nature, giant petri dishes of life. They have even become great patrons and protectors of that older, pre–urban nature. Office blocks are capped with green roofs, nested by eagles, while inner–city supermarket roofs transform into permaculture allotments, delivering "food from the sky."[2] Urban growing is exploding as agriculture joins culture on spare balconies, walls, rooftops, and disused railway tracks. Councils in England are increasingly mandating biodiversity—calling on homeowners to cohabit with other creatures and make room in their eaves for birds and bats. While English foxes are safer and better fed in London than anywhere in the British countryside, an unlikely "urban chicken" movement is sweeping across the United States (Block 2008). And everyone is awakening to the importance of bees, which are gifted designer homes everywhere; in London alone, they're lavished with the most exclusive addresses, from penthouse–flat roofs to the Royal Festival Hall's "People's Palace" on the South Bank.

biodiversity

ARTIFICIAL LIFE Vitruvius recognized our root in nature, but he also recognized our need for machines. His final chapter in the *The Ten Books on Architecture*, extolled an architect's role in designing machines of war. Homer identified early robotics as architectural—making the first mention of automata to describe automatic door openers. Our first stories of mankind vying to make life are tinged with automata. Prometheus—our heroic thief of fire, maker of man, and king of civilization—was sentenced to endless torture, his liver devoured daily by the *aetos kaukasios*, or artificial Caucasian eagle. Fast forward to the current day, where academic architectural labs are overflowing with robotic arms—giant hyper-powered simulacra of the old iconic architectural hand—drawing futuristic paths through space, groping for architecture.

robotics

It sounded bizarre when Robert Venturi first argued that a building should be a "decorated shed" rather than a "duck" – citing the simultaneously comic and eerie duck–shaped duck shop (Big Duck) on Long Island in New York (Venturi et al. 1977). But the legacy of ducks as rich cultural man–made artifacts[3]—epitomizing a fertile and febrile collision between engineering and biology—stretches back two centuries to Jacques de Vaucanson's celebrated Digesting Duck. Acclaimed as his masterwork (Voltaire argued that it symbolized the glory of France), the 1739 Canard Digérateur automaton claimed to be able to eat and excrete, though it actually ejected preprepared faux feces quite separately from the food it ingested. It wasn't until 2006 that artist Wim Delvoye invented a fully functional demonstrative digester—the useless, life–like, highly remunerative Cloaca machine. Shit sells.

engineering

---

2   See http://foodfromthesky.org.uk/.
3   *Big Duck* was added to the National Register of Historic Places in 1997, twenty years after Venturi first wrote about it.

Our post–mechanical, postindustrial times are indebted to preindustrial Vaucanson. The duck's intestines led to the invention of the world's first flexible rubber tubing—and Vaucanson invented the world's first automated loom six years later, using a punch–card system that formed the basis of modern–day computation. The industrial age ushered in the golden era of proto–robotic automata (roughly 1860–1910), whose descendants—virtual, cellular automata— emerged a generation later to inaugurate our current digital age.[4] They in turn paved the way for our quest for life simulation, via mathematician John Conway's seminal 1970 Game of Life – also simply called *Life*.

cellular automata

ARCHITECTURE AS LIFE I stare at the dictionary definitions of life and am astonished at how architecture's bid to life membership doesn't seem so distant or doomed. 1970s architecture claimed a Metabolist movement, though it used biology (as does so much architecture) metaphorically; but the building–management systems of contemporary architecture inch ever closer to a genuinely performative, functional metabolism, where the occupied building can change and adapt like a living organism. Buildings increasingly seek automated *homeostasis*, regulating their internal environments like life forms regulate theirs.

homeostasis

Another definition of life stipulates exactly what architecture epitomizes—organization, or the "structured arrangement of cells," which are ever more equipped to exchange rather than just merely abut. As sensing systems proliferate across our built environment, architecture conforms to life's traits of adaptation and responsiveness, its nervous system responding to stimuli and triggering looping feedback systems. Natural growth is perhaps not architecture's strong point, though self–healing materials and RepRap self–replicating manufacturing devices suggest this capacity is not far distant.

nervous system

Yet it is the biological act of reproduction that, for me, epitomizes architecture's kinship with life. Not only is the architectural blueprint almost synonymous with the genetic capacity for perfect reproduction (along with random mutation); not only has the history of "evolutionary architecture" found a rich legacy in generative, algorithmic code; but architecture's older history of insisting on culture beyond utility, architecture beyond shelter—and the primacy of people and pleasure— underline humanity's evolution of the reproductive act to encompass ingenious possibilities beyond biological duplication.

reproduction

LIFE ASPIRATIONS Our architectural and environmental work at atmos has touched on many of these versions and topics, often converging human, man–made, and nonhuman natures. Residential refurbishments like *Sensualscaping* (the

---

4   Academics have pondered whether the universe itself is a cellular automation (Llachinski 2001, p. 660).

Clapham House)[5] / fig.27 p.180 / attempt, in their simply quotidian way, to fuse nature and architecture, grown with the built environment in proximity and concert, the house and garden interchanging and intermelding, garden indoors and house outdoors, the building dancing in the corner with the tree, and plant–like systems reaching through the house, yet demanding humans to complete them—activating them through use. With the *Floating Forest*, / fig.28 p.180 / we cross–fertilized garden and machine, equipping a DIY catamaran with an electric outboard motor and a computer–cut ergonomic substructure that we then draped with flowers and grass, enabling London Eastenders to drift down its waterways on a detachable piece of parkland.

We've turned man–made weather into inhabitable environments by transforming the rapid transactions of the Frankfurt Stock Exchange into lightning storms within an old prison for *Incel*. We've piped real–time sunsets (and rhythmic satellite data) into an old observatory overlooking the harbor for *Weather Projection*, commissioned for Smart Light Sydney. We've proposed a global network of skycams in every capital city, relaying real–time qualitative (rather than quantitative) data back to a 300–meter–long responsive lighting sculptural occupation of Canary Wharf's Middle Dock for *Sunlands* in London's Docklands.

Lighthive saturated all 160 rooms of London's Architectural Association with swarms of sensors that fed back occupancy data to a room–sized chandelier that luminously mapped the real–time movements of everyone in the building / fig.29 p.181 // fig.30 p.181 /. *Lightfall* enabled this same sensed occupancy to trigger the public lighting illuminating Cutty Sark's Underground station—bringing light to life. *Lumiskin* offered a dark and dormant stage that sprung only to life with the presence of a moving human, its cameras feeding collocated cameras with projected particles that rapidly and precisely mapped the exact flutter of human figures onto a light fog, creating immersive, spatial follow–spots. And *Outreach* turned camera pixels into protrusions using an array of Kinect cameras to activate mechanical hairs sheathing the minimal volume surrounding the installation's visitor, each elongated in the areas where they extended their limbs.

Worldscape / fig.31 p.183 / offered a tumultuous CNC–cut table and seating landscape generated purely from world data—its tech–driven design and manufacture complementing a low–tech interactivity—hosting a pop–up restaurant every night of the 2012 London Olympics that was completed only by the participation and occupancy of its guests, nestling amid the towering mountains and twinkling cities. And our proposal for the Olympic monument—*The Cloud*, with Carlo Ratti Associati—merged digital and physical geographies with a proposal for an inhabitable series of inflatable observation decks laced with LED droplets that

---

5   See atmos studio's website (http://www.atmosstudio.com/) for more information on the projects discussed in this text.

veiled views with augmented reality and pulses of information fed both from top–down national broadcasts and bottom–up crowd sources.

EDIBLE, ERGONOMIC, ARBOREAL ARCHITECTURE The title of this essay puns on the architect's innate nature, to build; on the fact that we deploy natural materials to build; on our construction of life–like systems of design, generating buildings and information almost organically. And it neatly summarizes the final project I'll briefly describe that aspires to do all this—and also, literally, build a clump of nature.

We were commissioned by the City of London Festival to design a series of trees for a *Mobile Orchard*. The festival's mission is to unlock the spectacular spaces at the heart of London's oldest center—the "Square Mile" of its financial district—but also to celebrate the 150 natural parks and gardens peppered throughout it, and the year's theme of "trees." We designed a fantasy tree / fig.32 p.183 // fig.33 p.183 / that secretly contained a stair (a spiraling series of hidden, radial branches) that led to secret niches and harbors along its trunk, and to a throne "crown" at its peak. The branches (engineered to be rapidly removable for its nomadic journeys, yet robust enough to support the weight of the inevitable renegade climbers) were anthropo-tropic—deformed by the future imagined path of bodies, warped into cradling seats and loungers, and spliced with secondaries that held aloft real fruit—a trove of apples that was endlessly replenished, and itself endlessly fed a theatre of initial hesitation and grateful feasting.

Trees are systems as well as sculptures—tightly bundled fibers ferrying data and resources. Echoing the ubiquity of surrounding clocks and the mechanics of the city's financial community—its pinstriped automata—our tree was laced with electric xylem, its twelve segments (like a clock's twelve faces) each striped with a line of light that delineated the graphic wriggle of its growth pattern, but also pulsed out its own life–like rhythm; an artificial heartbeat, activated by bodies, its host eagerly awaiting, reflecting, and rewarding the life of lips and limbs.

references

+ Block, Ben (2008) "U.S. City Dwellers Flock to Raising Chickens." Worldwatch Institute, http://www.worldwatch.org/node/5900. Accessed: March 15, 2014.
+ Llachinski, Andrew (2001) Cellular Automata: A Discrete Universe. Singapore: World Scientific.
+ Venturi, Robert, Denise Scott Brown, and Steven Izenour (1977) Learning from Las Vegas: The Forgotten Symbolism of Architectural Form. Cambridge, MA: MIT Press.

A conversation between

Alex Haw,
Marco Poletto,
Dino Rossi,
Philip Beesley,
Claudia Pasquero, and
Simon Schleicher

Alive: International
Symposium on
Adaptive Architecture,
Zurich, July 8, 2013.

ALEX I find it quite salient how greatly everyone's work overlaps. There's so much common ground, so much sympathy between the works, and yet such oppositional tendencies, which are framed in quite radically different ways.
I'm wondering if everyone could address what level of synergy and what degree of opposition or diversions you most pointedly feel among yourselves. If you had to cross–fertilize with someone, who would it be? Whose family are you in, and whose do you feel quite different from?

MARCO I always like to take things from different projects, probably because of the way we [Claudia and I] craft our way through architectural experimentation, which is not very linear since we come from engineering and environmental design and have had a series of other experiences along the way.
Of course there are positions that differ but I think there are also elements that could be picked up quite easily by one another.
For me what is innovative and actually quite refreshing to hear is a clear push to overcome any form of reductionism in formulating sustainable design paradigms or projects. This is really stimulating because I have been to numerous events at which the paradigm of reduction was still extremely present, even in very sophisticated environments. I somehow have the feeling that among the different presentations there is a common sensibility even in the more—let's say, technical—aspects, which feels like the beginning to push ourselves beyond that paradigm.
The question now would be whether this is really a transition that is happening in the academic world or if it's just the work of certain individuals who are promoting this change.

ALEX Everyone has a certain contradiction that they play to. But it's interesting that you, Dino, maybe come across as slightly more concerned with an optimized form of things. And yet, when you were doing the tracking projects, you also said that there were moments when they flipped off from that adaptive, responsive, linear mode into other circuits of performance—which suggested that they were not directly aligned simply to the sun anymore.

CONVERSATION . **BIOINSPIRATION**

DINO Yes, I think I skipped one important point. What I'm actually trying to develop is more like an ecology of adaptive systems. So you have a shading system, an internal lighting system, and a climate–conditioning system, and these systems can all work together and adapt over time and change based on user interaction. The aim is not to optimize a building's energy performance, it's to balance energy performance with how people want to use their spaces. So really it's about creating flexible systems that can adapt to fluctuating environmental influences (building occupants included); in a way, it's actually the opposite of optimization.

MARCO But then optimization almost becomes a negative connotation, which I don't think should be the case. I think that optimization is something that's essential to life all the time. The question is rather, what is the conceptual framework in which these devices are installed or in which these algorithms run? That's where I think the real challenge lies.
Not that your devices are not interesting: I think it's great that you develop such a resilient system. The question is how we then use this kind of a newly found adaptiveness to challenge the way we think about the architectural envelope or, for instance, the way we treat the notion of boundary.

PHILIP It is tempting to speak of a tribal affinity in what is emerging as a language and in the pursuit of subtle functions.
With the beautiful *Flectofin* that Simon just showed, one can think of using it in a myriad of ways. It invites transforming the layers of a building. There's an absolutely lovely sense of learning

the anatomy and craft of biomimicry as an enabling set of languages and design methodology. Yet I have to confess some aversion to biomimicry as a general practice. I mean to speak of ambivalence. It's glorious to see that dragonfly's wing move. Yet at the same time, if I watch an animated X–ray of a human body walking, I must say it seems like an atrocity. That motion appears to involve constant falling, shambling, and lurching. It implies that the circumstance and resilience that nature uses can impart great suffering. The new language of resilience seems to work by approximation. It allows circumstantial, partial solutions to be coped with and to have their own local viabilities. That is both hideous and wonderful. Lucretius said that the purpose of something doesn't come out of grand design. The function of something doesn't come out of purpose; instead, it comes out of circumstance. Things work, and the resulting functions lurch up into existence out of that circumstance. To me, this makes a substantial inversion of our sense of a grand design and a religious reverence of nature.
Resilience seems a critical term for us all. It points to qualities of mediation and approximation, building competency into complex systems. At the same time I wonder about the capacity to include suffering or even a bloody mess as part of this practice. This, frankly, makes me want to avoid worshipping transcendent biomimicry practices. Instead, I want to keep in my back pocket brutal minimalist chopping and cutting and make something pure. Stepping very carefully in saying so, I suspect that mortality functions will be needed more and more as our ability to create resilience increases.

MARCO I think you're pointing at something that brings together a whole set of engineering notions, which can be extremely fascinating when applied to materials science or to architecture, but at the same time is easily useful as a way of justifying solutions.
And that's one of the problems with, for instance, many simulation engines or the way simulation is often applied in architecture. I feel that the problem really is that there is a widespread use of these metaphors or even more technical simulations as a way of justifying solutions and making

them acceptable, and these are often the sources of misunderstanding.

CLAUDIA For me biomimicry is almost like a tool, because it represents a very scientific, technological aspect of design. But the moment you bring it into a design concept you have to add something else, and all of us are adding different things. If you compare, for example, the work of Alex with that of Philip, both of them have a certain relationship with biomimicry, but they articulate it in two totally different ways. Philip is talking about the meta–aspect around the relationship between space and person, and Alex instead works with these geometries that are so refined in craft that they almost become a social activator. They go on the pop side of biomimicry and become this trigger between user and design and consumption.

PHILIP In the amalgam of disciplines you just described, it's tempting to speculate that creative space can produce a kind of license that is very different than a clean, optimal orderly space. It would in turn be tempting to say that we're acquiring a set of practices that impart resilience, fertility, and efflorescence. This allows us to take something wildly circumstantial, like an eccentrically, serendipitously formed building, and clothe it to become viable.
A voice from seventy years ago came from a hideous man who railed about the degradation of a mongrel kind of culture that came from intermixing things. He spoke, darkly, of his hunger for chopping and clearing instead. If we're going to chase this work, as we seem to be agreeing we are, then we're going to have a lot of mongrels. That may generate turbulence in the cultural reception of this work, turning biomimicry into something grotesque. We're going to have partial hiccupping messes that look like weeds and goats, clogged with jetsam and things which need to be cleared as well. We will need to have a tremendous confidence in the fertility, in the soil–like milieu, that this contributes to.

CLAUDIA But that's part of dealing with ecology, isn't it? We did a project at Smart Geometry once where we were working with a biologist who at some point said that there was no point in clean-

ing up bacteria because millions exist, and even if you remove 99 percent, thousands still remain. And what if you clean just the good bacteria and then the very bad ones remain and proliferate? So what you should do instead is to cultivate bacteria in order to develop an understanding of their ecology and then harvest their potential, like with cheese. One of the best cheeses from my area, Gorgonzola, is actually full of bacteria.
That's why sometimes I'm skeptical about engineering and zero energy, because zero energy does not exist.

ALEX What you're saying is interesting. I read Kevin Kelly's new book recently, *What Technology Wants*, and he talks about the end of biological development as being the invention of language and the beginning of technological development as being language. And so the sixth kingdom then takes over the seventh, which he calls the "Technium"; he says that the term "technology" alone is too bare, too scientific and not explicit enough. He calls it a range of technologies within which he encapsulates culture, whether it's Gorgonzola or Beesley on acid, or whatever form of "soil." There's a certain resistance to the purely scientific method and it feels that we're all teetering in the sort of schizo–land of being quite linear, quite digital, quite scientific, quite environmental, quite numerical somehow—yet deeply resistant—and enthralled by failure, error, and the haphazard. We constantly go back to the '60s and drugs and sex and war and difficulty. I wonder why this is. I mean, we live in an extraordinary age of revolt right now, protests that are united by their complete disunity. Bus fares or poverty, World Cup or football, what is it going to be?
I'm sort of returning to my initial question. Where do we position ourselves? Because every time we say we are technical, we mean that we are artists; and every time we say we are interested in death, we seem to be fascinated by infinite life. Are we straddling contradictions in a pure way? Are we authentically mad? Are we "zeitgeisty?" (*points to Simon*) You must answer!

SIMON Of course I cannot answer that. However, the aspect that fascinates me about biomimetics is that I continuously need to question myself about

my role and my position in our environment. This includes considering my role in the context of other artists and research, but also me as a human within and as part of nature. Exploring and reflecting these ideas requires a nearly forgotten dialogue beyond disciplinary boundaries. So in this time that you are describing, in which the ubiquitous presence of cross–connections generates an uncertainty that no longer allows us to maintain a one–sided identity, with an explicit affiliation to one discipline only, we are confronted with new burning questions.

In response to this situation, I do believe we are behaving according to a "Zeitgeist." After an era in which the priority was laid on the development of the individual, we now begin to understand ourselves as part of a greater whole. Being "mad" or developing a split personality might not necessarily be a bad thing though. For me, it seems more like we are becoming aware of our super–organism. From this perspective, we should feel positively encouraged to redefine our position, not only according to our personal strengths and interests, but also in respect to those of our surrounding colleagues and partners.

Materiability

"A new generation of architecture must arise with forms and spaces which seems to reject the precepts of 'Modern' yet in fact retains those precepts. We have chosen to bypass the decaying Bauhaus image which is an insult to functionalism. You can roll out steel—any length. You can blow up a balloon—any size. You can mould plastic—any shape. Blokes that built the Forth Bridge—they didn't worry."

David Greene, 1961.

CONTENTS . **MATERIABILITY**

Ludger Hovestadt — 62
Domesticating a World of Printed Physics

Manuel Kretzer — 72
Beyond Performance

Martina Decker — 78
Adapting Matter

Nicola Burggraf — 82
Bioluminescence: Toward Design with Living Light

Aurelie Mosse — 86
Smart Materials: Designing a Timescape of Interconnectivity for more Resilient Practices of Inhabitation

John Sarik — 92
The Unconventional Electronics Approach to the Internet of Things

Conversation — 98

Domesticating a World of Printed Physics

Ludger Hovestadt
/ Professor for Computer Aided Architectural Design, Swiss Federal Institute of Technology, Zurich.
/ Inventor of digitalSTROM® chip and Founder of several Spin-off Companies.

I want to talk about a special kind of physics, what I call *Printed Physics*.
This is a topic I've been thinking about for several years now. It became of interest to me when we moved away, at our Chair for CAAD at ETH Zurich, from empirical research into computing in architecture—namely generation of geometry, simulation, automation and production—towards a more basic research into a theory of architecture and information.[1]

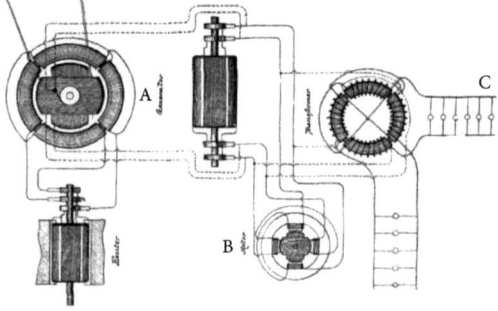

Fig. 1. Illustration of Nikola Tesla's US390721 Patent for a "Dynamo Electric Machine"

There is one technology which more than any other defines the 20th century; in fact it constitutes the very basis for it: *electricity*. We have got so used to electricity that we take it absolutely for granted and treat it as a natural part of our lives; we no longer marvel at its crazy behaviour. Take for example the above drawing of a patent application by Tesla, at the end of the 19th century.

What it "simply" shows is a specific arrangement of copper wires wrapped around some iron cores. But by this simple arrangement, you can turn axis A and somehow axis B will start to turn and lamps C start to glow. Nothing moves in between. There is no mechanical relationship. Just wires. Nothing is visible to the eye, except these wires, where nothing happens at all.

This goes against all intuition. It's a technical phenomenon beyond analytics and mechanics. But to me the most astonishing thing is that today nobody is in

---

1 You will find more on this in: Bühlmann, V., Hovestadt, L. (Eds.) (2011) Printed Physics, Metalithikum I, Applied Virtuality, Vol. 1 (Applied Virtuality Book Series), Springer, Wien.

the least surprised by any of it. That's quite different to the 19th century, when electricity was something new and "magical" that elicited an awed response from thrilled audiences. Today, we take it for granted, like something in nature, and we don't give it a second thought. Nor do we try to understand it, even though it is the technology most fundamental to our last century and even though it is founded in pure intellect.

If you look around, there is hardly a thing now without electricity. It's difficult to imagine that only 120 years ago there *was* no electricity. 120 years ago, there were just two applications of energy in our houses, and both were applications of fire: big fires for cooking and heating, and small fires, like single flames, for light. Today, we have not thousands but hundreds of thousands of electrical applications.

This is meant to be a short text, so I don't want to go into too much detail. Let's instead move on to the next step. These arrangements of materials that we see in Tesla's drawing and that are required to bring about electrical phenomena: let's imagine they could be printed and reproduced like books or newspapers. And just like books or newspapers, these arrangements, or patterns as we may now call them, get cheaper the more of them we print.

It would shift what "making" electricity is all about. It would now be all about the distribution of intellect: we know how to arrange these patterns and so we can now work out how to distribute what we get out of them. The primary issue would no longer be the consumption, movement, and fair distribution of the resources you need, to achieve mechanical motion in order to generate electricity.

Welcome to the world of today! It's a world of a new sophism (which first started with the establishment of phonetic alphabets) and of a new modernity (which first started with the invention of the printing press), and it is a world of an abstraction of both. This is today.

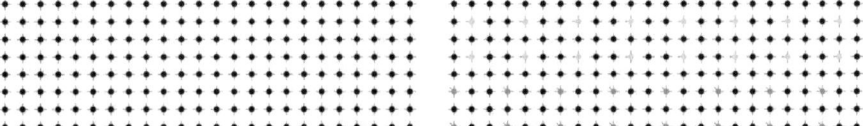

Fig. 2. A regular grid of silicon atoms (left) and the imprint of phosphorous and boron ions (right) create a photovoltaic cell.

Let's have a look at this "electrical printing," which in fact happens at a quantum level: we start, for example, with a "blank" sheet of foil layered with a regular grid of silicon atoms. By simply imprinting—the actual process is called "doping"—onto this layer some ions, in this case phosphorous and boron, we turn it into a solar cell.

energy

Now, if you expose this sheet of printed atoms to the sun, you get electricity. You don't use up any resources, you don't make anything move, you don't exhaust or consume anything. All you do is print atoms onto a surface in a particular way and then position your printed surface to face the sun and in return you get energy.

Enormous amounts of energy. The pool—or continuous stream, rather—that you now tap into amounts to roughly 10,000 times our overall energy consumption today. That's all of mankind, *everywhere*. And you do this just by using your intellect. It is true: by simply applying our creative thinking we can access an energy stream that offers ten thousand times the amount of energy we currently need.

abundance

So energy, the principal source of our existence, really is there in abundance for us. Simply because we know how to "write" or "draw" or "print" the right kind of pattern onto the right kind of material in the right way. This is incredible.

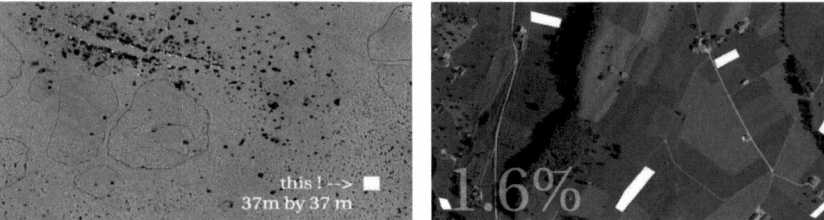

Fig. 3. This village in Ethiopia (left) requires an area of 37m by 37m of photovoltaic solar cells (equivalent to the white square; approximately) to cover all of its basic energy needs. The white shaded fields (right) mark the surface area proportional to the surrounding farmland that would have to be covered with photovoltaics (approximately 1.6%) in order to harvest enough energy to meet Switzerland's entire electricity needs.

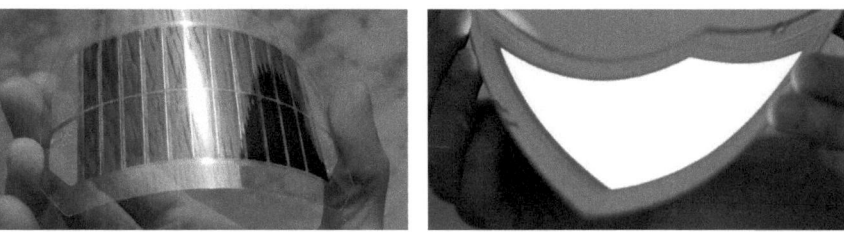

Fig. 4. Printed foils: a photovoltaic solar cell that converts the sun's photons into electrons (left); a light–emitting foil that converts electrons into photons (right).

physics

You can apply the same principle to all other types of physics: light, colour, motion, heating, cooling: whatever you want to achieve, there is a quantum printing configuration that allows you to sense and actuate it.

A simple way to illustrate the principle that is at work here is by taking a photovoltaic foil that converts the sun's photons into electrons, thus "generating" electricity, and a light emitting foil that—like any LED lamp that we're so familiar with—converts electrons into photons, thus giving off light.

On one side of the planet you can have a photovoltaic foil, and on the other side of the planet you can have your LED foil. At, say, 12 noon in the location of your LED foil, everything is bright and lovely. But as the earth turns and the sun sets, it gets dark all around. But at 12 midnight you can still have a bright warm glow here. Why? Because halfway round the globe your photovoltaic solar cell is exposed to the sun and sends electricity at very nearly the speed of light to your LED foil to light it up. So the new reality is that in fact in your LED location you always have light: during the day from the sun, during the night also from the sun, brought to you from the other side of the world. Install the reverse constellation and you can have the same in your solar foil location too. *The light is always on.*

In practice it is a little more complicated because in order for the principle to work you'll want not a couple of foils half a world a part, but a network of foils all over the globe, but still: your basic question is no longer "where do I get the resources to make sure I can have a light on?," the surprising new question now is "when and to what level do I turn off the light if I want to go to sleep?" So with this kind of printing technology, we experience a shift from resources to logistics, from how to keep the light on to when to turn the light off.

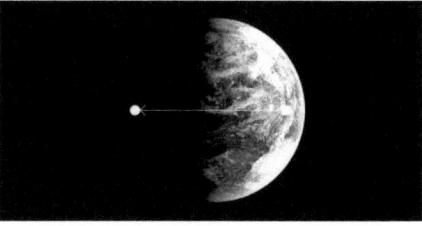

Fig. 5. A simplified illustration of the global interplay of photovoltaic (square) and light emitting (round) foils: the light is "always on."

This is what I think turns our world upside down. We no longer have to take things from nature, consume her resources. Instead, we negotiate an intellectual arrangement. It is a move from the scarcity of resources, and therefore the justice or injustice of distribution, towards the principle of abundance, owing to our intellect.

For those of you who are sceptical about our energy prospects and tend to focus the energy discussion on sustainability and a green planet, and who perhaps do not believe in this "simple" perspective, here is another kind of material doping that we are already using to great effect in our daily life: the *microchip*.

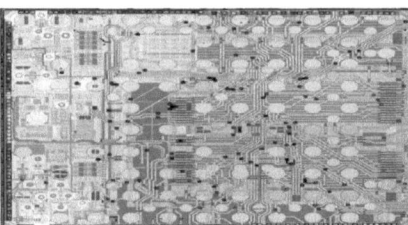 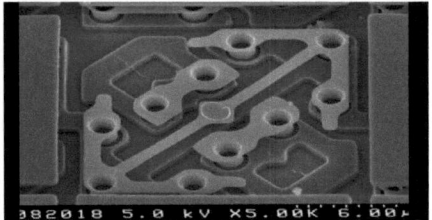

Fig. 6. The printed chip of a GPS System (left) and the printed piezoelectric mechanics of a DLR chip for video projection (right).

mobile phone

Take GPS, for example, or mobile phones. Their processors are printed products on a single chip. The same applies to piezoelectric elements used as microphones and speakers, such as you find in smartphones.

In the case of mobile phones, it took a mere fifteen years to saturate our planet with six billion of these printed pieces *and* to get used to them as an integral part of our life. Everybody and everywhere can and does own a mobile phone. Wherever they are on the planet. Rich or poor, from super developed mega–cities to remote African villages. Without cable. Simply because we know how to print it: it is pure intellect. Patterns of elements, written in a certain alphabet. And because it is printing technology, it gets cheaper the more you print.

printed matter

We currently see a price reduction of thirty percent per year in flat screens, mobile phones, GPS, microprocessors, storage devices, LEDs and also in photovoltaic foils, which are equally printed matter, and which we can use to power all these other printed devices. Very quickly, they become very cheap, if you print them in large quantities. Just like books or newspapers.

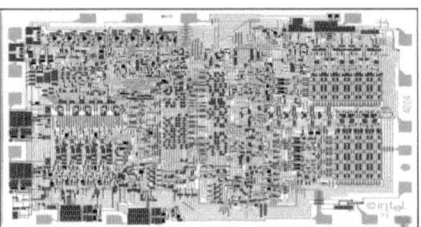 

Fig. 7. The first microprocessor (left), able to run the logic of any thinkable machine... (right)

microprocessor

Let's move on one level further. Let's leave behind the printing of sensors and actuators and enter the field of logic. *Body and mind*. A microprocessor is printed logic. It is able to run any machine you can think of, or think of thinking of, even in the future. And yet, it is nothing but a piece of printed material, and dirt–cheap. And this is exactly where we're at today: we can have any type of energy, any type of information, any type of operation at any point, anywhere in the world. This is really what we mean by "globalization." Our planet is no longer

information

a surface of resources, we are beginning to cultivate a generic network of logistics, connectivity and recycling.

But look at how we behave: we call it *World Systems Analysis* and its heroes are Al Gore, Immanuel Wallerstein, Manuel Castells, Antonio Negri, Michael Hardt. For $129 you can buy a piece of software called *CityEngine* and create your own multi–million people urban model within a few minutes. Rem Koolhaas calls this, a little sarcastically, the "generic city," or simply "junkspace."

If you take a step back, you will see that we've obviously entered a new world. Once you've connected everything to everything else, you run into strange paradoxes: you can't optimise or improve things any more by making them "better." Better social and political analysis, greater justice, cleaner design, more intuitive interfaces, none of these will actually help, we will still overheat within this paradox. In the generic game, things are already connected, and once they are connected they can't be connected any more than they are. The question today for architects, therefore, is: "What *should* I do, if I am capable of anything but I have no idea *what* to do?"

In relation to energy, we similarly have no idea what to do now, but we do know precisely what it is *not* about: it is not about resources; it is not about optimization; it is not about technology; it is not about sustainability; it is not about nature and it is not about autonomy. All this is just there, it is the essence or the surface of our new planet. And we as human beings can roam the planet and cultivate this new ground just by thinking.

If you were to ask me to define what mankind is, I would answer: "man is the creature who gets bored after three days." Which is why our world has always had been super rich, intellectually. Because we can't stand it if our world is not rich. The moment we find it isn't rich, we make it rich. And that means by definition that our machines are decadent. They always have been. *We* are decadent. We are not deficient animals with weak little teeth and a missing fleece. We are luxurious, with sumptuous bodies and super decadent.

What should our thinking be like then, if it is to cultivate the generic infrastructures of our new planet? It should be quantum thinking, because it is quantum writing and quantum printing that we use to create our new generic infrastructures with.

What we are afraid of is to leave behind the classical cause and effect model, the historical approach to writing and thinking that we have found in books for 500 years and that we've become so used to.

Fig. 8. The world upside down. In a mechanical world you have to worry about distribution within an environment of scarce resources (left). In an environment of electric indexality you decide what you don't want to have (right).

Quantum thinking is not about features that are certain or about precision in values. It is a little complicated to understand, but quantum thinking in a networked world is knowing all the others, and therefore being *not* like the others. In quantum thinking you cannot say who you are, you can only say who you are *not*. Not saying what or who you are keeps you rich. If, by contrast, you positively stick to the point, your quantum thinking is dead and you become part of the generic infrastructure.

identity

This inversion, creating your identity by being connected to the whole world, which is not you, is now what in fact maintains the richness of our world. As I have mentioned earlier, there is—if you want to calculate it in the old fashioned way—10,000 times more energy which we can harvest with photovoltaic quantum thinking from the radiation of the sun than we've been able to generate by means of classical thinking.

tragedy

There are two conservative attitudes with which we tend to confront this fundamental richness of intellect. One is to decelerate and protect what we've already got: our own rich cultural heritage. We do this with good reason and yet by necessity we lose. In theatre, this is tragedy: we have only the best intentions, but the deck is stacked against us, we can't win. Within the second principle, we are fascinated by the new potentialities and go all out to use them, as if there's no tomorrow. In theatre this is satire: we become strong, productive and immensely fertile, we are super–heroes, but we destroy all our cultural values, because we just don't care.

satire

comedy

So what is the way out of this disturbing theatre of confrontation? It is comedy. Laughter.

Let me explain: We've always had this theatre, it isn't new. Take for example colours: the human eye has colour receptors for red, green and blue. If you look upon this situation in a tragical way, you have the problem that there is no yellow. That is tragic. It is a great flaw to bemoan, and there is nothing we can do.

Fig. 9. The colour circle according to the three receptors of the human eye with missing yellow: float r = max (0, sin(rat*2*PI + 0*PI/4)*255); float g = max (0, sin(rat*2*PI + 4*PI/4)*255); float b = max (0, sin(rat*2*PI + 2*PI/4)*255);. And the colour circle with the fictitious colour yellow intermingled with the "real"'colours: float y = max (0, sin(rat*2*PI + 6*PI/4)*255); float r = max (0, sin(rat*2*PI + 0*PI/4)*255) + y; float g = max (0, sin(rat*2*PI + 4*PI/4)*255) + y; float b = max (0, sin(rat*2*PI + 2*PI/4)*255);

By contrast, the satirical stance is to say: "If this is how things are, colours don't really matter. I can use any colour I like, who cares?" It is satirical but also cynical: there is no value attached to any colour any more than any other; if there's no yellow, we'll just use red. Devil may care.

But as a comedian, you may say: "There's no yellow? Well, if there's no yellow, we *make* yellow! Here's a formula, let's create yellow out of red, green and blue." You laugh in the face of reality and make a new fiction in which things are the way you want them to be. You create yellow—the fiction—by mixing up the old realities of red, green and blue. And after a while we all get so used to the new fiction, it becomes as real. And nobody's laughing now. *Fictitious nature*.

fiction

Fig. 10. The cultivation of natural sources of energy (left); the cultivation of cultural sources of energy (right).

Take a look at the principle of photosynthesis. Here's how we describe this mechanism by which nature encapsulates the sun's energy and by which green stuff grows:

photosynthesis

$$CO_2 + H_2O + light \longrightarrow <CH_2O> + 2\,O$$

With electricity we can change the formula slightly to get the same result:

$$H_2O + electricity \longrightarrow 2\,H + 2\,O; \qquad 2\,H + CO_2 \longrightarrow <CH_2O> + O$$

organic chemistry

We call this the synthesis of sugar. It won a Nobel Prize in 1914 and it can be seen as the birth of organic chemistry. Again: fictitious nature. And if you want this expressed in the old fashioned way once more: using current photovoltaics to harvest electricity we can produce about 1,000 times more <CH_2O> with our "fictitious" nature than "real" nature provides.

In Switzerland you need 0.21 square meter of solar foils to harvest the equivalent of one liter gasoline per year. This makes our "fictitious" nature about 100 times more efficient than any "natural" plantation. You can do the same calculation with water or food: they all grow on "intellectual fields." And what emerges is a new and rather complex relationship between nature and technology: technology can now be seen as the thing that allows us to understand the nature of what we know.

Thus by "laughing" at the limitations of nature, we get 1,000 more "natures," with all the gas, coal and food that nature would provide. But laughing means we have to leave behind the classical space of analytical reasoning in time and enter a new plateau of thinking, which is about probabilities, attractions and vividness in quantum space.

So, if energy, food, information and health are just there, because we can think it, then, when we are faced with starving kids, people without access to education or medicine or clean water, we can no longer say, "sorry, there's nothing we can do," and refer to scarcities of resources and institutions out of their depth, nor can we say "it's free for all, nothing matters anyway." We have to laugh responsibly and create the world we want to live in.

intellectuality

Look at the current trouble in Egypt: this is not about resources, the economy or bad politics. I strongly believe it is a fight about intellectuality. People want to be part of the game. They want to talk as identities.

media

But why is it so complicated and dangerous to talk? In ancient times words were true if they were spoken by mythical individuals, who were referred to as "media." People trusted these media: they trusted the mythical entities, not the words.

Greek culture started out by writing down the phonemes of spoken words. In doing so, the ancient Greeks decoupled the words from their mythical origins, put them down on papyrus and carried them around to do fantastical things, which hadn't ever been talked about before. But why and how do we trust these writings? This is the birth of logic, which domesticates the fantastical possibilities of words.

In modernity, words again were decoupled from the cosmological medieval order to articulate individual projects in time. And with the arrival of the printing press, writing, like the world as a whole, became mechanical.

And for about 100 years now, with the emergence of quantum thinking, electricity and information technology, we've been leaving something else behind: the analytical order of time. We've invented new writings and new words of probabilities. And these words of probabilities again are decoupled from the things we used to think of as natural and real.

That is why I strongly believe that as architects we have to develop a literacy on a quantum level to be able to cultivate a world of *Printed Physics*.

literacy

Beyond Performance

Manuel Kretzer
/ Initiator of the materiability research network, Chair for CAAD, ETH Zurich.
/ Co–Founder and Partner of Responsive Design Studio, Zurich, Cologne.

INTRODUCTION The profession of the architect is quite varied and reaches into a number of different but often complementary disciplines. Besides needing an instinctive understanding for the complexity of spatial arrangements and human proportions and their combination based on substantial needs, personal interests, and individual behaviors, the architect has to be able to anticipate long-lasting usefulness and functionality combined with an aesthetically pleasing and appropriate form and appearance. Equally important is a general knowledge of historical, social, cultural, economic, and ecological aspects, sufficient understanding of structures and construction, the ability to communicate with clients and stakeholders, but also a continuous interest in the latest technological trends and developments.

knowledge

Obviously the intensity and importance of the different areas varies greatly depending on the respective design task, environment, context, and/or stage of the project, but in almost every case, at least if the expected results are to be of physical nature, an involvement with materials is inevitable. With the more traditional ones—concrete, steel, wood, glass, or even plastics—this is usually fairly straightforward since they are well established, painstakingly recorded, and often already introduced and experienced during an architect's education. Hence the architect can rely on extensive history and knowledge and thus confidently estimate what a material's limits are, in which situation and context it will perform best, and as such apply it in a very efficient manner.

education

SMART MATERIALS But then there are new and very different materials, materials that aren't static but that can adjust their properties dynamically, controlled, and in response to external stimulations. These materials are generally referred to as "smart materials" (Fox and Kemp 2009, p. 227). Because this activity is not based on a certain mechanical complexity but rather on chemical, electronic, and sometimes even biological interactions that occur in between specific functional layers or substrates, they don't require sophisticated, large, and consequently heavy and obtrusive support structures, which is the case with most other actuators—for example, motors, hydraulics, or pneumatics (Lochmatter 2007, p. 6). And since their response is often nonlinear and to some point even unpredictable, they bear a striking resemblance to soft, almost organic behaviors that generally only occur in a natural and living system, but that allow for a very intuitive and personal human

complexity

association and acceptance. The possibilities that these materials thus encompass for the creation of adaptive or interactive spaces are highly intriguing and encouraging. Architects, both in research and practice, are beginning to include them in their proposals and are speculating on how they could eventually enhance buildings to better deal with transient occupational demands and constantly changing environmental conditions (Lakenbrink 2012).

THE DILEMMA Due to the novelty of smart materials, the absence of precursors at an architectural scale, and accordingly a lack of applied knowledge in comparison with the above–mentioned, more established materials, architects are facing difficulties in using smart materials with a similar confidence and to a comparable extent. This struggle is certainly understandable since, due to their immanent dynamic activity, smart materials are fundamentally different from traditional materials. They operate within a predefined range of variable states, rather than just one particular setting. This additional dimension of time, variation, and decay as a material–defining tangible and visual property becomes a disturbing detail that can cause confusion and uncertainty since it stands in direct contrast to classical definitions of architecture, which tend to emphasize stability (Schofield 2009, p. 19), solidity, and durability (Le Corbusier 2008, p. 153), and is thus usually a fact that architects try to avoid at all means. Moreover the factors that drive the materials' transformation are not directly perceivable since they are based on internal reactions and processes. This is very different to, for example, mechanical actuators where one can see the parts physically change and hence easily anticipate their movement. Viewed in this context, the term smart *materials* is actually rather misleading and should maybe better be replaced by calling them devices, systems, or even phenomena.

novelty

decay

transformation

In an attempt to deal with this unknown territory designers tend to fall back on established schemes and approaches. Following the current attitude toward materiality in architecture, they focus on the materials' visual and aesthetic surface qualities, very similar to the use of textures in 3–D CAD programs (Jeska 2008, p. 25). Such an approach might be feasible when dealing with conventional materials, since with a bit of experience one can probably anticipate and predict certain properties. But when dealing with smart materials, their evaluation, standardization, and categorization to make them fit into existing design palettes and catalogues becomes a rather hindering practice since by doing so their defining active and variable properties have to be ignored or seriously simplified.

standardization

Additionally, architects tend to attach smart materials to rigid structures, which constrain their intrinsic abilities (Oxman 2010, p. 83), use them to replace prevalent technologies and devices without addressing material specific characteristics, or apply them in gimmicky and superficial sensational contexts. In order to overcome these limitations and propose novel, more innovative solutions, it is important to identify and analyze their origins in a bit more detail.

Albeit the fact that smart materials, in comparison to other materials, still play a niche role, a major problem is their large, constantly growing number and their varying properties and appearances. Many of them are still very young and far from being market ready, but all of them are designed for a specific function and tuned to exhibit a certain performance. Usually they are not developed for architectural purposes, since the expectations of the building industry in terms of longevity and consistent efficiency are pretty demanding compared to other areas—for example, the car or entertainment sectors. Consequently architects end up with materials that were initially developed for very different applications and they then have to (somehow) try to integrate them into their designs. And even if these materials might have been designed to exhibit their best performance within a specific situation, this is not necessarily the only way they can operate. For example, solar cells are usually sandwiched between two sheets of glass; the same goes for liquid crystal displays, electroluminescent screens, or organic light–emitting diodes. But interestingly all of them could also be produced as flexible foils, which might decrease their performance, longevity, or UV resistance, but in return offers a completely new range of applications and possible spatial scenarios.

performance

The development of a new material, from a research prototype to a commercially available product, can additionally take decades if not centuries. Combined with the concomitant scientific mystification and general lack of comprehensible, in–depth communication between disciplines, this leads to greatly slowing down the creative process and restricts designers to work and think within established boundaries and conventions. Quite surprising however is the realization that the fabrication process of many of these materials is actually not that complex. As long as efficiency and durability are not crucial factors, they can easily be replicated with a bit of sensitivity and training. The most demanding part constitutes finding the necessary ingredients, tools, and correct recipe or assembly instructions, after which the process is surprisingly similar to cooking. Depending on how the parts are mixed together or how the substances are printed on top of each other, the results can vary strongly, allowing the emphasis of very different aspects of the composition.

mystification

To summarize, part of the initially mentioned problems could be solved if architects and designers not only have to work with finished products that are intended for a very specific and often different context, but if they could gain access to novel material developments at a stage early enough to induce architectural requirements. Consequently a rise in demand for architectural smart materials would also decrease production limitations and related costs.

cost

THE MATERIABILITY RESEARCH Such an approach requires not only the will to collaborate and exchange across various disciplines and professional levels in a nonhierarchical manner but especially access to information in a way that architects can understand and comprehend and hence the development of knowledge in order to communicate and mediate across the complementing fields.

The materiability research emerges from collaboration between the Chair for Computer Aided Architectural Design at ETH Zurich and various academic and industrial partners in the areas of materials science, interaction design, textile design, product design, engineering, and robotics. The aim of the research, which began in 2010, is to develop a more general understanding of smart materials through looking at where they come from, how they work, and especially how they are made. Rather than prescribing specific scenarios or applications, the focus is on cultivating a general understanding and practical methods to approach novel material developments with a strong interest in mediating ways for self–education and independent progression. By not concentrating on improving a certain material performance or property but rather revealing the process, prototype, and development, this method allows one to be fairly fast and flexible in responding to new advancements and also cover a relatively broad field.

collaboration

self–education

In an effort to open up this didactic approach to a larger audience and to encourage borderless experimentation and critical thinking, the materiability research network[1] was established as an Internet platform in 2012. The network is essentially an educational community site and constantly growing database, which reveals these materials both on a theoretical level and in a DIY hands–on approach as basic tutorials. The aim of the network is to reveal potentials and opportunities, to provide open access and inspiration, and to offer a stage for its members to actively engage in the discourse by displaying their own experiments and reviewing each other's work.

open access

Currently the collection includes details and tutorials on ferrofluids, thermochromics, bioluminescence, aerogels, soft robotics, dye–sensitized solar cells, electroactive polymers, bioplastics, polymorph plastics, electroluminescent displays, piezocrystals, and algae photobioreactors. Since the materials come from various areas of research the aim of this database is not to clearly identify and categorize them as such but rather to demystify and reveal their complexity while fostering interdisciplinary exchange and cooperation; in a broader sense, empowering people to become intellectually independent from industrially available resources.

SMART MATERIAL PROJECTS To test and evaluate these materials and fabrication techniques a number of speculative smart material installations have been realized during student courses and workshops. The following projects emerged from a rather naive curiosity in technological progress and scientific phenomena and were created in a context during which real–world limitations were deliberately avoided to provide space for playful and integrative experimentation.

workshop

---

1 See http://www.materiability.com/.

SHAPESHIFT (2010) *ShapeShift* looked at the use of dielectric elastomers to create dynamic spatial applications. While the main application of dielectric elastomers is to produce artificial muscles, the students focused on highlighting their quality as dynamic surface material. Each element within the structure consisted of a pre–stretched film that was attached to flexible acrylic frames and sandwiched between two compliant electrodes. Once a high DC voltage (3–5 kV) was applied, the film was compressed, which led to a planar expansion of the membrane. Since the membrane was attached to the flexible acrylic frame, the frame bent when the material was in its relaxed state and flattened out when the tension was removed during actuation. Through connecting a multitude of components together, a dynamic configuration could be achieved that resulted in a feasible self–supporting structure / fig.34 p.185 /.

artificial muscle

PHOTOTROPIA (2012) During *Phototropia* the focus was to self–produce all materials that were used in the project to prove a certain independence from industry and the market. This included the making of electroactive polymers, electroluminescent displays, eco–friendly bioplastics, and thin–film dye–sensitized solar cells. The elements were combined into an autonomous installation that generated all its required energy from sunlight and responded to user presence through moving and illuminating elements. The produced energy was stored in batteries below a base platform and distributed via microcontrollers to the respective elements. Since all elements in this project were self–made, their durability and performance did not reach their maximum potential. Consequently a number of industrially produced dye–solar cells had to be integrated in order to achieve the required voltage / fig.35 p.185 // fig.36 p.185 /.

solar cell

RESINANCE (2013) The formal design of *Resinance* was strongly influenced by the behavior of basic organic life forms and particularly the formation of cellular colonies. It consisted of forty active elements produced from a polyester resin and enhanced with thermochromic pigments that were touch–sensitive and had the ability to change their surface color correspondingly. The color change was achieved through heating and cooling a liquid inside the hollow elements. The temperature inside the containers was constantly measured, which allowed it to be mapped precisely onto certain color schemes. The state of each element was perpetually communicated to its nearest neighbors. Therefore the tactile input not only changed the touched element but was also transmitted throughout the whole assembly, resulting in steadily evolving patterns / fig.37 p.187 /.

color change

RESINANCE 2.0 (2013) *Resinance 2.0* was the successor of *Resinance* and built upon the initial installation with improved behavioral complexity and technical and material resilience. The layout of the installation was changed to a linear arrangement consisting of ten clusters, each containing three elements. The sensing capabilities of the individual elements were simplified by embedding a capacitive metallic mesh into the polyester resin walls. Moreover the exchange of information between the individual clusters was changed to wireless communication and a visual interface graphically represented every element, its current temperature, how often it had been touched, and what its status was in the network / fig.38 p.187 // fig.39 p.187 /.

CONCLUSION The world, environment, and society are constantly changing at an ever–faster pace. Borders are dissolving, whether they're political, cultural, or sexual. People are becoming educationally and vocationally more flexible but yet specific, less geographically and domestically committed but at the same time increasingly addicted to continuous medial input, social connectivity, and an abundance of information. Since architecture is omnipresent and permanent during every stage of life, it carries a great responsibility to address and respond to these advancements. This not only means the incorporation and adaptation of new technologies, among which smart materials will certainly play a lead role, but also the effort to reach beyond dogmatic paradigms like longevity, stability, and performance for the creation of softer, more dynamic environments. Such progress is hard to implement since it has to arise from intrinsic aspirations and not imposed sanctions; thus new models for education and especially interdisciplinary collaboration and communication are necessary. The proposed materiability approach provides a viable method to reveal innovation in an open way and develop a language for open exchange based on emerging techno–social phenomena.

references

+ Fox, Michael and Miles Kemp (2009) Interactive Architecture. New York: Princeton Architectural Press.
+ Lochmatter, Patrick (2007) "Development of a Shell–Like Electroactive Polymer (EAP) Actuator." PhD diss., ETH Zurich.
+ Lakenbrink, Hubert (2012) Smart Building Materials for the Future Smart Material Houses. Available from: http://www.iba–hamburg.de/en/themes–projects/the–building–exhibition–within–the–building–exhibition/smart–material–houses/projekt/smart–material–houses.html. Accessed: January 21, 2014.
+ Vitruvius (2009) On Architecture. Trans. Richard Schofield. London: Penguin Classics.
+ Le Corbusier (2009) Towards a New Architecture. Miami: BN Publishing.
+ Jeska, Simone (2008) Transparent Plastics: Technology and Design. Basel: Birkhäuser.

Adapting Matter

Martina Decker
/ Assistant Professor, College of Architecture and Design, NJIT, Material Dynamics Lab.
/ Partner, Decker Yeadon LLC, New York City.

Adaptive architectures that can react to a variety of inputs, whether they originate from human interventions or the natural surroundings, have been greatly advanced by emergent materials—in particular, smart materials. What distinguishes smart materials from traditional architectural materials is that they can react to an external stimulus with a very particular material response. They can utilize inputs such as thermal differentials, light photons, chemicals, magnetic fields, or electric currents. The material response that ensues is a significant transformation of their properties, resulting in, for example, a change in color, luminosity, shape, volume, or the production of an electric current.

Artificial muscles, such as dielectric electroactive polymers, are polymorphic smart materials that consist of a polymer core sandwiched between two electrodes / fig.40 p.188 /. They respond to the electrostatic forces that are applied to these electrodes with a significant shape change. They have inspired architects and designers to create a variety of architectural interventions, such as smart facade designs. The *Homeostatic Facade System* by Decker Yeadon LLC can guide daylight into our buildings or control solar heat gain[2] / fig.41 p.188 /. The lightweight actuator design that is embedded in a double–skin facade system can flex and bend through the application of a high–voltage differential along any point of the ribbon–like installation. The design affords us a very high degree of control over the amount and the direction of sunlight that enters into the building through architectural glazing / fig.42 p.188 // fig.43 p.189 /.

Shape–memory alloys are another example of a polymorphic smart material and have also been proven to control the amount of solar energy that enters into our interior spaces. They react solely to ambient room temperatures and can control solar heat gain without needing computing devices, sensors, or electricity. The material itself has all these functions programmed into its matter on a molecular scale.

Working with these material motors is quite unlike working with mechanical actuators that architects and designers have been utilizing in their respective

---

2 "Homeostatic Facade System by Decker Yeadon LLC," last modified December 30, 2010, http://www.youtube.com/watch?v=7CThFRt95aI.

disciplines. Nanotechnology has afforded us a detailed understanding of materials at an individual molecular scale and is of great assistance in designing with these emergent material technologies. Comprehending the inner workings of these materials is of the utmost importance, especially when we are designing interactive and reactive environments in which high–performance materials are fully integrated into material assemblies in order to perfectly position them to perform as expected.

For instance, the previously mentioned shape–memory alloys gain their memory from their particular crystalline structure that is transformed when the ambient temperature changes. The packing arrangement of the atoms can be deformed at low temperatures by one to eight percent and will return to its original state upon reheating the material. The resulting deformation can be put to great use, but the nickel titanium alloy has to be protected in the actuator assembly from external forces. If the alloys are excessively deformed their lifespan is greatly reduced and their memory can only be restored in an energy–intensive process by heating up the material to its annealing temperature. This process will force the atoms back into their pristine crystalline packing order.

Beyond the point of merely understanding a material, nanotechnology has also brought us the power to actively manipulate matter at the minute scale. We now have the capability to adapt matter if we think the performance of a particular substance is lacking, and the examples of newly designed materials and composites that are being developed in laboratories worldwide are impressive. Great advancements have been demonstrated in the area of flexible electronics in the last decade. Sensors, for example, can simply be applied to flexible substrates in an ink–jet printing process. And the abovementioned dielectric electroactive polymers would not exist without the flexible and even stretchable electrodes that are essential for their performance and at the same time determine the extent of their shape change. As designers, we do not have to contend only with a material palette that has been used in the discipline for decades. We can now, in collaboration with the STEM (science, technology, engineering, and mathematics) fields, work actively on the future of architectural materials and explore the new possibilities they afford us.

Active and reactive materials can create new interfaces between architecture and their environments that rise beyond the electromechanical gateways we are accustomed to. Emergent material interfaces can establish an extension to our own bodies or connect our buildings with their surroundings. They can create environments that are deeply rooted in intimacy and touch, as Philip Beesley's work quite exquisitely demonstrates, or offer a physical manifestation of digital public spaces by transforming building facades into media–rich digital landscapes (Zarzycki 2010). But one of the most significant promises of emergent materials in adaptive architectures is in the challenge set forth by climate change (Roaf et al. 2010). This largely human–induced trend transforms our global weather patterns with severe consequences for our society, economy, and the environment. Our cities and buildings in particular will have to respond to more frequent extreme–weather events such as thunderstorms, tornadoes, heavy or freezing rain, heavy snowfalls, high wind speeds, extreme temperature, or hurricanes. It is of great importance that we adapt our architectures to these upcoming changes in global weather patterns to create new, resilient buildings. Smart materials that harvest energy from a variety of sources in their environment can serve as embedded systems of redundancy that do not rely on existing urban infrastructures. This could significantly improve the resilience of cities, while not losing track of the fact that we can no longer squander our resources or add to the atmospheric carbon that contributed to the climate issues in the first place.

Whether our intentions for the use of novel materials are born out of the desire for a new intimacy with our built environment or out of the necessity to preserve and protect our cities, it will require an effort across many disciplines to implement these emergent material technologies. The next generation of designers and architects would have to adopt an interdisciplinary vocabulary and language that has to be developed by, and will be grounded in, an interdisciplinary cooperation. To create future adaptive architectures we must be prepared to open up the design process to greater transparency and make it easily accessible to the multiple disciplines from the STEM fields as well as the construction industry.

Interdisciplinary endeavors that strive to accelerate the evolution of advanced materials are seen in projects such as the Materials Genome Initiative, undoubtedly inspired by the well–known and well–established Human Genome Project. This unprecedented research effort successfully completed its international and highly collaborative undertaking in early 2003 and created a sequence and map of all human genes. While the human genome is the complete and extraordinarily complex blueprint for our own body's growth and development, the materials genome will be a blueprint for materials innovation and advancements. As announced by the United States National Science and Technology Council in June 2011, the Materials Genome Initiative will devise new methods of collaboration and create new tools and research infrastructures. They include computational tools for advanced simulations, experimental tools, a digital collection of materials data, and collaborative networks. One of the goals is to optimize the process of discovery, development, property optimization, systems design, systems integration, certification, manufacturing, and deployment in order to cut down the time it takes to implement new materials by at least fifty percent. Another objective of the undertaking is to significantly reduce the cost of the entire materials–development continuum from the laboratory to the commercial marketplace (NSTC 2011).

The desperately sought–after data transparency and communication strategies for the materials community that the Materials Genome Initiative can offer will equip innovative architects and product designers with tools that go well beyond the advanced materials libraries that we use today. Apart from becoming merely informed about current standards, we will also be able to participate in the creation of a new generation of architectural materials that have been developed explicitly for our upcoming global challenges in architecture.

references

+ National Science and Technology Council (2011) "Materials Genome Initiative for Global Competitiveness." Washington DC: Executive Office of the President.
+ Roaf Sue, David Crichton, and Fergus Nicol (2010) "Designing Buildings and Cities for 3°C of Climate Change." In: Adapting Buildings and Cities for Climate Change. Second edition. Oxford: Architectural Press, pp. 344–68.
+ Zarzycki, Andrzej (2010) "Wall to Wall: the Digital Landscape." In: Architecture Boston, 13(3), pp. 28–31.

Bioluminescence:
Toward Design with Living Light

Nicola Burggraf
/ Product Designer and Bioluminescence Artist.
/ Graduate with distinction from the University of Art and Design (HfG) Offenbach am Main.

---

lighting design

Current lighting design primarily deals with artificial electric light sources. As the incandescent light bulb is phased out in favor of more energy–efficient alternatives, it clears the way for light emitting diodes (LEDs), light sources that have a very long lifetime while using a fraction of the energy of a light bulb. Light sources such as LED can be digitally controlled and connected in networks, which allows the designer to create a scenography of light that adapts to various situations and is accessible only when needed. As a result, lighting design heads toward individualization and adaptivity, using light only where and when it is needed. Innovative lighting will interact with the user and will adapt automatically instead of waiting for manual impulses (Müller 2006).

Bioluminescence, the ability of living organisms to produce light, offers a novel approach to design with light. No artificial illuminant so far can compete with bioluminescence in terms of energy efficiency. The following essay discusses the potential of bioluminescence for design as well as the constraints and chances in working with "living material."

BIOLOGICAL ILLUMINANTS All known phenomena of bioluminescence are based on a chemical reaction within the cells of the organisms, and can be therefore categorized as chemoluminescence. Most bioluminescent reactions are based on a luciferin/luciferase principle. The substrate luciferin combines with the enzyme luciferase (acting as the catalyst) and oxidizes under the presence

cold light

of oxygen. The released energy is given off as cold light (Pieribone and Gruber 2005). Bioluminescence can either be primary, when the organism is able to produce light itself, or secondary, when the organism lives in a symbiotic relationship with a biological illuminant (e.g., bacteria). The female anglerfish, for example, is a deep–sea predator that attracts prey by a glowing lure dangling in front of its mouth—a modified dorsal–fin spine containing a packet of luminescent bacteria at its tip (Pieribone and Gruber 2005). Bioluminescent organisms are rather rare on land—there are, among others, the well–known fireflies (*lampyridae*) and luminous fungi. However, in the complete darkness of the deep sea, over ninety percent of the animals are bioluminescent (Pieribone and Gruber 2005). Marine bioluminescence mostly occurs in the blue/green light spectrum as those wavelengths travel the furthest in seawater. Biological light is a means of optical communication to manipulate the behavior of other organisms. Its main functions are searching for prey, finding mates, deterring predators, or camouflage. The following sections concentrate for the most part on marine bioluminescence.

communication

STIMULUS With the exception of bacteria that glow permanently, all luminescent marine organisms have precise control of their light emission. In the complete darkness of the deep sea, producing light at the wrong time can be a deadly mistake (Latz 2009). Thus, more advanced bioluminescent creatures developed complex mechanisms to enhance their light output. Specialized cells or organs can block, filter, reflect, direct, or channel the light. Creatures that harbor luminescent bacteria keep them in special organs with a shutter that can be opened and closed to control the emission of light. Single-celled organisms, such as dinoflagellates, emit light in all directions. The light originates from microsomes, "scintillons," which are distributed within their cell (Pieribone and Gruber 2005). The research into the potentials of bioluminescence presented here centers around the marine organism *Pyrocystis lunula*, which belongs to the diverse clade of dinoflagellates / **fig.44** p.191 / that populate the illuminated zones of the ocean. Ninety percent of the species are phytoplankton, some of which are also bioluminescent. Each cell is able to produce multiple flashes of bluish light until all of the luciferine is oxidized. One flash lasts for about one tenth of a second. "The time from stimulus to light emission is less than 20ms, making it one of the most rapid cellular processes known" (Latz 2009).

Pyrocystis lunula

Dinoflagellates emit light when they are disturbed. Their bioluminescence is an immediate cellular reaction to certain hydrodynamic movements—e.g., created by fish, dolphins, divers, ships, or breaking waves. Normal seas do not trigger a light reaction, as it would be inefficient for the organism to permanently light up. Due to their microscopic scale and slow motion, dinoflagellates experience the movements of the ocean as shear force. It used to be assumed that the light reaction could only be triggered by the quickly changing and chaotic properties of turbulence. However it is now proven that laminar flow can trigger bioluminescence (Latz and Rohr 2000). Dinoflagellates can therefore be considered tracer particles that flash only when suitable levels of shear stress are present, whether the flow field is laminar or turbulent (Latz and Rohr 2000). To instrumentalize bioluminescence, underwater shear forces need to be produced synthetically. During my research, different mechanisms to trigger turbulences have been empirically explored (Burggraf 2009), ranging from tilting, shaking, stirring, pouring, and rotating various containers filled with a salt-water medium containing Pyrocystis lunula in differing cell densities. The bioluminescence of dinoflagellates is controlled by a circadian rhythm: it occurs at night, while in daytime, the organisms perform photosynthesis. In the lab, this rhythm can be shifted so that the organisms emit light when needed. However, there needs to be sufficient hours of illumination and recovery. Furthermore, dinoflagellates require nourishment provided by an enriched salt-water medium. The potential of dinoflagellate luminescence is not

turbulence

photosynthesis

brightness. Measurements that I took during tests with 200 ml of dinoflagellates showed an illuminance of 0.6 lx (Burggraf 2009). The brightness may vary with cell density and the amount of liquid agitated.

TRANSFER In the following section, I present two design projects that derived from the insights of the preceding research, utilizing dinoflagellates as a living light source. They differ in the setup as well as the trigger mechanism.

BIOLUMINESCENT FIELD, 2010 The installation was presented during the *Luminale* 2010, the Frankfurt Lighting Culture Biennale / fig.45 p.191 /. Visitors entered a darkened room with a field of eighty thin poles carrying delicate glass vials filled with a salt–water medium that contained a dense concentration of dinoflagellates. A reactive floor passed the visitor's movements on to the poles, which produced slight turbulences in the vials. The algae immediately responded with ephemeral flashes of blue light. Each cell acted as a motion sensor to the disturbance caused by the visitors. Visitors could be seen as intruders in a "bioluminescent minefield," activating the cells to set off alarm signals whenever they detected movement.

INTERFERENCE, 2012

> "In attempting to observe the phenomena of vibration, one repeatedly feels a spontaneous urge to make the processes visible and to provide ocular evidence of their nature. [...] However great the power of the ear to stir the emotions, [...] the sense of hearing cannot attain that clarity of consciousness which is native to that of sight."
>
> Hans Jenny, 2001 (p. 21)

Whereas in *Bioluminescent Field* the light emission was triggered through interaction with the visitors, the project *Interference*, designed for the *Luminale* 2012, sought to explore the possibility of triggering light reactions via acoustic waves and vice versa, rendering sound visible. Visitors witnessed a scenography of biological light deriving from a cube in the center of a darkened room / fig.46 p.193 /, as a dense population of bioluminescent algae in 3.2 liters of a salt–water medium was exposed to a composition of acoustic impulses. Specific frequencies stimulated the microorganisms to emit punctuated flashes of bluish light as an immediate response to the sound. In otherwise complete darkness, the audience experienced sound waves as they were rendered visible by the living organisms / fig.47 p.193 /. Activating frequencies ranged between 12–35 Hz and were combined with higher–frequency sound elements, which did not trigger light emission but helped to create a holistic sound experience. To prevent depleting the cells' ability to emit light, each sound cycle lasted for 3:39 minutes followed by a pause of fifteen minutes. Constant stimulation with maximum light output was avoided in favor of a subtler composition of alternating frequency levels. Interference explores the threshold of frequencies that create enough force to stimulate a light emission. Each microscopic organism can be seen as a small–scale autonomous sensor making vibration visible in real time.

POTENTIAL A novel approach to lighting design introduces the possibility of working with biological light sources. The actual material—that is, the organism— stays untouched in the process; the light output is indirectly controlled by designing the organisms' environment and the interaction with the trigger mechanism. Therefore, the designer needs to follow a more systemic methodology, managing environmental input, visual output, and the system's internal parameters, such as vital necessities.

biological light

Both installations presented here work solely with biological light and display a unique visual light experience. Glowing dinoflagellates perform as luminous pixels or particles giving real–time feedback of fluid flow patterns. Although they are purely biological, both installations have a very digital appearance.

Implementing bioluminescent organisms in design applications is possible, but within limits. It calls for a sensitive approach, always bearing in mind that the "material" is a living organism. Considering all the parameters presented here, bioluminescence offers a potential for future light design that requires a higher degree of interdisciplinary collaboration.

collaboration

references

+ Burggraf, Nicola (2009) Bioluminszenz. Zur Gestaltung biologischen Lichts. Offenbach am Main: Hochschule für Gestaltung.
+ Jenny, Hans (2001) Cymatics: A Study of Wave Phenomena and Vibration. Newmarket: B&W Publishing.
+ Latz, Michael (2009) "Dinoflagellates and Red Tides." Available at: http://siobiolum.ucsd.edu/dino_intro.html. Accessed: July 15, 2009.
+ Latz, Michael, and Jim Rohr (2000) "Flow–Stimulated Bioluminescence." In: Proceedings of the 11th International Symposium on Bioluminescence and Chemoluminescence. Singapore.
+ Müller, Vanessa Joan (2006) "Effizienz und Energie." In: Peter Weibel & Gregor Jansen, eds. Lichtkunst aus Kunstlicht. Ostfildern–Ruit: Hatje Cantz Verlag, pp. 684–89.
+ Pieribone, Vincent, and David F. Gruber (2005) Aglow in the Dark: The Revolutionary Science of Biofluorescence. Cambridge, MA: President and Fellows of Harvard College.

Smart Materials: Designing a Timescape of Interconnectivity for more Resilient Practices of Inhabitation

Aurélie Mossé
/ Textile Designer & Researcher, CITA, Royal Danish Academy of Fine Arts, Copenhagen.
/ Part–time Lecturer, École Nationale Supérieur des Arts Décoratifs, Paris.

---

interactivity

This essay is an abridged versions of two chapters integrated in the PhD thesis *Gossamer Tales: Designing Self–Actuated Textiles for the Home*, developed at the Royal Danish Academy of Fine Arts, School of Architecture. It explores the conceptualization and materialization of smart materials for the design of a more sustainable home. In the first part of the text, I emphasize the intellectual framework of interactivity through which smart materials have been traditionally appropriated and its inappropriateness in a sustainable context. Through the description of *Reef*, a self–actuated ceiling changing with the wind, I suggest the concept of interconnectivity as a more fruitful framework for appropriating smart materials in the perspective of more resilient practices of inhabitations / **fig.48 p.194** // **fig.49 p.195** /.

#48
#49

DESIGNING WITH SMART MATERIALS Smart materials represent a relatively new set of technologies that are progressively being integrated into everyday life. They define a very unique field of research and innovation concerned with the development of performative materials that are enriching traditional families with a new set of dynamic possibilities. Changing color or shape, emitting light or sound, producing electricity, among other functions, they inherit their active capabilities from recent advancements in material science and engineering. As they transform themselves over time, these behavioral materials not only offer new functions and new modes of expressions but they also affect, as with any technology, the perception of the world: how it is conceptualized and experienced.

material science

By introducing movement and change—and therefore time—as an essential dimension of their presence, smart materials not only challenge the traditional categorization of man–made artifacts, they also challenge the practices of design. In contrast with dancers or musicians, designers and architects are not usually trained to express ideas through temporal concepts and qualities. Bound to static materials and modes of representations, traditional design methods—from drawings to prototypes—privilege the development of ideas in space and matter (Addington and Schodek 2005). In this context, the temporality of the design object is rarely questioned, except concerning its lifetime. In architecture, this primarily relates to the resistance of the building to passing time and the desire to inscribe it in a logic of permanence. In the design industry, the temporality of materials is essentially apprehended in terms of its endurance to use and its relationship with trends. Smart materials stand outside of the temporal conventions of these two fields. They are conceived as intrinsically dynamic, developed through longer cycles of production, and inscribed in a logic of adaptation. Yet, as soon as materials are perceived as behaving in time, the design process can hardly be restricted to questions of form, function, or aesthetics, and it inevitably questions the temporal characteristics of the object: how it unfolds in time, at which pace and rhythm, through which typology and patterns of movement, etc. Designing with smart materials therefore implies an investigation into the concepts, methods, and know–how through which designers can explore the temporal dimensions of their creation. The question encompasses not only how designers design when materials become dynamic but also what kind of time they are designing through these materials. This latter question is of prime interest in a sustainable context, since contemporary philosophers, sociologists, and environmentalists have pointed out the instrumental role of industrial conceptions of time in harming the environment. Yet designers rarely question the impact of their creations on the construction of the social timescape and their consequences for the environment. In the light of the increasing pressures on nature and society—embodied, for instance, in climate change and the disappearance of fossil fuels—it therefore becomes essential to question the kind of time we are inserting into the everyday while designing and implementing smart materials.

TIMESCAPE OF INTERACTIVITY To do so, I propose to use the notion of timescape developed by Cardiff University professor of social sciences Barbara Adam. She defines the concept as "the record of a reality–generating activity" acknowledging "the space–time–matter interdependency of human reality while foregrounding its temporal dimension"; in other words, a cultural representation of reality focused on time (Adam 1998, pp. 11, 54). This means that technology is understood not only as the appropriation of a scientific fact into a series of techniques or applications that can be acquired but also as a cultural medium, an agent of social reconfiguration affecting all dimensions of human experience. Beyond the internal dynamics at stake within smart materials, I therefore propose to discuss time as a sociocultural perception shaped by specific theories, tools, and habits.

The timescape induced by smart materials has been traditionally conceived through the intellectual framework of interactivity, which is to say the whole set of interactions made possible by embedded computing. Interactivity emerged as a concept in the field of cybernetics to describe the capacity or extent in which two systems exchange information, particularly referring to computer–human interactions. In the context of the home, interactivity became a reality when the computer was democratized and personal and portable devices were integrated in the 1980s as domestic–monitoring systems that allowed, for instance, to control lighting or heating remotely. (Addington and Schodek 2005; Fox and Kemp 2009; Riley 1999). Today, this domestic interactivity is taking an architectural dimension as smart materials and embedded computing make possible the materialization of an architecture that can adapt to changes in the environment (Beesley et al. 2006; Bonnemaison and Macy 2007; Bullivant 2006; Fox and Kemp 2009). In this perspective, the home becomes increasingly perceived as a "permeable structure, receiving and transmitting images, sounds, texts, data" (Riley 1999, p. 11) up to the point that sociocultural commentators talk of an extroverted perception of the home.

> "What we call home is increasingly defined by what is outside, not by what is within—including inputs from all kind of communication networks. Home is the place where we ingest all this information [or imported goods], all of this foreignness."
>
> David Morley, 2000 (p. 195)

INTERACTIVITY IN A SUSTAINABLE CONTEXT When it comes to addressing the stakes of sustainability, smart materiality becomes particularly problematic. Within the field of design and architecture, sustainability is predominantly understood as a practice aimed at reducing and minimizing the impacts of human actions on the environment. Yet sustainability is not only an issue of space and matter but more fundamentally a temporal aspect: that of "[understanding] what we are sustaining, for how long and in whose interest are we sustaining it for" (Devall 2008). In this context, the ways we understand and appropriate time become critical. Despite efforts to develop energy–harvesting and energy–generating materials emphasizing the potential of renewable energies, smart materials still have a very low visibility within the sustainable design debate. This can be largely explained by the fact that smart materials are hardly recyclable; often made out of rare or toxic materials, they rely on energy–demanding processes of fabrication or actuation. Yet I argue that the way we conceptualize and appropriate smart materials' interactive properties is equally problematic.

Traditionally, interactivity within the home embodies a set of experiences essentially concerned with a user–oriented time–space based on human–machine dependences. It has been used as a commercial argument without a real technical foundation to promote more intimate relationships between humans and machines (Guéneau 2005). If interactivity represents for the home a door opened toward the exterior, this openness is rather selective. It is much more concerned with semiotic consumption, commercial transactions, or sociocultural exchanges than a permeability opened to the temporality and context of nature.

In fact, such experiences of interactivity ritualize a timescape inherited from the Industrial Revolution in which time is apprehended as a standardized, abstractable, and measurable reality completely disconnected from the rhythms of nature. They have been notably conveyed into the everyday by the clock, the computer, and their associated practices. Together, they have contributed to the construction of the postmodern timescape as an overstimulating, deterritorialized, and compressed experience of time (Adam 1998; Hoffman 2009). Despite the implications of this temporal framework in the development of ecological problems, smart materials remain primarily informed by theories, intentions, and values that have underpinned most technological developments since the Industrial Revolution—in short, the understanding of technology as a mean to control and overcome the limitations imposed by nature. These assumptions have consequences that stand in opposition to the dynamics of earthly existence. Thereby I argue that as long as smart materials are informed by disembodied and deterritorialized conceptions of time, they will continue to take part in the development of environmental hazards.

technology

REEF: IMAGINING A TIMESCAPE OF INTERCONNECTIVITY

The design experiment *Reef* reflects on these temporal issues by exploring how values of interconnectivity can be embodied at the core of smart materiality using the home as a design context and an electroactive polymers cloud as a supporting technology. It is an attempt to appropriate smart materials through a more sustainable framework for thinking their interaction.

interconnectivity

Grounded in the context of a dynamic architecture, *Reef* builds upon architectural practices that understand the built environment as the design of an ecology and interaction beyond issues of control. As a tale, *Reef* explores the idea of a self–actuated ceiling changing with the wind. The name is inspired from the world of sailing—evoking the part of a sail that can be tied or rolled up to be smaller in a strong wind. Between sky and earth, the installation embodies a space of mediation where, like the sail subject to the unpredictability and variation of air, *Reef's* components fold and unfold as they sense wind. It works as a metaphor seeking to explore new ways of conceptualizing actuation. As opposed to the sail designed to control the speed and stability of the ship, *Reef* explores territories beyond functionality, where the primacy of the user fades to imagine a landscape of negotiation, of shared respirations.

ecology

functionality

As a material system, the architectural installation is a journey across scale from the exchange of electrons to the design of active components and their orchestration as a dynamic environment. At the molecular and component level, the installation relies on the design of adaptive minimum–energy structures. These structures are made out of dielectric elastomers, a specific family of electroactive polymer that change and stretch when they are exposed to high voltages. Hanging from the ceiling, these structures compose the central element of this aerial canopy. Digitally crafted, the ceiling gathers both active and passive structures. Passive structures shiver by responding to indoor airflow, while active structures open and close according to wind fluctuations in the exterior environment. They are materially distinguished by the black conductive coating, allowing active structures to become dynamic. To make the active structures respond to wind speed, an interactive digital circuit was developed. The circuit is based on an anemometer, sensing the speed of the wind. This information is translated into digital inputs for a microcontroller unit to regulate two high voltage amplifiers. These devices directly control the actuation of the electroactive network of adaptive minimum energy structures / fig.50 p.195 /.

From a design perspective, the issue was not so much to explore how to build the installation as to question how to design its temporal qualities. Intentions lay in developing a direct and instantaneous translation of outdoor dynamics through a cloud of electroactive polymers opening and closing according to wind speed / fig.51 p.195 /. The intention was to reconnect the home with natural temporality. This was tested through the building of an architectural demonstrator developed as a 210 x 310 cm surface composed of fifty–two passive and active minimum energy structures. These structures were developed across five sizes ranging from a diameter in flat configuration of ten to about fifty centimeters. The pace of aperture and closure of the structures embodies the velocity of the wind in the exterior. Within this setting, light wind conditions were translated by the aperture of the two biggest component sizes. Medium winds ranging from a strong breeze to a gale were embodied by the opening and closure of the three smallest structure sizes. Strong wind conditions were transposed by the activation of the whole set of the adaptive minimum energy structures. Each wind family (light, medium, strong) was itself subdivided into more refined transcriptions.

CONCLUSION As an experiment, *Reef* works as a way to pose questions on the construction of our everyday timescapes and the values through which smart technologies are appropriated, as much as it works as a possible solution for materializing interconnectivity within the home. By embodying a home that feels, breathes, and quivers at the pace of nature, *Reef* seeks to promote a renewed intimacy with nature by reconnecting the interior with an awareness of its exterior environment. By materializing the presence of the wind within the interior, *Reef* operates a transfer in which the inhabitant is not in control of, but exposed and subject to, the rhythms of nature. This shift expresses the need for technology to synchronize with the time of nature as a means to reintroduce a culture in which technology is less human–centered than interconnected with the earth. Here technology becomes the medium through which the natural world can make its voice heard, affirming its presence in a space from which it has long been excluded. *Reef* reconnects the same technologies—which, irrespective of natural temporalities, have contributed to a disembodied and deterritorialized experience of time—with the variable and unpredictable dynamics of nature. As such, *Reef* contributes to the thinking of an architecture that is alive by suggesting that the concept of interconnectivity—understood as interactions framed by an embodied temporality underpinned by earth–life interdependences—is a more relevant framework for thinking the design and appropriation of smart materials in the perspective of more sustainable practices of inhabitation. It highlights that sustainability is in the first place a temporal issue that cannot avoid going beyond modern assumptions—the concepts, theories, values, and experiences through which time is usually grasped in Western societies. Ultimately *Reef* emphasizes that an architecture that is alive is not only one that is dynamic, but one that is aware of its interdependencies with nature and its inhabitants.

sustainability

references

+ Adam, Barbara (1998) Timescapes of Modernity: The Environment and Invisible Hazards. London: Routledge.
+ Addington, Michelle, and Daniel Schodek (2005) Smart Materials and Technologies for the Architecture and Design Professions. Oxford: Architectural Press.
+ Beesley, Philip, Sachiko Kirosue, Jim Ruxton, Marion Trankle, and Camille Turner (2006) Responsive Architectures, Subtle Technologies. Cambridge: Riverside Architectural Press.
+ Bonnemaison, Sara, and Christine Macy (2007) Responsive Textile Environments. Halifax: TUNS Press.
+ Bullivant, Lucy (2006) Responsive Environments: Architecture, Art and Design. London: V & A Publications.
+ Devall, Bill (2008) "The Unsustainability of Sustainability." Culture Change. Available from: http://www.culturechange.org/issue19/unsustainability.htm.
+ Fox, Michael, and Miles Kemp (2009) Interactive Architecture. New York: Princeton Architectural Press.
+ Guéneau, Catherine (2005) L'intéractivité: une définition introuvable. Communication et langages 145, pp. 117–29.
+ Hoffman, Eva (2009) Time. London: Profile Books.
+ Morley, David (2000) Home Territories: Media, Mobility and Identity. London: Routledge.
+ Riley, Terence (1999) The Un–private House. New York: Museum of Modern Art.

The Unconventional Electronics Approach to the Internet of Things

John Sarik
/ Electrical Engineer at Xenex, San Antonio.
/ Co–Founder of Lumiode, Inc., New York.

Moore's Law

Technological progress in the electronics industry has been traditionally measured by transistor counts. In 1965 Intel cofounder Gordon E. Moore observed that the number of transistors on integrated circuits doubled approximately every two years, and thus Moore's Law was born. Conventional, silicon–based electronics technology has mostly followed Moore's Law and the results have been revolutionary. Advances in non–silicon–based, unconventional electronics have been often overlooked. Unconventional electronics are an important complement to conventional electronics and the combination of the two will enable new smart materials and smart objects that will transform our environment.

open–source

The Columbia Laboratory for Unconventional Electronics (CLUE), led by Ioannis Kymissis, creates optoelectronic and sensing devices based on organic and other thin–film materials. Unlike devices based on conventional electronics, these devices can be large, flexible, nonplanar, or grown directly on unusual substrates. CLUE has developed a collection of devices, such as transistors, light–emitting diodes, photodetectors, photovoltaics, batteries, and piezoelectric and ferroelectric elements, which can be easily integrated into complex systems. Additionally, CLUE is working to make these devices accessible outside of the traditional laboratory environment using novel materials and fabrication techniques and open–source software and hardware (Sarik and Kymissis 2011; Sarik and Kymissis 2010). Developing unconventional electronics isn't just about using non–silicon materials; it's also about imaging new approaches to designing, fabricating, and using electronics.

Internet of Things

Proposed Internet of Things solutions demonstrate the difference between the conventional and unconventional approaches. At the 2014 International CES consumer technology fair, Intel demonstrated the Edison, an SD card–sized computer with a 400 MHz processor and integrated Wi–Fi and Bluetooth. The conventional vision for the Internet of Things is to connect everyday objects directly to the World Wide Web. The upside is the ability to autonomously perform computationally expensive tasks and communicate directly with a server; the downside is increased complexity, cost, power consumption, and size of the necessary electronics. Moreover, objects that are constantly connected to the Internet raise significant privacy and security concerns. The unconventional electronics vision for the Internet of Things is to only connect everyday objects to each other and their users. This can be accomplished using smaller, lighter, less power hungry electronics that can be better integrated to match the form factor of everyday objects. Creating more ubiquitous local networks will give users more control over their environment and the objects within it.

To enable these networks, CLUE and collaborators are developing Energy Harvesting Active Networked Tags (EnHANTs), a new type of wireless device in the domain between RFIDs and traditional wireless sensor networks (Gorlatova et al. 2009; Margolies et al. 2013). EnHANTs will be small, flexible, and self–powered devices that can be attached to objects that are traditionally not networked. Like RFID tags, EnHANTs will be attached to everyday objects, such as books, keys, or clothing. However, EnHANTs will be active devices with their own power sources and communicate in a distributed multi–hop fashion. Compared to traditional wireless sensor networks, EnHANTs will operate at lower data rates, consume less energy, and transmit mostly ID information. The envisioned form factor for EnHANTs is shown in figure 1.

RFID

Fig. 1. A physical mock–up of an EnHANT that includes a functional thin–film solar cell and a functional thin–film battery.

EnHANTs will be used to permanently track objects' locations and their proximity to other objects. They will operate continuously, achieve pervasive coverage with multi–hop networking, and report on themselves and the EnHANTs around them. These EnHANT capabilities will make objects searchable and significantly simplify the organization of physical objects. For example, books in a library could be equipped with an EnHANT encoded with a unique ID. Nearby books would exchange ID information and the ID of any book that was not similar to its neighbors would be forwarded through the network of books to a sink node. This would allow librarians to quickly and easily identify books that are mis–shelved. In general, EnHANTs can be used to determine if a set of objects are in a desirable or undesirable configuration. Other examples include real–time inventory tracking, locating misplaced items, and locating survivors of disasters such as structural collapse.

Recent advances in ultra–low–power microprocessors, ultra–wideband (UWB) transceivers, and thin–film energy harvesting and storage devices will enable the realization of EnHANTs in the near future. To survive on harvested energy, EnHANTs devices will have to spend significantly less energy than Bluetooth,

energy harvesting

solar cell

Zigbee, and IEEE 802.15.4a devices. Light is typically the most abundant energy source, but the intensity of indoor illumination is three orders of magnitude less than the intensity of outdoor solar illumination. An EnHANT deployed in an indoor environment and equipped with a thin–film solar cell would only be able to harvest 1 J/cm^2 of energy per day (Gorlatova et al. 2011). Fortunately, the ultra–wideband impulse radio (UWB–IR) transceiver using an EnHANT will achieve energy consumption of less than 1 nJ/bit to transmit and 2–3 nJ/bit to receive, compared to 10–100 nJ/bit to transmit or receive for competing technologies. Based on these estimates, the tag shown in figure 1 would be able to support a continuous data rate of 10 kpbs, which is sufficient for the envisioned tracking applications.

The EnHANTs project can be divided into three main research areas: developing the energy harvesting, storage, and management system; developing the UWB transceivers; and developing energy–adaptive networking protocols. To fully understand the cross–layer interactions between these research areas the EnHANTs prototypes are being built from the ground up to integrate the new components and protocols. For example, when using a UWB–IR transceiver the energy required to receive a bit is higher than the energy required to transmit a bit. Legacy wireless networking protocols assume the opposite and therefore completely new protocols must be developed. The current prototypes, shown in figure 2, use thin–film pho-

multi–hop network

tovoltaics optimized for indoor light harvesting, form multi–hop networks using ultra–low–power UWB–IR transceivers, and implement novel energy harvesting adaptive networking protocols. While there is still much work to be done miniaturizing and productizing the EnHANTs prototypes, they demonstrate the viability of the unconventional Internet of Things approach.

Fig. 2. A current EnHANT prototype. The EnHANTs prototypes can efficiently harvest indoor light energy, form multi–hop networks, and implement novel energy harvesting adaptive networking protocols.

Ubiquitous, customized EnHANTs will enable smart spaces that will be populated with tags tailored to the specific needs of the space and its users. Consider the following vision for a smart research laboratory. The CLUE research laboratory is located on the main campus of Columbia University in Manhattan, where space is always at a premium. The lab is a shared space used by dozens of students, postdocs, and visiting researchers, and includes many different types of equipment, from a multimillion–dollar thin–film deposition system in a nitrogen glovebox to ten–cent resistors and everything in between. Keeping track of these objects in a shared space with users coming and going is extremely difficult, but it is necessary to ensure the lab remains functional and safe. All the chemicals in the lab must be tracked (currently this is done manually) to ensure that everything is stored and labeled properly, expired chemicals are properly disposed of in a timely manner, and the lab is in compliance with fire and safety regulations. Tagging all chemicals, electronics components, tools, and fabrication equipment with EnHANTs would greatly simplify and improve lab management.

But not all objects are created equal. Different objects will require tags with different functionalities and form factors. A tag for a chemical storage container needs to know its location in the lab, the amount of chemical left, and the chemical's expiration date, but it only needs to last until that expiration date. A tag for a hand tool only needs to know its location in the lab, but it needs to last for the entire life of the tool. A tag for shared equipment could use low–power, bistable display to tell the current user how much time they have left and who the next user will be. Where the objects are stored and used in the space will determine the environmental energy available to the tags. Tags on objects stored in fixed locations, such as tool chests or chemical storage cabinets, could harvest energy from fixed RF transmitters. Tags on objects that move around the lab could harvest energy from ambient light or their motion. Some spaces with large windows will receive copious amounts of natural light, but other spaces, such as the CLUE lab, have no windows and only receive fluorescent light. These energy–availability estimates are important to consider when designing tags to provide the right balance of the form and function.

tag

energy

Ultimately EnHANTs will be a building block in a larger Internet of Things ecosystem. Once the underlying technology has been refined and productized, continued research will focus on creating a modular, accessible platform. One prominent example of this platform approach is Arduino, which provides a complete, flexible, easy–to–use hardware and software platform that is widely used by artists, designers, and hobbyists of all experience levels. Novice users benefit from the numerous tutorials, extensive documentation, and robust community. Arduino is also powerful enough to enable more advanced users to develop complex systems. This has allowed the community to create a collection of "shields" and software libraries that extend the functionality of Arduino. The success of Arduino highlights the importance of accessibility, community, and an open–source approach.

Arduino

community

Many other platforms, such as Microsoft Gadgeteer, BugLabs, littlebits, and SeeedStudio Grove, are expanding on this plug–and–play approach to hardware development by developing a series of standardized modules and connectors. In the conventional electronics approach, the hardware modules are designed, fabricated, and then sent to the user, who must manually connect the modules for their application. The end user only has control over the connection process. Unconventional electronics will enable users to go beyond connecting modules and take control of the design and fabrication process. This will be made possible

plug–and–play

<aside>3-D printer</aside>

by the combination of two emerging technologies: 3–D printing and printable electronics. Today desktop 3–D printers that allow users to print a wide range of mechanical structures are affordable and accessible. Printable electronics based on unconventional electronics are well positioned for a similar mainstream adoption. Advances in materials and fabrication techniques will continue to increase the performance and affordability of both technologies. These two technologies have been largely independent, but combining them would enable exciting new possibilities that extend the personal factory concept to functional objects (Sarik et al. 2012).

<aside>collaboration</aside>

Ultimately, unconventional electronics will enable a new paradigm for smart spaces and the Internet of Things. The tags will adapt to the objects, not the other way around. This opens up many exciting possibilities for architects to integrate these technologies into the environment. As an engineer, I am excited by these technological advances, but I am even more excited to see these technologies deployed outside of the lab. It is imperative that engineers and architects establish strong collaborations to make this vision a reality. The role of engineers will be to create technology platforms that are robust, scalable, and accessible, and the role of the architects will be to understand the potential and limitations of these technologies and work to integrate them into the environment.

references

- Gorlatova, M., P. Kinget, I. Kymissis, D. Rubenstein, X. Wang, and G. Zussman (2009) "Challenge: Ultra–Low–Power Energy–Harvesting Active Networked Tags (EnHANTs)," ACM MOBICOM.
- Gorlatova, M., A. Wallwater, and G. Zussman (2011) "Networking Low Power Energy Harvesting Devices: Measurements and Algorithms," IEEE INFOCOM.
- Margolies, R., L. Pena, K. Kim, Y. Kim, M. Wang, M. Gorlatova, J. Sarik, J. Zhu, P. Kinget, I. Kymissis, and G. Zussman (2013) "An Adaptive Testbed of Energy Harvesting Active Networked Tags (EnHANTs) Prototypes," IEEE INFOCOM.
- Sarik, J., and I. Kymissis (2010) "Lab kits using the Arduino prototyping platform," IEEE FIE.
- Sarik, J., and I. Kymissis (2011) "Building interactive systems using unconventional electronics," ACM TEI.
- Sarik, J., A. Bulter, N. Villar, J. Scott, and S. Hodges (2012) "Combining 3D Printing and Printable Electronics," ACM TEI.

A conversation between

Philip Beesley,
Ludger Hovestadt,
Martina Decker,
Manuel Kretzer,
Areti Markopolou,
Kas Oosterhuis, and
Ruairi Glynn.

Alive: International Symposium on Adaptive Architecture, Zurich, July 8, 2013.

PHILIP Throughout the various presentations I was struck by an emphasis on precision of performance in new instruments and new processes. This could raise a fundamental question about collaboration, about what an architect can offer when tuning and optimizing these processes requires such a specialized practice. Could you comment about your collaborations and on what you as architects are contributing? What model of practice emerges?

LUDGER Let's look at the Internet of Things as an example. Some years ago I founded the company digitalSTROM, which produces a small piece of silicon that is able to communicate directly over the power line and as such proposes a single–chip solution for all the principal electrical devices in your living environment. The problem is that in your apartment or room you have one– or two–hundred electrical devices, which you want to control. But it's unclear how to control these buildings or environments as a body of functions since you are faced with complicated diagrams and dialogues—for example, your smartphone interface—and people do not like that.
So our solution is the inverse. We are no longer interested in a mechanical or dynamic way of interacting with our environment in the form of functions, like saying, "I want this." Instead, we've rearranged the setup around activities. Now we are saying, "I am doing this." And we're moving with our activities from one place to the other, so the building or the cloud of intelligent things is then adapting their functionality to these activities.
The interaction then is simply "I'm reading," "I'm sleeping," "I'm chatting," and so forth, and the functions around us are adapting. The only interaction with the environment on a functional level is the negative one, training the system by saying, "I don't want this amount of light if I'm sleeping," or "I don't want music on if I'm making a telephone call." The interesting thing with this inverted interaction is that it remains super simple by not talking about abstract technical functions but about concrete personal activities. This inversion greatly reduces the complexity of the environment. I believe that this is the new role of architecture, and that we have to learn this kind

of language in order to abstract a pure functionality from it.

MARTINA On the topic of collaboration, the most intriguing interactions that I had over the last couple of years were with a number of different scientists. I found that representatives from the sciences are equally fascinated with the architectural and design disciplines as we are with theirs. Many of them are quite eager to collaborate with us. Working in disciplinary isolation can be counterproductive to exploring a rich variety of possible applications. In order to carry a material invention right through to implementation they really appreciate interdisciplinary discourse and input from architecture, industrial design, and art. Probing emergent materials and technologies in this manner can greatly inform the broader impact on our society at large.
I would really encourage everybody to develop a steady communication with the numerous different disciplines from the STEM fields. It can be an extremely stimulating process that offers an invaluable source of inspiration and can influence the design process greatly. But remember to keep your own field accessible to others, too. As designers and architects we have to communicate in ways that an outsider can understand.

MANUEL I am curious about something I believe all your presentations touched upon: the importance and use of printing technologies, like printing substrates with different properties onto flexible materials, some of which light up, some that produce energy while others store it. What is your opinion on how this will actually affect architecture? So far I haven't really seen any kind of spatial concepts dealing with these new properties. Of course there are ideas out there,

like Kieran Timberlake's SmartWrap, which was already developed some ten years ago—a foil that combines OLEDs, organic solar cells, thin–film batteries, phase change materials, etc. But architecture is essentially the same as it was before; nothing has changed fundamentally. Where do you see the true potentials of such technologies for our discipline?

MARTINA My fascination with the various printing techniques is connected to precision, ease of production, and cost–effectiveness. Particular substances, especially if they are born out of nanotechnology, have fascinating properties that are hard to scale up to our macro–world. Ink–jet printing can offer an invaluable tool for that, even on flexible substrates.

ARETI I think when you speak about printing you refer to the nanoscale fabrication of flexible or smart materials as the ones presented by several of the guests. But I would also like to think of printing in a wider vision because the technique of additive manufacturing is a quite new technology in our discipline compared to others such as CNC cutting or robotic fabrication, which exist since the Second Industrial Revolution.
Additive manufacturing is revolutionary but, of course, we shouldn't forget that it is a rather slow technique from the nanoscale to the construction scale. I consider it a very important research field that opens up possibilities not only for architectural purposes, but by bringing these different disciplines together, also for new applications that are part of a different logical conception.
This means that it is not so easy for the kind of architecture we have been building up until now to accept the use of new techniques that are also connected with a new mode of thinking and operating.
That is probably why these applications will need a bit more time to evolve; it gets complicated when you need to face the various agents and layers of traditional design and construction. However, mentalities and requirements are shifting faster than ever, which will eventually allow new methods to enter the architectural discipline. I am certain that additive manufacturing on all scales will form new ideas and models of what

architecture means. So we might just need to continue exploring patiently.

LUDGER In my perspective, it is very challenging to know about all these new technologies and still stay focused on the very kernel of architecture, which I think remains, as always, about space, wood, and stone. But our view about space, wood, and stone will change drastically because of digital media and new printing technologies, which will make things that used to be scarce and expensive, available and cheap.
A very interesting parallel is the Middle Ages, where we had a world of words. But with the invention of the printing press, a mechanical method was developed for reproducing these words. The mechanization of traditional writing made books accessible and affordable to everyone and introduced the functional world in which we currently find ourselves. And in the Middle Ages before the printing press, as well as during the Renaissance, Baroque, and Enlightenment, with the existence of the printing press, buildings were made of stone and wood. Nothing had changed on first glance. But the buildings were erected in completely different worlds: one was the world of words and the other was the world of functions. Currently, with actual printing technology, we face a similar step. Instead of printing words, which opens up to modernity, we now are able to print functions. Basically it's the same situation: stepping out of a framing worldview.
And as we did in modernity, we start to develop new words, new languages, and a new literacy toward a new world. Therefore I think it's instructive to see how the notion of stones or of space changed during the Renaissance, because we have to expect similar changes today. It's not directly the printing that is interesting for architects. The printing is an enabler: it changes the economy and the politics of things and opens up a new plateau for architecture—which will still be about space and stones.

MANUEL But when we look back at the '60s or '70s, we see all these inflatables, performances, and social experiments—all these crazy utopias that were thought up. They had new materials, new types of plastics and fabrics, computers, and cybernetics, and then they came up with all these fabulous ideas. Somehow I'm not seeing this kind of radicality anymore, even though we're now in a similar time. We also have all these very prominent new tools and materials and I can feel a similar frustration with the existing architecture and with social and political structures, at least among younger people. I didn't live in the '60s so I don't know if that vibe was actually so strong and present back then or if it's just because we are now romanticizing it in hindsight, but I miss such innovative, radical, and especially thought-provoking experimentation with new technologies today.

LUDGER I think it's the whole twentieth century that we are talking about, for these changes happened at the beginning, not in the middle, of the twentieth century. I would see the '60s as some kind of lab for globalization. Things got symbolically capsuled and cool, ready for global distribution. Cybernetics came up and all these famous organic materials and experiments spread very successfully all over the world. This is the vocabulary we are working with today. I think our current architecture would not have been possible without this terminology. But today, I would say, we are more on the side of developing a new language than creating a new vocabulary, so architecture is more a logical interplay than a drastic articulation of new elements.

ARETI Then it will be an outcome of, let's say, several revolutions at a time. It's not only the one in architecture that will fall with this kind of radical change. There is also input from other changes—the ICT advancements for instance, the Internet 2.0, or the way we communicate, socialize, and organize people around ideas that all influence the way we perceive space and function within everyday life. Those parallel changes will also foster some more radical obligations and experimentations.

LUDGER But in relation to that—I mean, I really like the work you do at IAAC, but I have a question, for example, with this pavilion you showed for Madrid, the *Fab Lab House* that you did for the Solar Decathlon. If we are in this connected

world, if we have this kind of indexability, why do you follow these environmental parameters? Why do you follow, for example, radiation, shadows, and so on, and say that this is your parameter of design?
With smart materials, in principle you don't have to care about ventilation any longer, since for example if you have solar foils, you don't have to care about energy. Energy is out of the equation for your building. So I don't exactly understand why you are following these lines of the environment, of nature, if you have this new technology that allows you to do whatever you want. It would be cheaper to have solar panels somewhere else and just work with the incredible amount of energy they produce, rather then following the lines of solar radiation and trying to use as little as possible.

ARETI I see what you mean and agree that it's an interesting contradiction. But at the end of the day, it's always one step at a time. Current construction has limitations of budgets and feasibility. That was our one–step contribution toward a principle we focus on. Our work is based on the idea that a building is a tree. Building components are like the leaves of a tree that follow the path of the sun. It's not like a plugged–in, secondary materiality that allows properties and performance to happen, but it's the same organism that is adapting itself to environmental conditions. Of course, the next step would be that such an organism itself could be able to move or follow different sets of inputs. But the idea that it's formal is out of the context, since part of the concept is that it is alive.

LUDGER This might be good for the flora. But in contrast the fauna, all the animals, are not following the sun, they are playing around with it. And I think that we as intellectual beings we should also play around with the sun.
There is another point that I'm always struggling with: the idea of code as a source of nature. I think there is no code of architecture or nature, but we are thinking in terms of code and we see and describe our environment as code, which is what we have with DNA and so on. For fifty years now people think in code, but some two

hundred years ago there were different methods to describe the world. I don't understand why we say this is a source, because if it's a source then we are in a functional world. This is a functional understanding of a genealogy of things that is following specific paths of developments. And this thinking is in clear conflict with the notion of code, which is able to articulate discontinuities. Therefore I think speaking of source code in this combination with nature and cultural artifacts is simply a shortcut.

ARETI But then values or numbers are also not necessarily information. You can work with code also as a process of different values so that you can have valuable information as a starting point to understand these specific numbers. It's not only about numbers; rather, it's about processed numbers within certain logical conceptions and different contexts. A value is only a number. But processed numbers within contexts and concepts become information.

KAS I would like to hear some comments from you on the building industry. Of course, the use of insulation is on the rise: in relation to solar parts, it's definitely a much larger percentage, and maybe in the end a building will be one hundred percent insulation. You could think of a strategy like that, but it will take a while. But to be able to get there, you would like to actually introduce the building industry into these new schemes. So in order to change the buildings you need to change the building industry. And the building industry produces buildings like the one we are currently in, and 99.9999 percent of buildings are produced like this one. So what is your strategy to change this tendency?

MARTINA I believe our best strategy to influence the building industry is collaboration, and to introduce representatives from various disciplines and the construction industry very early on in the process. This could be as early as the point when we invent or tweak materials and their properties, since we can either adjust the materials or the way we build with them. During my presentation I introduced the *Homeostatic Facade System* and I mentioned that the particular artificial muscle

that is being used is quite fragile in the context of contemporary construction. The material itself would have to be greatly improved before it could become a viable candidate for our architectural construction process, but we can also consider the design of the environment that hosts the materials in a more protective way. Involving various trades, architects, and the STEM fields to address a problem early on can help us find solutions.

MANUEL Well, I think it's somehow a vicious cycle. First, a lot of people don't even know about these technologies, and second, they are usually not developed for architecture, where we have very distinctive boundaries and definitions. So there is no demand in architecture to really introduce them. And if there is no demand they are not going to get cheaper for architectural applications. But then, when we look at other industries, like the entertainment field or the car industry—BMW's Gina concept, for example—they are much more progressive and experimental and dare to take bigger risks. Of course they have completely different requirements, with scale representing a major factor, as well as longevity. A car doesn't need to last for a hundred years, maybe only ten, and a phone, computer, or TV set, probably only five.

KAS I think you have a very good point there. We should design buildings that don't last so long. This is the discussion you, Ludger, are having with Areti. If we dive into this sustainability issue we will lose, because then buildings have to be made so they last longer. Actually, we kill our own ambitions.

LUDGER Well, the building industry is super conservative; they hardly do any research, even though it's the biggest industry with the largest turnover. In order to change that you can't approach it technologically because it's not a technologically driven industry: it's made up of principally *craftsmen*.
My suggestion in the current situation would be to simply leave energy out of the equation of buildings. It's cheaper to have energy produced somewhere else and to burn energy with the environment you want to cultivate. Actually, for some

three or five years now, it's cheaper to buy solar trackers in Spain than to renovate a building in an energy efficient way in Switzerland. And through this you can focus on experiments around materiality, adaptability of buildings, and these new technologies.

RUAIRI I don't think that the building industry will respond and take the lead. My sense is that changes will rather be led by the consumer market. All sensors that we need in buildings will infiltrate through new objects that are purchased. I don't think architects will necessarily be responsible in any way for building those smart sensory structures. If you look at the city, most of the computing intelligence is in a certain location, specific behavior, or how your devices are controlled. But it's mostly done in servers in Scandinavian and various other cold places. So it seems like the sensing and the computation is being lifted out of the actual spaces and that we're out of the responsibility of those who build the spaces anyway. What might be left at the end is more of the feedback into the environment, the actuation of the spaces. Perhaps that's where architects still have particularly interesting roles to play, where they can take a lead. The building industry is not going to take a lead because it doesn't like to take risks, and for the most part it's much easier for a building to be designed with a fixed number of sensors and a set series of algorithms that run predictably in a certain series of outputs that are predictable as well. It's a very close–looped reactive model. But I think what some of your ambitions say about truly adaptive, interactive architecture would suggest things that are much more resilient, much more distributed. I don't think that the building industry will be particularly responsible for solving these problems; they will rather be solved by a much more distributed ecology of disciplines that are currently working on them. I think architects only feature a very small part into that conversation. But perhaps the most interesting aspect is that kind of physical feedback into the environment itself.

PHILIP The sense of the durability of things—needing to last—can sometimes seem an ethical obligation. Durability can appear as a core of sustainability. That might be the elephant in the room. Perhaps it leads us to interrogate the processes that we've just been offered. For example, the fluxing, opening, and closing constructions that Martina was showing us in her *Homeostatic Facade System*, cladding the skyscraper, immediately raises questions when it's tested against a storm like Sandy or a cycle of freezing and thawing.

Yet I wonder whether we need to assume that making something durable is an ethical imperative. It seems that might be based on an ancient religious sense of emplacement as much as in an actual exchange of effectiveness and involvement. Making something as light as possible that uses itself up quickly with its performance could, I think, be an effective way to contribute something to sustainability. Perhaps a different paradigm might be conceived that fosters innovation through a flexible approach to mortality, rather than the seemingly pervasive attitude that mortality is always to be feared.

Now, when these thoughts are shared they could be dangerous, because they could imply an excuse for waste and cynicism, a disease-based model. But I do wonder whether there could be a different set of equations than ones based only on permanence and restriction of consumption. When I look at that cladding on the skyscraper building it seems to me to foster a kind of involvement and exchange. Perhaps the potency of that exchange could be increased by designing it to serve a four- or five-year model rather than insisting on a forty-year duration.

MANUEL The question of temporality in architecture is an interesting one. Since the beginnings of humanity we actually had both—very temporary and flexible shelters like tents for a nomadic lifestyle, and then caves or stronger structures to protect from the environment and animals. But then of course architecture is not only about shelter or protection. It's also—and in some cases even more—about culture, society, and religion, and in such a context the question of temporality and also decay takes on a completely different relevance. How would a culture or religion represent itself if its churches or temples would only hold up for five years?

PHILIP But why not build in dissolving and evaporation? And have those kinds of mortalities as positive potencies and intensities rather than flaws.

MANUEL Yes, certainly, but I think this is much more complex. It's all of humankind that is somehow fixed and attached to these iconic, never–changing things. Of course a lot has already evolved in that respect. We don't posses that many physical objects anymore, memories become more digitally related, and values change. But nevertheless, until architecture reaches such a point it will take either an extremely long time or maybe a much more radical approach. And simply a shift from physicality to digitality is not really a solution either.

RUAIRI I would say that my Apple Mac laptop deliberately dies every three years. I think there are already plenty of devices that dissolve and break down very intentionally out there. In terms of software though, the principal thing for me in trying to bridge the divide between the building industry, which has its platforms and systems for responsive buildings, and the platforms that we are talking about, is really trying to find those open–source protocols that allow exchange between a set of buildings they are installed with and a set of other technologies that infiltrate whether the architects like it or not. So for me, it really becomes about certain software resilience as much as hardware resilience.

LUDGER This conversation I think is very near to the discussion of the functionalists in the '60s, with Cedric Price, for instance. And with that we are proposing the generic and following the driving forces of globalization. The question today should be how to deal with these flexibilities. If you want to develop a culturally deep language, you need to look at what we have and what we can articulate. And therefore spatial stability has an enormous impact, because this is what we have culturally in our masterpieces and thus we can identify ourselves with it.
And I think it's not possible to solve this problem of cultural stability only by software or smart materials. We rather have to tell big stories, and refer

to the existing stories of our cultural heritage. We have to retell those in a new language with a certain substantial stability.

ARETI But there is a moment when we also need to overcome some kind of cultural limitations. Like the first car we ever built as humans, it had the form of a horse, and that's simply because it was very difficult for people to understand that something that moves them around doesn't need to look like the animal that used to carry them. So this kind of cultural limitation that is strongly related to the iconic, the symbolic, or the aesthetic also needs to be profoundly debated, so that we can be honest in looking for a new step, if this is what we are actually trying to do. While some things should be totally reformed, others should be left in the past and some new ones will arise and form a different way of thinking. I am not sure whether the future buildings should look like the ones that we inhabit today or whether the church should be different from an office building, or whether an office building will even exist in ten years. We do need to make an effort and try to rethink the iconic and aesthetic symbolism of our architecture and try to cross cultural limitations using technology as a method to redefine forms, functions, and interactions.

KAS I would assume that we have to find a way to the consumer more directly. All the examples you give are consumer products—cell phones, etc. So it's a "want to have" thing. I want to have it. It's one to one: one person wants to have it. But the building industry is completely institutionalized. So we should not talk about these representative buildings, but we should talk about if we can change the building in a way for it to relate better to the consumer, which is someone who works somewhere, someone who lives somewhere, someone who maybe even worships somewhere. This is a different condition than we had before. And I agree completely in this idea of wealth or richness, abundance, and that all this is available to the individual consumer. So *that* will turn around the building industry eventually. It is of course still a difficult point because it's such an institutionalized self–defensive system. But I think the twist is in the consumer, in reaching out there and creating something that the individual consumer can afford to *want* and to *have*.

LUDGER This brings me to one of my favorite lines of argumentation. In the nineteenth century under the notion of capitalism and industrialization we had the creative individual, a political person, who was free to move within this framework of the national state economy. So the politics was with the people, and the specificity respective to the economy was, for instance, with the built environment.
This setup seems to be inverted today; now the consumer is a stable point that is powered by the generic, logistical infrastructures. And the environment, including the architecture, now needs to negotiate politically. Therefore I would not say that the consumer acts politically and is economic, whereas the individual is political and acts economically. We as consumers have to articulate our activities, and the environment will react to that politically. The game is not any longer about framed functions and designed products, it's about interesting activities and convincing attitudes.

Intelligence

"It's gonna be stormy weather for the next thirty years. And at the far end of it, I think there's gonna be a cognitive revolution. People are going to combine the computation thing and the genetic biological thing and are going to start actually tinkering with people's thought processes in an industrial fashion. And if you thought LSD was a lot of fun, wait until this really works."

Bruce Sterling, 1998.

5

Kas Oosterhuis — 114
Caught in the Act

Stefan Dulman — 120
Spatial Computing in Interactive Architecture

Jose Sanchez — 125
Polyomino: The Missing Topology Mechanic

Jason Bruges — 129
Architecture and Audience

Tomasz Jaskiewicz — 133
Approaching Distributed Architectural Ecosystems

Conversation — 140

Caught in the Act

Kas Oosterhuis
/ Director of ONL [Oosterhuis_Lénárd] bv, Rotterdam.
/ Professor of Hyperbody, Department of AE&T, Faculty of Architecture, TU Delft.

human brain

The Society of Mind, coined by Marvin Minsky in his eponymous 1988 book, where he described how our brains operate, based on his expertise in computing and robotics, is loosely referred to as a template for today's Internet of Things and People. Connectivity rules societies of a different kind. The digitalization of everybody's home and the connectivity between all devices and their users parallels the connectivity of cells in the human brain. The home has become the brain in which you live. To reach such a level of connectivity, one needs a critical mass of the number of connected components. Such a critical mass can be obtained in a Society of Plots, as is described in an imaginary master plan concerning the radical reorganization of the Noordoostpolder municipality in the Netherlands, based on numerous plots that are members of the same swarm, thereby facilitating mutual connectivity. Only when taking the swarm as a point of departure can the next level of intelligence be achieved. Society of Products, Society of Building Components, Society of Experts.

swarm

home

SOCIETY OF HOME Your house is the home of the Internet of Things and People. Data from economic surveys show that things one buys for the home are getting cheaper, while things and services you purchase for outdoor activities are getting more expensive. This a remarkable trend but more or less expected. Think of it, where do you use your tablet? Mostly at home. Where do you play Wii or Kinect? Most likely at home. Where do you watch interactive TV? At home. How do you want to feel while working professionally? Right, you want to feel at home—that is why the working places of today are converted into quasi–homes, to provide for that lounge feeling. Home merges with the working place in a continuous activity that is sometimes labeled as private life and other times as professional work. You can feel at home when traveling; you may work when at home. The bigger commercial market for connectivity with new gadgets is the home, and the wearables that allow you to feel at home wherever you are. The 2012 Philips Hue Program, for example, connects your smartphone to programmable LED lights to customize to your personal preferences.

So will we become super–consumers, fulfilling the meaning of life through interactive play? Not completely, since we will play with our 3–D printers as well, becoming cocreators and codesigners of customizable products. We will codesign our homes, everything we surround ourselves with. And these customized products may be immersed with intelligence, establishing conversations among each other and with you. Within ten to twelve years, you will live in a Society of Home.

SOCIETY OF PLOTS In the United Arab Emirates each citizen is entitled by birthright to own a piece of land of one thousand square meters. The right to own the land forms part of the identity registered in the citizen's ID profile. This forms the basis for interactive living. To build interaction on the scale of a country, all players should be able to be identified as unique, as a member of the same swarm—such is the assumption for the dynamic of a swarm system. Every member must have an identity, equal but not the same. No one was asked to be born; therefore it seems a good thing to get not only an identity as a citizen, but also the right to obtain a solid basis for living your life on a free property. It is up to the citizen how to build upon those rights, how to expand and acquire more property, but not at the expense of others. Not expanding your property should not lead to poverty and a poor life. Nor should one be allowed to sell the base property. Swapping with others should be possible as to get closer to friends or relatives. One should also be able to choose to either inherit property or get a new one on a new location.

identity

Twenty years ago I saw a TV documentary on psychiatric patients in China. One man made some remarkable statements that I will always clearly remember, since it was so perfect. He described the program he would implement to improve of the People's Republic of China. Point 1: Better food. Point 2: Clothes made of wool. Point 3: Transportation via limousine. Point 4: China as one big villa park. Brilliant; such an elegant political statement. This guy was not so crazy after all.

Suppose we map this strategy on the Netherlands. The country measures 41,543 km^2 and hosts a population of 16.82 million people, which works out to 2,470 m^2 per person, including the surfaces that are taken by water, cities, and roads. Naturally we cannot reallocate all property in the Netherlands but we could propose a radical change. Simple rules may form the basis for a truly interactive society, based on negotiations. A quick calculation informs us that if everyone were entitled to own 500 m^2 of land, we would only need to assign one fifth of the country for redistribution. Five hundred square meters is enough to support oneself in terms of food and shelter, so this would be a fair assumption. After negotiations with another party, two persons living together could own 1,000 m^2 of land, which is already very generous in terms of actual ownership of land in the Netherlands today. To see things in perspective, the area of agriculture grassland in the Netherlands covers one fourth of the country. So if we could agree on eating less meat, we basically could find the space to redivide approximately sixty percent of all Dutch grassland in lots of 500 m^2 to unfold this bold strategy.

agriculture

This is the power of design by law—rule-based design. It is that simple to realize the four points of the visionary Chinese patient: all plots of land with unique

rule-based design

homes and workplaces, transportation with electric luxury Teslas, organically grown food in robotic biospheres, clothes made to measure using CNC cutting and sewing machines. We could start with the Noordoostpolder municipality and turn this polder into a giant villa park. The Noordoostpolder measures almost 460 km², which would be able to host 552,000 people when taking into account that we will only use sixty percent of the land. As the twenty–first–century Broadacre City, we can call it the "NOpolder." The Dutch Vinex neighborhoods of the late twentieth century are too small; the NOpolder will have enough critical mass to become a true metropolis with over 500,000 inhabitants. Urban interaction would be based on the one–to–one interactions between one plot and the other, between inhabitants and other inhabitants, and between plot and inhabitant, like the Internet of Things and People (IoTaP), playing the urban interaction game in the Society of Plots. Complexity will grow naturally from this extreme form of distributed interactivity, leading to a critical mass of complex relationships that opens for unexpected combinations and configurations / fig.52 p.196 /.

SOCIETY OF PRODUCTS / fig.53 p.196 / It is now more than ten years ago that I drafted this brief for my Hyperbody students at the TU Delft: Build an application for interactive shopping with the target location being the Lijnbaan in Rotterdam. We were working in the game development software Virtools, with which we simulated the interaction in real time. The interactive–shopping design brief suggested to retrieve information from the exposed products while walking around in the shop, thereby making printed price tags obsolete, and interacting with the built structure as well as opening doors and drawers and activating screens. We imagined a give–and–take situation: the consumers retrieve their information from the products simply by coming closer or keeping their eyes focused on the product for some seconds. This presupposes that both the product and the viewer are tagged. The products would be provided with RFID tags and the consumers would use the apps on their smartphones via Wi–Fi signals to read the info. A challenging interaction design exercise then, a societal debate today.

Journalist Bas Heijne showed his concerns in his weekly column in the Dutch newspaper NRC on January 25, 2014, naming this situation Little Brother. He is concerned that all Little Brothers (like the electronics retailer Dixons), crowdsourcing people together—their potential clients close to their shops—will eventually shape a Big Brother who is watching you. What should we be concerned about? A fair situation would be to agree on a bidirectional information exchange, and not one–sided information harvesting. It should be a give–and–take situation, where the consumers have access to relevant information on exposed products in exchange for allowing them access their coordinates. Moreover, it should be a simple choice one can opt for or not—whether or not to be open for such information exchange—and not a choice that only tech–savvy users can manage in their smartphone settings. It should not be *Brother* that is monitoring *You* but also *You* checking out *Brother*, setting preferences to what extent one wants to both be known and share information, whereas the rule could be that the most rigorous threshold set by one of the negotiating parties will be the mutually accepted basis for the data exchange. If one does not want to be seen, she or he does not get access to augmented information from the other party either. One could imagine a world where one can choose the desired level of connectivity. As a consequence of a desire for more privacy one would be more excluded by other parties as well.

privacy

Bidirectional data exchange is a mandatory basis for interaction. How could an information stream from individual consumer to reseller and vice versa become an interactive dialogue? To inform and be informed is not interactive. Interaction means mutual response: the receiver processes the incoming information and sends new information, maybe with a similar intent but different and unpredictable for the other party, which forces the receiving party to process again and come up with something new and refreshing. Can you imagine that a consumer and a reseller would embark on such a constructive dialogue? Only if the product sold changes with the conversation. Only if the product is made to measure in real time (or close to real time), only if the outcome of the dialogue has had serious consequences for the configuration of the negotiated entity. Only then will the commercial market adopt to the IoTaP. Such interactions and negotiations will probably no longer exclusively take place in the shopping mall, but more likely in a digitally augmented environment—perhaps in your virtually augmented home or in an interactive shopping experience.

real time

The Society of Products is now transformed as to make every person on earth a *Little Big Brother*. Ultimately all people will have access to data from Wi–Fi signals; everyone could in principle execute the crowdsourcing. Why should it be unethical when a commercial company like Dixons dives into crowdsourcing, while scientific researchers use similar tracking and monitoring systems to perform their behavioral studies, without you knowing that they do?

SOCIETY OF BUILDING COMPONENTS Scaled between the product, the home, and the plot is the building—the built environment at large. How can we map the IoTaP to the stuff of which buildings are made? At the first *Archilab* conference in 1999 in Orléans, France, I presented a three-minute video of *Trans–Ports*, which was a built structure that changes shape and content in real time. I made that animation as response to Greg Lynn's 1998 collection of essays *Folds, Bodies & Blobs*. In the book he accepts the methods of freezing animated forms, and he even accepts the discrepancy between designers' space and contractor space. The *Trans–Ports* project took animation one step further. I wanted to keep the process going, I wanted to keep the animated body alive. I knew how to realize this from previous experience with the real behavior of the *Waterpavilion* and earlier exercises with virtual reality and responsive environments in the *Sculpture City* project. Rather than being a fantasy, it was an explicit possibility to consider buildings as dynamic systems displaying real-time

animation

virtual reality

behavior. Freezing the process like Lynn and his peers do did not seem logical to me—by doing so you only show an instance of a process, which does not in any way represent the animated version. Freezing the animation is just as poor as representing the body with only a section of it. Using animation software is a good thing to generate millions of instances, but a poor thing when the process is arbitrarily stopped—film reduced to a photo. Although it must be considered a professional skill to take the snapshot at a particular moment in time as to capture the action, the action itself is always on a whole different level. A living bird is more interesting to watch than a dead bird.

Now how can that building body be kept alive, that programmable building body that can change shape and content in real time? The answer is just as simple as it is difficult to obtain using standard building components available on the market. First of all, all building components must be actors that can perform given tasks and, another level up, improvise when executing their tasks. Let us try to describe that first level up, which is the level of interactivity. The basic assumption for any interactivity is that the interacting things or people are not completely the same. There is no interactivity possible between exactly similar entities, since there is nothing to exchange: what you send comes back is exactly the same thing. No two snowflakes are the same, since one out of every three thousand molecules is not water but deuterium. Precisely because of the unpredictability of the position of these deuterium molecules each and every snowflake will be unique. Thus, each and every building component in an interactive building must be unique—at least slightly different—with an unique identity to be able to be addressed either in its program or in its parametric system. Identifiability in the design process as well as its lifecycle is a mandatory feature of any interactive building. The acting capacity of these building blocks expresses itself in either the ability to exchange data in real time or the ability to actuate its shape, to change its shape in real time. Now we can speak of a Society of Building Components, free from Marvin Minsky's brain theory. The built environment, whether your home or your city, becomes a connected brain where your life unfolds inside the IoTaP / fig.54 p.197 /.

SOCIETY OF EXPERTS Connectivity is the basis of all societies. Human brains are connected in order to shape humanity; a single brain, not connected to other people, is useless. Brains have evolved through their connectivity: human societies have evolved through the collective intelligence of all people, not excluding a single person. All people have been instrumental in reaching the extremely complex configuration society has achieved. All tools—starting with language—including all constructs that have ever been built, especially the banal and the generic ones, have been instrumental in shaping our cities, machines, agricultural systems, computers and their operating systems. This could only have happened because all our brains are virtually connected, all seven billion of them, each one knowing the other via no more than an average of six degrees (the uncle of my neighbor's doctor has a friend that knows a classmate of President Obama, etc.). Only by this collective effort of the global brain has this been possible. Exceptional individual achievements are the hubs in this grand web of evolutionary play that stitches human brains and their tools and machines together to form IoTaP, which has always existed, but is now experiencing an enormous boost since the exponential growth of the digital.

Experts in the design process have always worked together in some form of delayed connectivity. Now since the introduction of the digital in the profession of architectural design we can connect experts in real time. The expert swarm operates in a state of immediacy, instantly writing each design decision to a dynamic database, informed by a sensor network that pumps their data in real time to the dynamic database, thereby continuously refreshing all parameters acting upon the design scheme. Any change in the design as proposed by any authorized expert, including clients, users, quantity surveyors, climate designers, structural designers, stylists, and the expert, formerly known as the architect, is immediately administered in the dynamic database. Any mass model (Level Of Detail 000–100), any surface and specified space (LOD 200–300), and any building component or detail (LOD 400–500) in the design is informed by real–time environmental data, instantly checking its performance during the design process and beyond in the operational facility management phase. Anyone in the expert swarm that retrieves data from the database at any moment in time is, per definition, bound to work with instant data. The connected expert team literally operates as a swarm, always changing its configuration, always adjusting direction, always with another leader taking temporary lead. They form the informed Society of Experts, the design process is caught in the act on a permanent basis.

immediacy

Spatial Computing in Interactive Architecture

Stefan Dulman
/ Researcher at CWI, Amsterdam.
/ Co–Founder of Ambient Systems BV and Hive Systems, Delft.

---

distributed computing

Distributed computing is the theoretical foundation for applications and technologies like interactive architecture, wearable computing (Starner 1996, pp. 618, 629), and smart materials. It evolves continuously, following needs rising from scientific developments, novel uses of technology, or simply the curiosity to better understand the world around us. The pace of evolution is fast: in a short span of time distributed computing helped the Internet develop into how we know it today and overcame the dynamics of the large spread of mobile wireless communication. Soon, we will see the effects of distributed computing in the rise of the Internet of Things.

systems theory

Interactive architecture brings a specific set of requirements to distributed computing (sheer number of devices, specific dynamics, resources, control constraints, etc.). The mapping between the requirements of interactive installations and distributed systems theory is well understood. Architects are already acquainted with concepts such as emergent behavior and swarm behavior and use them in their designs. Nevertheless, despite the availability of all the constituent ingredients, the number of large–scale installations employing distributed behavior in hardware and software is very small. The vast majority of systems are still controlled from a central computer that creates the desired behavior and that faces obvious issues of scale. This is the main research question that I would like to tackle in this essay.

smart city

Before going into details, let us contemplate for a moment the larger picture, making abstraction of the technological barriers. The dream of large–scale interactive systems responding and adapting instantly to the user's desires will come one step closer to actualization. For example, the myriad inputs triggered by the crowds inhabiting a city will be translated automatically through extensively equipped intelligent surroundings. Aspects of control, safety, and privacy will be automatically dealt with in real time. Humans will have a new understanding of the world around them, which will simply adapt to suit their needs. Smart cities and the Internet of Things will finally become a reality.

SPATIAL COMPUTING Computation evolved from single powerful mainframes to the interactions taking place in networks of multiple small intelligent sensing devices embedded in the world around us. *Spatial Computing* is a term coined to express this novel trend in computer science, addressing the specifics of integrating computation with communications and sensing activities. Computation becomes intertwined with the properties of the space where it's located—distance, connectivity, and density become common attributes that influence results.

network

In some aspects, this transformation can be perceived as natural. Computation techniques have found a source of inspiration in nature for a long time already— one of the most visible examples being ant–colony optimization, a technique inspired by the activity of insects. Adaptation based on processing information using a distributed environment happens all around us, with examples including schools of fish, flocks of birds, or morphogenesis at the embryo level. Consequently, a number of fields evolved alongside each other, trying to mimic and exploit our surrounding nature: amorphous computing, cellular automata, Lindenmayer systems, particle systems, genetic programming, etc. (Abelson et al. 2000).

adaptation

Areas dealing with mobile ad–hoc networks, wireless sensor networks, and swarm robotics are flourishing at the moment (Akyildiz et al. 2002, pp. 102, 114; Dorigo and Stützle 2004). They are perfect constitutive elements for the community of interactive architecture, which has already been employing them for a number of years, and they are at the forefront of creating the sought–after interactive spaces. Technology will keep advancing with miniaturization and cost reduction; the embedded network around us will increase in size and provide novel features.

cost

Spatial computing can be found at a multitude of scales and in highly diverse systems from the perspective of resources employed. Field–Programmable Gate Arrays (FPGAs) are chips consisting of a collection of basic elements ("gates") that can be connected by the user to create a specific functionality in the chip. There is also a current increase in the use of processors containing multiple cores. At the opposite end of the spectrum are crowds equipped with smartphones or intelligent cars, cooperating to achieve their desired goals. All these examples rely on the same underlying concepts—computation performed in a distributed spatial manner with specific requirements imposed by the physical separation of the constituent elements.

BREAKING DOWN THE CONCEPTUAL BARRIERS Despite the aforementioned work, today's large–scale interactive systems are still in their infancy and don't fully take into account the distributed computing techniques available. Among the main causes here are the following two obstacles: the unavailability of a programming paradigm relying on high–level behaviors, and, secondly, the availability of a distributed user interface.

user interface

functionality — Programming devices is well understood—both bottom–up and top–down methodologies exist, with formal methods being developed to describe and guarantee the behavior of the device under discussion. Development of complex systems has led to a series of practices, predominant among which are the separation of concerns and layers of functionality. The Internet is such an example, with its architecture being described by the seven layers of functionality of the Open Systems Interconnect (OSI) model. The lower layers deal with physical aspects linked to transmitting information via a physical medium prone to error, while the top layers deal with interaction with the user and specifics related to applications.

emergence — Despite the strict formality brought in by such approach, when the system exceeds a certain size, top–level emergence occurs. Emergence has a large number of definitions, a common adopted one being: "The whole is greater than the sum of its parts" (Laughlin 2005).

Interestingly enough, applications built on top of large–scale systems can be decomposed in the interaction of a number of emergent behaviors rather than with the primitives suited for writing programs on a regular computer. Specific programming languages employing emergent behaviors as primitives are rather few and highly specialized. I argue that a change of perspective is necessary (Beal et al. 2012). Programming spatial systems should be performed from the top down rather than bottom up. In other words, instead of writing code for each of the devices in a network and hoping that the final operation will not be too affected by unforeseen emergent behavior, a system designer should first look at the bigger picture. The *behavior* — desired global functionality should be decomposed in a series of stable behaviors that are known and understood. The program should merely specify how these primitives interact, the compiler having the task to automatically create the code needed for each individual device.

Experiments in this direction have already been carried out, leading to a number of initial promising results—the Origami Shape Language being such an example (Nagpal 2001). To the best of our knowledge, these results apply mainly to static systems—an extension to systems with mobile elements is still needed. Intuitively, *crowd* — this will allow the programming and control of systems, such as crowds of people interacting with smartphones in a fully distributed manner to create light patterns (i.e., a crowd attending a concert) or to perform useful computations (i.e., computing the crowd density and flow in certain congested locations to detect and signal possible stampedes).

The second obstacle to be overcome is the availability of user interfaces for large–scale complex systems that can be accessed by a myriad of users at the same time. Emergent behavior in the way the users interact with the system and design decisions based on it should be taken into account, rather than having techniques put in place to prevent it.

Large–scale systems such as the ones described above should be self–adapting. The dynamics involved in such systems are complex and, most importantly, change with time. Users tend to learn the system capabilities and find new uses, changing their requirements and the way in which they interact with the system. The system itself also changes, by employing new hardware and software components that allow new functionalities and behaviors. Adaptivity becomes necessary at all levels: the user interface, the behavior of the system, and the way users interact with the system.

PUTTING IT ALL TOGETHER: HIVEKIT Interactive architecture is an interesting field for distributed computing. It presents a set of novel challenges, but most importantly, it is deeply integrated in our daily life—allowing continuous experimentation and being available to everyone rather than being constrained to specialized research labs. The users of this application can provide feedback in a variety of ways, from taking an explicit action to letting the system learn and react to their daily activity patterns.

The need for novel programming interfaces led us to the creation of *HiveKit*, a software toolkit that allows for the programming of large–scale interactive systems using a top–down approach.[1] The software is provided as a plug–in for the Grasshopper suite of the Rhino 3–D software package. It allows the use to specify the desired behavior of the network and automatically generates the embedded software and the communication protocols for a network of Arduino Due devices. Sensors and actuator behavior are reduced to simple numbers, the user being able to employ a large range of devices with no overhead on his side / fig.55 p.198 // fig.56 p.199 /.

The advantages of using this software tool do not rely on the specific features offered, which are subject to change based on user feedback. The main gain a designer obtains from this approach is the tremendous speed–up of the design cycle. Traditionally, after the first draft of an installation is completed, the implementation of the software for the system can easily take a few months. With the HiveKit software suite, complex behaviors can be implemented in less than an hour. Features such as automatic and viral deployment of the code in the network and the use of off–the–shelf standard hardware enable the designer to experiment with the system right away, greatly speeding up the typical development cycle.

Seina / fig.57 p.199 / is an interactive installation designed for the Princess Maxima Hospital in the Netherlands.[2] It is controlled by a distributed system, reacting to human presence and engaging with the audience via light patterns. Several

---

1   See http://hive–systems.net/hivekit.
2   Seina, www.seina.nl, Minor Interactive Environments, IDStudioLab, Delft University of Technology, Fall Semester 2013.

behaviors were explored and programmed in the installation and this was also possible because of the fast prototyping capabilities offered by *HiveKit*. The authors were able to explore a large number of behaviors very fast and also gained additional time because they did not have to become concerned with the technical details of the underlying network.

Decades of interdisciplinary work will eventually come to an end and bring the words and vision of Mark Weiser to fruition:

> *"Ubiquitous computing names the third wave in computing, just now beginning. First were mainframes, each shared by lots of people. Now we are in the personal computing era, person and machine staring uneasily at each other across the desktop. Next comes ubiquitous computing, or the age of calm technology, when technology recedes into the background of our lives."*
>
> Mark Weiser, 1991

references

+ Abelson, Harold, Don Allen, Daniel Coore, Chris Hanson, George Homsy, Thomas Knight, Radhika Nagpal, Erik Rauch, Gerald Sussman, and Ron Weiss (2000). "Amorphous Computing," Communications of the ACM. 43 (5).
+ Akyildiz, I.F., Weilian Su, Y. Sankarasubramaniam, and E. Cayirci (2002) "A Survey on Sensor Networks," Communications Magazine, IEEE. 40 (8).
+ Beal, J., S.O. Dulman, K. Usbeck, M. Viroli, and N. Correll, (2012) "Organizing the Aggregate: Languages for Spatial Computing." In: Marjan Mernik (ed.) Formal and Practical Aspects of Domain–Specific Languages: Recent Developments. IGI Global.
+ Dorigo, Marco, and Thomas Stützle (2004) Ant Colony Optimization. Cambridge, MA: MIT Press.
+ Laughlin, Robert (2005) A Different Universe: Reinventing Physics from the Bottom Down. New York: Basic Books.
+ Nagpal, Radhika (2001) Programmable Self–Assembly: Constructing Global Shape Using Biologically–Inspired Local Interactions and Origami Mathematics. PhD diss. MIT Artificial Intelligence Laboratory.
+ Starner, T. (1996) "Human–Powered Wearable Computing," IBM Systems Journal 35 (3 and 40).
+ Weiser, Mark (1991) "The Computer for the 21st Century." Scientific American, special issue on "Communications, Computers, and Networks," pp. 94–104.

Polyomino:
The Missing Topology Mechanic

Jose Sanchez
/ Assistant Professor, University of Southern California, Los Angeles.
/ Director of the Plethora Project.

The following essay presents research developed with students at the USC School of Architecture as part of the *Gamescapes Agenda*, directed by Jose Sanchez.

While the current conversation within technology circles in architecture seems to focus on ideas of robotic manufacturing and precision control, it is important to point out counter–paradigms that offer parallel ideas of the future of conceptualization and manipulation of matter within the discipline.
The ideas behind robotic manufacturing suggest that the mechanism of manufacturing has become digital and that computer control allows for an infinite differentiation of designs while matter itself remains analogue, being pushed around by machines of precision. The model is that of a continuous system where material detail will always surpass the capacity for us to compute it.

The opposite idea, as promoted by Neil Gershenfeld (2012), is that matter itself could become digital. It is important to understand the definition of digital in relation to a discrete model, in a framework of unit–to–unit communication. Gershenfeld's argument is that the Lego block is smarter than the kid assembling it. The unit contains a coordinate system and correction for assembly. Each Lego can interface with another Lego as part of the same system. For some time, this paradigm of a kit–of–parts has been rejected as something that the discipline is trying to overcome, being a remainder of serialized fabrication, standardization, and the Industrial Revolution. But a newer computational version of the kit–of–parts idea has slowly been building up, especially since the advent of computers: similar parts could be rewired to perform different tasks. There is a fundamental difference between this and an automobile made out of industrialized parts and operational units that could be combined and recombined in differentiated topologies. What is understood by this model is that the "data" that describes the topology of a system is of great value, and a system that could crowd–source its body plan could perpetually transform in the hands of its users.

This was clearly understood by Braun when they introduced the Braun Lectron kit in 1966. The Braun Lectron is a kit of electric circuits in the form of a game that would allow a user to learn and experiment with electronics safely. Several units are the same, but are combined in different ways, to allow for many different circuits / fig.58 p.201 /.

It is precisely the data of the missing topology of the system that allows a user to explore and learn. The key concept behind the Braun Lectron system is the encapsulation of complexity to enable playful exploration. You don't need to be an electrical engineer in order to play with the system because the system has been designed to intuitively correct the errors or help you avoid them. The graphics and symbols encode the information you need to consider to generate a specific outcome / fig.59 p.201 /.

social agent

The Braun Lectron is the precursor to a series of products such as Cubelets or Little Bits, and games such as Minecraft or SpaceChem, that have understood the power of this mechanics. The missing topology mechanic accounts for a social agent that will tinker and explore the possible outcomes of the system. It is a discrete kit of parts that needs to be coupled with an iterative search and exploration force.

interactivity

To some degree this kind of system could be considered "interactive." But yet again we need to clarify the kind of interactivity we are addressing. Traditionally, we would understand interactive architecture as an architecture that reacts or behaves in relation to the user. This paradigm has certainly been developed through many projects, but I will argue that it has reached an apex with the HypoSurface by dECOi. In such a project, the relation between the actuation of the wall and the sensing of a user happens almost immediately. The result—sometimes reactive, sometimes purely behavioral—lives in a parametric space of possible interactions. While we could argue that a reactive approach to this kind of project is not as interesting as a behavioral approach, where the wall or unit could demonstrate its own "attitude" to the environmental stimuli, we could still mathematically define them as deterministic prepackaged responses. The parametric space that defines them is limited by a clearly identifiable domain.

game

A discrete kit–of–parts, such as those found in games, is what I call the *missing topology mechanic*, and it's fundamentally nonparametric and actually combinatorial. This means that the missing element is not a number or parameter in the system but rather the topological diagram that puts them together. While a parametric system can be altered in magnitude or intensity, a combinatorial system can change in *nature*.

voxel

This argument is the central premise conceived in the *Polyomino* research agenda. Using references such as the Braun Lectron, we set out to design a geometrical tile set that could be recombined in many different ways. Such a unit would have to live in a 3–D data structure, a voxel. For this, we studied the systems that could create perfect 3–D packing, and finally decided to use a truncated octahedron and its hexagonal packing as both the geometric and data structure.

While the truncated octahedron is perfectly symmetrical in every direction, the initial studies with students started by describing a unique topological connection of each unit. Similar to the game of domino, each paper unit would contain data that would allow it to connect to other units. In this way, we could start differentiating the potential connectivity of each unit.

connectivity

Suddenly the perfect voxel data structure became far more complex as each unit would not only describe connectivity, but would also block the connectivity of adjacent units. The design iteration over the connection types present in a unit would allow us to describe a diagrammatic aggregation model prior to conceiving the final geometry.

The work at this stage was done by trial and error, by iterating with folded–paper models. The connection of units enabled us to consider clusters or sequences that could also be recombined at a higher order of scale, and describe their particular connecting nodes, very much like the way letters describe words and words describe sentences.

While pure aggregation seems like a good initial strategy, students detected the necessity of having two different kinds of units. These two color–coded units would allow two "players" to peruse different interests in a generative aggregation game, where each unit would become complementary to each other. This idea of symbiotic agencies within the structure allowed us to completely repattern the aggregations negotiating two opposed interests / fig.60 p.201 /.

aggregation

symbiotic agency

Finally, understanding that the paper models would only represent a topology diagram, it was time to develop the geometry that would encapsulate such connectivity and constraints. The final units developed by one of the teams would identify the agencies of structure and porosity, allowing some units to describe a much stronger connection, while others would diffuse the light and allow for porous channels throughout the fabric. At this point, the final formation would start blurring the notion of the tile, generating assemblies that would operate at a larger scale. The aggregations could bridge between linear and surface formations and from surface to volumetric configurations. The underlying topological diagram would enable simulations of structure by pure propagation of forces between units. It would also enable us to quantify costs or provide for the framework for additional calculations / fig.61 p.203 /.

The idea that the brick or unit configuration constitutes a data structure allows us to speculate on the future of how materials could become digital and describe a discrete relation to each other. The research points to a self–conscious fabric of architecture, one that could self–regulate by detecting the intrinsic topology of its units.

data structure

We are still at the very beginning of this study into which algorithms could coexist with a persistent digital assembly; however, it is certainly a step forward to connect the current passive state of matter into a possibly computational entity.

object–oriented design

This methodology is what I argue we should call *object–oriented design*. The term has garnered diverse appropriation from different sectors, and is influenced by both an object–oriented programming paradigm and a newly coined object–oriented ontology in philosophy circles. However I would argue that object–oriented design needs to develop and demonstrate itself through projects that operate at a discrete level, emphasizing the role of objects in their autonomy over their relationality. This would be a practice where the definition of identity comes before the process of formation. It is in these terms that an object–oriented approach goes against a Deleuzian framework of morphogenesis whereby everything is always in flux and in formation.

Polyomino celebrates an object–oriented methodology where units are reinstantiated as building blocks, where units are no longer simply parts but operational entities. It is perhaps in the pre–actual state of such an agenda, where the definition of the list or inventory of units is more relevant than the implementation itself. Similar to how code libraries generate computational objects that can be combined in different ways, the model adopted is that of a "sandbox" where an inventory of

potentiality

pre–actualized design units exists in pure potentiality. A list of objects, before any relation, allows us to understand different agencies in design and this is perhaps one of the few mediums that allows for contradictions. As Ian Bogost (2012) presents it: "Lists remind us that no matter how fluidly a system may operate, its members nevertheless remain utterly isolated, mutual aliens" / fig.62 p.203 /.

#62

The *Polyomino* agenda reflects on the mechanism of negative entropy that we possess as designers, and it tries to broaden the repertoire of techniques, incorporating elements of game design. The inevitable inclusion of a social agency in game design has allowed games to develop a much more sophisticated idea of control, and develop notions of design that are far more probabilistic and speculative. The ultimate goal is to cater to a collective intelligence in design that could benefit from lucky or persistent individuals as well as from designers in the traditional sense. *Polyomino*, as part of the *Gamescapes* research, questions authorship and the politics of production, and gambles on an open–source network and a

game design

knowledge

promiscuous proliferation of knowledge / fig.63 p.203 /.

#63

references

+ Bogost, Ian (2012) Alien Phenomenology, or What It's Like to Be a Thing. Minneapolis: University of Minnesota Press.
+ Gershenfeld, Neil (2012) "How to Make Almost Anything: The Digital Fabrication Revolution." Foreign Affairs, Volume: 91.

Architecture and Audience

Jason Bruges
/ Creative Director and Founder of Jason Bruges Studio, London.
/ FRSA BA(HONS) DIP ARCH.

Designing for audiences is about creating an architecture that is interactive, responsive, and dynamic. As a studio we are interested in creating environments and objects that have the power to change, transform, and update in some way. We use a diverse palette of materials, which might even be borrowed from an entirely different area, and which is future facing or tried and tested over the last twenty years. We use our in–house workshop to hack into these materials, pull them apart, rebuild and reconfigure them, or design them from scratch. We create prototypes and design iteratively, through making. Nothing that we create is abstract; everything is designed to have a living and animated, unpredictable entity interacting with it. Like the theatre, our work is about the collective human audience and creating artworks and installations that delight, entertain, and encourage. Whether we are creating a spectacle, a large–scale public performance, or an individual interaction, we focus on the subtleties of the interaction within its specific environment.

environment

theatre

The studio's work is hugely varied and can be something that is designed to only last a few seconds in the real world—a piece that is filmed and shown on television for thirty seconds, for example—or something that has an eighty–year design life and must be robust enough to withstand significant changes in temperature. This means we constantly have to consider how technology and interaction can be updated—not just in the near future but longer term as well. And this can have a dramatic impact on how a design might develop, adding several layers of complexity to a project, and perhaps even determining the broader parameters that shape it and the way that we want our audiences to interact with it.

complexity

We find that audiences can also respond in unexpected ways to pieces; reactions and ways of seeing are not necessarily what you predict or intend. Projects can take on a life of their own. Our O_2 *Memory Project*, a digital site traveling around the UK filming different spaces, was focused on the community. This digital twist on a cyclorama was intended to film landscapes and townscapes, project images of them inside as digital panoramas, and prompt thought and discussion around the temporary nature of our digital memories. We found that communities were treating it as a portrait machine; people were jumping up and lifting one another to capture images of themselves. This happened in spite of the fact that it hadn't been designed for this purpose and the height parameters were completely off,

community

making it rather difficult to achieve this. The project essentially developed into something bigger and more intimately connected to people than we had originally anticipated. This kind of transformation and evolvement is something we find incredibly exciting—it reiterates that our pieces are living, breathing works. It also underscores our fascination with taking photos of ourselves.

Different environments provide different kinds of opportunities for audience interaction. As a studio we are interested in exploring the street or urban context, what could be seen to be analogous to street theatre or performance. These contexts provide incredibly rich environments—everyday and familiar spaces and places that passersby can actively engage with. The *21st Century Light Space Modulator* was a temporary piece we produced in 2012 for a site on London's Southbank, beneath Hungerford Bridge. The artwork paid homage to Lázló Moholy–Nagy's *Light–Space Modulator* and explored interaction and performance with a network of Microsoft Kinect sensors. It essentially looked at something we call accidental or inferred interaction; how pedestrians interact with artworks. We looked at how the piece could be made to respond to individuals, pairs, and groups of three, seven, twenty, and up to fifty people. We had to ask ourselves how we could build systems that would cope with varying audience sizes and densities, and individuals of different height, too. We explored how we could choreograph a series of very different performances and how these performances could manifest themselves in this environment. The result was a piece that breathed new life and light into an underused, dark, and dingy space. It was an artwork that captured people's imaginations; a playful intervention that dramatically changed the place it was in for the duration of its time there.

A gallery or enclosed environment provides a different kind of opportunity and is a space where the attention or focus of the audience is almost guaranteed. People come to this environment to look and to take part, and the interaction that takes place here becomes something altogether different in its nature.

One of our pieces, *Panda Eyes* (2010) / fig.64 p.204 /, is interesting to consider because it was created for this kind of space and in a sense re–evaluates the relationship between viewer and object. *Panda Eyes*, for the World Wildlife Fund for Nature, is made up of one hundred of the charity's iconic panda collection boxes. Designed to raise environmental awareness, the artwork sees the bears arranged in a grid and rotate autonomously, tracking the presence of visitors to the space in which the piece is displayed. The piece responds directly to the first person that it tracks, fixing the collective gaze of the pandas on this individual and then following them as they move around the space. The piece gave us the opportunity to really think about concentrated two–way observation and to look at this as a meeting place for, effectively, a two–way audience. Panda Eyes has been hugely successful in the way that it tells the WWF story. It is a captivating artwork that invokes a highly emotional response in the viewer. How and what we embody and imbue technology with is also a fascinating area of study that is raised by this kind of project.

For *Mirror, Mirror* (2009), a piece originally designed for the Decode exhibition at the Victoria & Albert Museum, the studio looked at the idea that an individual can be both audience and performer. The piece comprises a number of white–dot matrix panel modules carefully arranged within a pond that individually record and play back to the viewer what they are doing. The composition is arranged and built around capturing a person of full height in filmic–quality resolution, and then creating a reflection in the water. This recording and playing back is a popular theme in the studio's work. Digital narcissism is an area that is gaining ever–increasing popularity; we find that people are becoming more and more interested in seeing themselves reflected in one shape or another, digitally.

Showtime (2010) / fig.65 p.204 / is a media facade artwork situated in London's Leicester Square. When we were first given the brief for this artwork, we looked closely at the history of the area and felt that we wanted to respond to it. Leicester Square has a rich history of buildings that were designed to entertain. Its theatrical and cultural provenance dates back to the nineteenth century with experiences such as Burford's Panorama and Wyld's Globe, spaces that allowed visitors to explore scenery and imagery in ways and at scales never seen before. Building on this, the studio decided to work with the kind of frequency of performance that a cuckoo clock in a town hall might have; something that has presence and is part of the feel of a space, but at the same time isn't overbearing. Using cameras mounted on the roof of the building, the artwork captures the skyline and interprets this as short performances that are then displayed on the facade of the building during the hours of darkness. As London's first responsive, illuminated facade artwork, this piece allows the facade to tell a story about the area and to relay it to the huge numbers of people that visit and inhabit the area.

Another type of audience—the commuter or moving audience—also has a colorful history, including spaces such as elevators, train, and cars. These environments provide very different vantage points and opportunities. In 2005 the studio created *Litmus*, a set of four artworks that are interlinked and act as markers in the landscape on the A13, one of the major roads into London. The twelve–meter–high sculptures are located on separate roundabouts and respond to local environmental stimuli. This includes the light and tide levels, the volume of traffic, and the power generated by a neighboring turbine. They are carefully sited so as not to surprise or distract drivers along the road, and yet at the same time they symbolize and build on the regeneration of this area of Greater London. The discussions and questions that these pieces raise to those traveling along the A13 are what make them interesting to us as a studio.

augmented reality

Working with audiences that use different types of technology to view the world—mixed reality and augmented reality—has changed dramatically over the last few years. Smart devices now empower audiences to see the complete effect and composition of an artwork that is otherwise "invisible." For Beck's *Green Box Project* (2011), the studio was asked to design and build a series of illuminated "green boxes" to act as physical symbols and keys to the beer brand's new augmented reality gallery. Passersby were encouraged to download Beck's *Green Box Project* app, which enabled the user to view uniquely commissioned artworks from some of the world's best artists. The really fascinating part was that the studio produced reality keys for a large number of different sites around the world, which were actuated at similar times. So, in effect, the project had a global audience that was actively engaging with the physical and digital overlays at the same time.

touch

Engaging audiences through physical touch is also something that the studio enjoys exploring. One of our pieces at Tate Britain, *Dotty Duveen* (2005), looked at how people move through space and invited them to touch objects within this space. Our sense of touch is incredibly underused in the world of artworks, installations, and interactive spaces, and inviting people to touch, interrogate, and move through objects allows for a very different kind of experience. This piece is about creating an immersive experience without being entirely immersed; it allows people to inhabit a space and engage with objects in that space without being beholden to it, as engagement is voluntary. As part of the project, the studio also filmed and tracked people in the space to capture and record the changing space syntax.

distraction

For the Great Ormond Street Hospital for Children, the studio created a digital texture that was mapped behind wallpaper. The piece, *Nature Trail* (2012) / fig.66 p.205 /, was commissioned as a distraction artwork for children on their way to surgery. It is intended to create a calming and yet engaging space. As children and adults move through the corridor, animals come to life that sequentially match the half–tone wallpaper. The artwork highlights a variety of uses when considering audiences and performance; in this case it is about distracting, delighting, and entertaining those that come into contact with it. The piece has been hugely successful so far and the studio has been commissioned to create two further artworks for the hospital.

conversation

The above examples show that the studio is keen to explore many different kinds of audience, interaction type, and space. Conversations with our environments play a central role in how we experience our world. At Jason Bruges Studio we seek to tease out these conversations and focus on the subtleties of our interactions. People are key to our projects; our work needs occupants, observers, and passersby. Without an audience, our works are incomplete.

Approaching Distributed Architectural Ecosystems

Tomasz Jaskiewicz
/ Assistant Professor, Interactive Design Prototyping, Industrial Design Engineering Faculty, TU Delft.
/ Co-Founder Hive Systems, Delft.

IMAGINING ALIVE ARCHITECTURE What does it mean for architecture to be "alive?" If we were to take the notion of "living" literally, it would mean buildings that are animate, that actively react to external stimuli, grow, reproduce in some way, and, most importantly, can sustain themselves. Being "alive" also implies buildings that play parts in larger ecosystems in which they may interact with each other and with other natural or artificial "living" entities.

Such a vision of alive architecture can initially evoke various pictures in our minds. One could think of living buildings from fairy tales, such as a house walking on chicken legs from the Slavic folk legend of Baba Yaga, or of countless haunted houses featured in horror stories and films (think Stanley Kubrick's The Shining). One could conjure images of buildings made of living plant tissue, reminiscent of root bridges found in the Indian Meghalaya province / fig.67 p.206 /, trees that have grown over centuries through the ancient Cambodian Angkor Wat temples, or artificially grafted plants grown by horticulturalists such as Axel Erlandson (Erlandson 2001). One could also think of popular science-fiction examples of architectural spaces controlled by vital forces not of a metaphysical or natural sort, but that emerge out of man-made technology. Films such as 2001: A Space Odyssey or I, Robot, where artificial intelligence takes charge of human habitats, instantly come to mind. Yet it's not just singular intelligent buildings that science-fiction stories evoke. In countless sci-fi examples, protagonists are immersed in environments full of innumerable "smart" devices that interact with them, ranging from flying cars and robots to omnipresent interactive displays and all kinds of embedded sensors and control systems—a future that, in the contemporary world of smartphones and unmanned military drones, does not seem too distant.

THE FEAR OF "ALIVE" What links all of these seemingly different visions of habitats coming to life is the combined feeling of fascination and fear that they evoke in the public imagination. Featured narratives often involve humans losing control of living environments. As writers and movie makers have conditioned us to believe, whenever one gives up or loses such control, things tend to end up messy, at least until a hero steps in and puts us humans back in charge at the end of the story.

Yet when we imagine a building with hundreds of inhabitants and millions of various kinds of movable elements, light units, controllable climate zones, dynamically adjustable acoustic membranes, and opacity–changing walls, floors, and ceilings, we instantly realize that direct and simultaneous control of each one of those elements would be counterproductively laborious. Whether performed by some powerful control unit or a human supervisor, such micromanagement of a large number of devices would most likely cause significantly more problems than benefits. Current automation systems allow choreographed control of many devices embedded in buildings, however relatively little interaction between individual users and these systems is then allowed. This results in inhabitants being frustrated by the lack of influence on their surroundings. Despite the natural fear of giving up control, the idea that such buildings could instead "come to life"—as balanced systems of people and devices directly responding to each other while maintaining efficient global performance—comes across as a compelling alternative. Yet it requires a change of perspective in the way we think about buildings. If traditionally we would compare a living building to a single tree, maybe we should think of it as an entire forest instead: an ecosystem of various artificial "plants and animals" forming a habitat that sustains itself as a whole, along with its inhabitants.

SHIFTING FOCUS: FROM TECHNOLOGY TO BEHAVIOR

Such a change of perspective may coincide with the more general trend in contemporary culture. Daring visions of dynamically changing buildings and cities have been appearing since the 1950s. The conceptual designs of architecture studio Archigram or the architects Cedric Price and Yona Friedman have had a seminal influence on much of contemporary architecture and modern architectural thinking (Cook et al. 1999; Friedman 2006; Price et al. 2003). Yet none of these projects have been turned into reality, despite apparent technological means to do so. Why should the situation today be any different?

When investigating early ideas of transformable buildings and cities conjured by Cedric Price or Archigram, what strikes us at first glance is the exposed technology. Large cranes, rails, and movable capsules clearly convey the fact that these structures are to operate more like robots than traditional buildings as we know them. The actual underlying social process and rationale of their transformations and reassemblies seem less relevant. The ephemeral yet provocative visions of the artist Constant and more pragmatic, yet still conceptual, schemes of Yona Friedman focus less on technology. Although their drawings and models present ideas of how a city could look, which were equally novel for their time, the social aspects and their inner workings draw more attention here. It is in these social models that the real questions seem to be buried. Given that a city can be continuously transformed with relative ease, how should these transformations be decided? Who should be in control and to what extent? How are we to deal with ownership of space, when no space is truly permanent? While Constant turns these questions around to emphasize the vision of the ludic society that lives primarily in the present, Friedman proposes an IT–driven system for "booking" three–dimensional lots and connections to infrastructure. Similarly Price, in the Fun Palace project, extensively elaborates on a control system that moves the building's modules based on the demands of their users. This very empowerment of the inhabitants to trigger rapid transformations of their surroundings was arguably the most profound innovation of these projects and serves today as a conceptual foundation of alive architecture.

THE INTERNET OF ARCHITECTURE Today, after more than four decades, these visions still amaze. Not only technology has become significantly cheaper and more accessible, but we have also entered the era of hyperconnectivity, where information is being exchanged globally and instantly, where software is gradually more valued than hardware, where consumers are being replaced by contributors, and where users have become makers. The Internet of Things, connecting everyday objects to people and other objects via the Internet, is the technological trend recognized by the largest companies. Watching promotional videos by IBM or Cisco makes us feel that the future of fascinating ecosystems comprising people and interactive digital artifacts is just around the corner.[3] It seems that alive architecture will take architects by surprise, appearing not out of a visionary master plan, but through networks of devices filling up, augmenting, and eventually reshaping our habitats. Yet there is a disconnect between the promise of the inspirational ideas used to promote the Internet of Things and what actually is taking place.

hyperconnectivity

This dissonance can be clearly illustrated by an analogy with natural ecosystems. Natural systems are not governed; they self–stabilize through negative feedback loops. There is no hierarchy or any form of top–down control—only a flow of energy, matter, and information. On the other hand, the Internet of Things' applications, as they are being commercially developed now, use the ability to control as their main selling point. They provide users with the remote control of thermostats, the centralized monitoring of power meters, or the reception of mobile–phone notifications when the dishwasher is done, among many other examples. Much of the Internet of Things' discourse orbits around the topic of big data, collecting large amounts of information in the cloud by large companies or governments, driven more by the need to control or manage citizens, or target advertisements to individuals, rather than create better social models or empower individuals.

hierarchy

the cloud

Architecture appears to offer a surprising opportunity to reconcile the dichotomy between the bottom–up promise and current top–down direction of the Internet of Things. While in the virtual space of "the Web" everything and everyone can be

---

3   See http://www.ibm.com/smarterplanet/us/en/overview/article/iot_video.html; and http://www.cisco.com/web/solutions/trends/iot/overview.html.

connected with few restrictions, the physical space of architecture organizes these relationships and helps to attribute concrete meaning to them. If architecture were to be more involved in the discussion on the Internet of Things, the locality and proximity of things would certainly gain prominence, allowing stronger focus on end–user benefits of technologies related to the Internet of Things.

EMBRACING THE BOTTOM–UP Giving up the requirement of centralized control or data gathering allows a stronger focus on local interactions between people and what constitutes their habitats. Such a shift then positions the idea of alive architecture in a different perspective, from which the key question is not of such architecture's form, but of its content. We can assume that technology exists for dynamically transformable architecture to be made and we can imagine many ways in which such architecture may look. Yet we know little of the mechanisms by which it should work. We may only gradually assemble its constituents along with interactions among them, and evaluate whether it improves the operation of the architectural ecosystem as a whole, allowing it to sustain itself and flourish. We can assume that such a system is unlikely to be developed in a top–down, centrally governed, choreographed, or in any other controlled fashion. We may guess that an approach artificially replicating the mechanisms of evolution and adaptation would yield better results.

In this, we can't expect artificial devices to breed and evolve just yet. However the trends set by the maker movement set new paths (Hatch 2014). With know–how exchange platforms (like instructables or materiability), highly accessible technological prototyping platforms (ranging from Arduino and 3–D printers to the network of fab labs), and crowd–funding platforms (Kickstarter or Indiegogo), we are already experiencing an unprecedented proliferation of new kinds of interconnected devices. Projects such as the WikiHouse or Fab Lab House show the potential these trends bring to the built environment. The recent success of Philips Hue lights or Nest thermostats also shows that there is large interest from the general public in making their living environments more dynamic and "smart." However, none of these products or developments provides solutions to architecture that would exhibit the characteristics of an ecosystem.

D/E/FORM Installations such as Philip Beesley's Hylozoic Ground or Daan Roosegaarde's Dune help us imagine and to some extent experience what an artificial architectural ecosystem could be. Yet we still know relatively little concerning how such ecosystems could actually work on a larger scale of both time and space, how could they sustain themselves, and how could they be intertwined with the lives of the people inhabiting them.

The project *D|E|Form* has been an attempt to identify mechanisms on which artificial architectural ecosystems could operate. The concept involves an architectural space made up of triangular elements that can be added, removed, or reassembled to modify an architectural environment. Each of the elements contains a microcontroller and can be equipped with a set of sensors and actuators. Preliminary sensors include infrared proximity on both sides of the panel, light intensity, temperature, and a set of capacitive touch triggers. Actuators include electric linear actuators, servo–driven shutters, and RGB LED lights. Additionally, elements can communicate with each other through a physical connector or a built–in radio module. Elements have been designed to be easy and fast to fabricate using a CNC router and then disassemble and recycle.

microcontroller

The system has been envisioned to allow the creation of spatial constructs that continuously transform over time. The transformation can be either done by users of that space, or, to some extent, by the installation elements on their own. The system was implemented in such a way that it is impossible to draw a clear distinction between transformations of the installation performed by the users or by the installation itself. What's more, the installation has not been designed as a whole, but as a system of individually operating elements. Each element has been programmed to analyze its own "success" using a utility function of the rate of occupancy as well as the rate of occupancy of neighboring panels. Simple buttons were added to panels to allow users to express approval or disapproval of a panel's location. A panel with low utility would initially try to change its state or position though its actuators. If this would not lead to an increase of utility, it would mark itself for removal, indicated by a slowly pulsing red light. Similarly, panels with high utility would pulse with green light if they had open connections on their sides. Users would then be given an option to trigger a new element to be added to that connection / fig.68 p.207 /.

occupancy

Both virtual simulations and limited physical tests have indicated that such behavior leads to a growth–like phenomenon of the installation as a whole. In this process, places found by people to be useful, interesting, or beautiful are enforced, and the dull useless ones gradually disappear.

growth

With its open–ended, behavior–focused design, the *D|E|Form* system ventures into a new territory for architecture. It was clear that the prototyped behavior of panels only scratched the surface of possibilities. Many pitfalls have also presented themselves. Behaviors of panels have easily grown overly demanding, requiring the use of artificial learning. What's more, the complex nature of the system and its open–endedness needed many iterations, tests, fail–safe mechanisms, and, above all, the continuous testing, modification, and improvement of behaviors. The introduction of a large number of autonomous elements that interact with each other has also meant that such a system could exhibit emergent properties and utilize algorithms researched in the field of "spatial computing." The initial tests have also shown that the cultural and social aspects of the system are equally challenging. Not only the design of interfaces, but also ways to engage people in the making and transformation process are critical to further the system's success.

spatial computing

As the system develops and evolves, its users also grow accustomed to it, learn new ways of interacting with it, create new social models and come up with new expectations.

NEW TOOLS FOR MAKERS OF ALIVE ARCHITECTURE

The *D|E|Form* project has shown that to realize living architectural ecosystems, new approaches and new tools are needed to facilitate the design, evaluation, and deployment of behaviors for complex distributed architectural systems. *HiveKit* is a software solution that I co–developed to answer this need. It provides several constituents, namely a graphic environment for scripting behaviors of complex networks of elements, a simulator to test behaviors in a virtual environment, a virtual machine that runs on individual devices constituting the system, and a mechanism for instant "viral" programming of scripted behaviors onto large networks of devices. A version of *HiveKit* has also been developed as a plug–in for the Rhino/Grasshopper suite. This permits seamless integration of the simulation with generative design models and digital fabrication routines / fig.69 p.207 /.

One of the main features of *HiveKit* is the inclusion of spatial computing primitives. These are well–studied algorithms that allow for the creation of predictable behavioral patterns onto complex networks of devices. An example of such primitives is "firefly synchronization," which ensures that all elements develop a shared notion of time without any form of centralized coordination. Another example is "gradient," which provides each element with information on the network distance ("hops") to the nearest element activated with a given trigger / fig.70 p.207 /.

The *HiveKit* has been successfully tested with installations such as *Hive Panels* by Hive Systems and Chris Kievid Design (see the article *Spatial Computing in Interactive Architecture* by Stefan Dulman in this volume for further reference), or *Seina* by the students of TU Delft's Interactive Environments minor program. An interactive floor and facade, among others, have also been implemented, in all cases providing a wide array of novel functionalities. The rapid development and unprecedented ability for multiuser interactions have been largely appreciated by designers and prospective customers of the system.

WRAP–UP The vision of alive architecture seems less distant today than ever before. Yet with much of designers' focus being on the technological and material challenges, the possibly biggest challenge often seems to be overlooked: the ways to develop the mechanisms for artificial ecosystems to sustain themselves, develop, adapt, and ultimately flourish in tight symbiosis with their users.

This essay has briefly sketched an approach where living architecture is being developed as a distributed ecosystem of devices and users, without the need for a centralized control system. Such systems seem natural in many ways, above all in their promise to sustain themselves, develop, and evolve. The *D|E|Form* project has been used as a general example, and *HiveKit* introduced as a new kind of design tool allowing for the fast development of behaviors for these kinds of systems. Yet all these developments only indicate one direction into a vast new territory that lies ahead of designers and architects. If we are to embark on the quest of actualizing the vision of alive architecture, a significant amount of work still needs to be done.

territory

references

- Cook, Peter, et al. (1999) Archigram. New York: Princeton Architectural Press.
- Erlandson, Wilma (2001) My Father "Talked to Trees." W. Erlandson.
- Friedman, Yona (2006) Pro Domo. Barcelona: Actar.
- Hatch, Mark (2014) The Maker Movement Manifesto: Rules for Innovation in the New World of Crafters, Hackers, and Tinkerers. New York: McGraw–Hill Education.
- Price, Cedric, et al. (2003) Re:CP. Basel: Birkhäuser Architecture.

A conversation between

Tomasz Jaskiewicz,
Kas Oosterhuis,
Jason Bruges,
Ruairi Glynn,
Ludger Hovestadt,
Stefan Dulman,
Areti Markopoulou, and
Philip Beesley.

Alive: International Symposium on Adaptive Architecture, Zurich, July 8, 2013.

TOMASZ In the topics addressed, I find it interesting that, on the one hand, we are talking about incredible design tools that allow every single piece of a building to be customized until that building is realized—yet it is such an immensely slow and difficult process to introduce these techniques in the industry. On the other hand, we are looking at very temporary installations, which are incredibly responsive and interactive, and which can change multiple times per second. So I am wondering where and how these two worlds will meet?

KAS I think it is simply payback time. If it pays back in one day, we can invest in a project that pays back in one day. If it pays back in fifty years, then it takes fifty years. In other words, it's a commercial thing. Money is an important factor and so far I haven't heard anyone speak about it yet.

JASON Well, I think there are two questions in this type of interactive, responsive, time–based work. The first one is obviously around maintenance: Who is going to look after these systems? These things can break, and they don't necessarily have longevity, but that part can be planned, and risks can be discussed and included in the process. And finally certain elements can also be repurposed and recycled.
The second question is about budget. In our studio in London we really try to look at equivalence, but how do you quantify it? You can of course apply certain algorithms, which the advertising industry uses, for example, like tracking the number of pairs of eyes looking at something. So then you can try to quantify how successful your facade or structure might be in drawing attention and getting people to look at it, and therefore you can put a certain value to it. Obviously that is another way of looking at things, at mapping budgets to criteria.
The involved technology and the designing and engineering are yet another line on the quantity–surveyor spreadsheets, and are quite often not even singled out as a different item. But luckily this is becoming more and more apparent. I am thinking of a project we are working on at the moment, the new station at York University in Toronto, in which we are looking at a very small

uplift over two thousand square meters of cladding on the station concourse, and the value of what it brings to the station versus the cost is a nominal uplift essentially. But again, it is more about the thinking, the intelligence, the interrogation of the space and the collaboration between the designers to make it happen. So it can be deemed expensive or it can be something that is very carefully integrated and thought about during the inception of a project.

RUAIRI Jason, you just showed us your lovely *Panda Project*, which is perhaps the simplest thing you have ever built, yet one of your most successful pieces, probably because it uses one of the most fundamental techniques in puppetry—the gaze—which creates a very visceral, very meaningful reaction in a person. So when comparing this to Tomasz's and Stefan's *HiveKit* I wonder about the kind of interactions and sensations that you can have in such a distributed system, whether you can create a similarly meaningful interaction with something that is emerging and potentially so intricate or if it gets lost in its own complexity?

TOMASZ Well, in our system, whatever complexity of interactions you want to create is really up to you. Yet I think the possibilities of *HiveKit* unfold only when you want to have very large numbers of devices. If it is only ten, or maybe even fifty devices, like with the *Panda Project*, it doesn't really make sense to work with distributed algorithms. But if you are thinking of ten thousand devices embedded in a building facade or scattered in a park, and you want to achieve an experience that is not only about the interaction of one person and one device, but involves a lot of people and all these devices at once, then you have to figure

out a way to do it. So far I haven't found a feasible way to do it in a centralized manner, especially if you really want to scale things up.

LUDGER But especially then, if you have these ten to twenty thousand elements on a facade and you want to project videos or other very simple things, it is impossible with this kind of technology.

TOMASZ The *Protodeck* project—the interactive floor at Hyperbody—was actually a very good learning experience for us in that sense. Having a distributed system doesn't mean that you cannot have a centralized one operating in parallel. So actually, for testing and debugging next to these distributed swarms of devices and the local communication among them, we cheated a little bit by having a communication bus connecting all the devices. This essentially allowed us to do two things at the same time. If you want to stream a video to however many devices you have, you can do it, but then on top of that you can use distributed logics for other purposes.

STEFAN One more thing following from your previous question: if you have such a tool that allows you to design a new system, a new software behavior in minutes or days, you can think of reconfiguration.
The structure of the building is going to stay for twenty, thirty years, but the behavior of the building at the software level can change very fast.

And if I'm thinking of the number of eyes that get attracted by your particular construction, well, people get bored looking at the same thing over and over again. But if you can change the behavior very fast or if you allow the community to change the display by connecting with a smartphone or whatever, this makes it interesting and opens up new possibilities.

ARETI What mainly intrigues me and where I see the biggest potential of interactive design is in applications for activating and transforming public space. The public space is the soul of the city. It is the area of overlap, the stage where socialization and exchange of information happen. The

information society is now bringing to the scene not only new technologies but also new principles of operation—for instance, how streets and parks behave or what a certain public space looks like. If we are able to collect and monitor the invisible layer of information within urban environments then we will be able to use this information for both bottom–up and top–down processes, for a more efficient way of inhabiting public space. It makes me think that cities could soon be looking after their citizens thanks to a well–designed urban operating system. At the same time, as a citizen, I must be able to choose the shortest or most comfortable path to bike to my office or share information with others at high speeds. All this could happen through the most important aspect of those advancements, which in my opinion is the democratization of a big part of software and hardware involved in these technologies.

JASON In London we have actually been looking at permeability throughout the city and being able to intervene in different ways so people are able to orient and navigate better. But we can also look at the overlap between digital systems, personal systems, and the environment, essentially de–clustering space through a certain editing that makes the environment more pleasant. And particularly in London, layers of things are constantly being added to the environment—signs and furniture and other stuff—that you possibly want to get rid of, and I wonder if you can have a multifaceted system that becomes part of that palette in terms of public space.

PHILIP If Vitruvius was your muse you would be following durability above all. The work that you are doing would be an internal counter–form to our living anima. Ruairi, calling your work *Anima* perhaps captures it. The vivid temporal qualities in the work of all of you suggest that there needs to be quite a new paradigm that requires a new set of skills and strategy. How can this material survive? What kind of response do you give to the question of durability, of maintenance, and of survival? I wonder if you could speak directly about durability.

RUAIRI Regarding Vitruvius, a lot of people think that his books are exclusively about how to create buildings, but the tenth book is entirely about how to make machines. And so machines result as architecture. Not included in those machines are automata, which very much were attempts to build architecture that had anima that performed. I believe that the machine and the automaton and that particular history of architecture are completely compatible with the notions of durability. The fact that things perform and people get emotionally attached to them actually encourages people to look after them. Look for example at how people cry when their Tamagotchi dies. These relationships are very fascinating and they are more likely to occur as things develop degrees of goal–directed behavior and perceivable intelligence. And perhaps people are going to build new relationships with these objects and value them differently, which might lead to another kind of a durability that emerges from these new connections.

JASON Considering durability I should mention the *80 Year Project*. We are building a series of granite monoliths and the client has stipulated that they want them to be there for the life of the park they are sitting in. The Vitruvian waterway is actually a good point to look at in this respect. If you break down a system like that, the bronze infrastructure and the metals within the gears and axles would probably last hundreds of years, but the wooden paddles would wear down and have to be replaced. So you basically go through a kit–of–parts and you look at how long they last. The operator, thirty–five years, the wood, fifty years, some of the bronze infrastructure, even longer. And we've essentially done the same, looking at the granite cladding and the metal infrastructure: eighty years, with some of the fixing possibly less—we're doing a major refurbishment of the electronics every fifteen years. And then we've been putting the piece in a rapidly accelerating testing environment for three months. So we have been trying to break the glass, granite, and electronic interfaces at eighty–degree Celsius temperature shifts over very quick cycles. This is how, in the studio, we are gearing up to put things in the real world and give it some form of

accreditation.
It remains a very difficult question, and it's interesting to consider our attitude toward conserving things, which we want to see kept in a certain way, like we do now with buildings and environments and with listing and protection. That same level of protection gets afforded to the things that we are creating now, regardless of how long they might actually want to last.

LUDGER I would say that we are looking at very different ways of thinking. Vitruvius was about orchestrating matter and space, having spatial order and keeping it stable, which to him meant durability. With modernity came a focus on the repetition within time, and this was called durability. And today, durability is about identity, about having certain places and different investigations to keep a stable identity of these places, of these brands. And I agree that it is completely within the idea of Vitruvius. If we connect durability directly to matter, for example, we are back to the durability of the Egyption pyramids, which even Vitruvius disconnected from and developed a level of abstraction by talking about orders in space.
To make a connection with this conference and the very impressive applications that we have seen, and also with the Swiss environment, which I'm working in, is that here we don't like to show things as expressively as you tend to do in the UK, which I find fantastic with your work and a little frustrating with our work. Just as with the building we are in right now, which is from the '50s and was recently renovated while trying to change as little as possible. We expected a kind of interactive environment, so we have hundreds of sensors and actuators, all completely distributed but hidden and not visible. By changing the setup through basically an inversion of all these building services, the building is now much more comfortable and uses radically less energy. There is no opposition anymore between the system and us. We are within the play. But we can discuss it in the same way as we do with all these very expressive and interesting applications that we have seen earlier today, but it's the exact opposite. Therefore it is a little strange that we can have such different attitudes toward the exact same thinking.

RUAIRI I am really interested in designing those kinds of systems and think that there is a beautiful symmetry to the thermostat, which is either below or above a certain level, and thus either turns itself on or off—that sort of simplicity. But then something like the images Philip showed of the thermal behavior of people's skin offer such a rich quality of sensory data that it urges you to have responses that pose a similarly high definition. But I wonder if it is even possible to design things with the same kind of requisite variety. I think this is a question of whether we are hyper–reductive or whether we expressively embrace this complexity.

LUDGER This is what I find really striking: that you can do the exact same thing and be either very expressive or reduce it to the minimum. The Swiss way is to do it, to understand it, but to not show it.

RUAIRI Maybe that truly is the difference between the Swiss way and the English architectural education, which is to show it and celebrate it. Yet these are both very interesting and important ideas. But I think these kinds of performance pieces encourage people to think about it in a very different way than they perhaps would if you said, "This is completely invisible, but you have to trust me that it's working."

Branko Kolarevic
/ Chair in Integrated Design and Co-Director, Laboratory for Integrative Design.
/ Professor, Faculty of Environmental Design, University of Calgary.

Outlook

Over the past decade we have seen an increasing interest in exploring the capacity of built spaces to change—i.e., to respond dynamically, and automatically, to changes in the external and internal environments and to different patterns of use. The principal idea is that two-way relationships could be established among spaces, environment, and users: the users or the changes in the environment would affect the configuration of space, and vice versa. The result is an architecture that self-adjusts to the needs of the users. Different terms have been used to describe such architecture: adaptive, dynamic, interactive, responsive, etc. As I will argue in this paper, the principal idea behind it—facilitating and accommodating change—is not new; what has changed are the technologies (and materials) to accomplish it.

IT ALL STARTED IN THE 1960s The first concepts of an adaptive, responsive architecture, as it is understood today, were born in the late 1960s and early 1970s, primarily as a result of developments in cybernetics, artificial intelligence, and information technologies. Such architecture, however, was first envisioned in science-fiction. James Graham Ballard, a British novelist, described in a short story from 1962 a "psychotropic house," a machine-like, mood-sensitive house that could respond to and learn from its occupants, becoming "alive" as it was occupied. The imagined responsive house was made from a material Ballard referred to as "plastex," a combination of plaster and latex that allowed the house to change its shape as needed. The house also had many "senso-cells," distributed all over it, which were capable of "echoing every shift of mood and position of its occupants." While Ballard was among the first to envision an "alive," responsive, adaptive house, Gordon Pask, as an early proponent of cybernetics in architecture, is often credited with setting the foundations for interactive environments in the 1960s with his concept of "conversation theory," intended as a comprehensive theory of interaction. Pask's ideas had a tremendous influence on both Cedric Price and Nicholas Negroponte, with whom he collaborated. Price adopted concepts from cybernetics to articulate the concept of "anticipatory architecture," demonstrated by his seminal Fun Palace and Generator projects. Negroponte (1975) proposed that computing power be integrated into buildings so that they could perform better, turning buildings into "architecture machines"—i.e., "evolving mechanisms" that are "'assisted,' 'augmented,' and eventually 'replicated' by a computer." At roughly the same time that Negroponte was working on his architecture machines, Charles Eastman (1972) developed the concept of "adaptive-conditional

Adaptive Architecture: Low–Tech, High–Tech, or Both?[1]

architecture," which self–adjusts based on the feedback from the spaces and users. Eastman proposed that automated systems could control buildings' responses. He used an analogy of a thermostat to describe the essential components: sensors that would register changes in the environment, control mechanisms (or algorithms) that would interpret sensor readings, actuators as devices that would produce changes in the environment, and a device (an interface) that would let users enter their preferences. That is roughly the component makeup of any reactive system developed to date. Not much happened then in the 1980s and 1990s, with the exception of Jean Nouvel's Institut du Monde Arabe (figure 1), completed in 1987 in Paris, as the first significant, large–scale building to have an adaptive envelope. A number of dynamic, mechanically actuated building skins were completed over the past decade. Enric Ruiz–Geli's Media TIC building in Barcelona, completed in 2011, stands out for its large–scale, pneumatically activated adaptive facade, which is made of lightweight ETFE air cushions that provide sun shading (figure 2).

Fig. 1. Kinetic curtain wall at Jean Nouvel's Institut du Monde Arabe (1987) in Paris, made from over 30,000 mechanically activated apertures.

Fig. 2. Media TIC building in Barcelona, by Enric Ruiz–Geli (of Cloud9), features a dynamic facade made of "breathing," pneumatically activated ETFE air cushions.

---

1   Parts of this paper were published previously in reForm(), Proceedings of the 2009 ACADIA Conference, edited by Tristan d'Estree Sterk and Russell Loveridge.

Much of the recent surge of interest in responsive environments stems from the introduction of an inexpensive open–source microcontroller board called Arduino (figure 3), which was released in Italy in 2005. It can be connected easily to a variety of sensors detecting light, motion, touch, sound, temperature, etc. and by reading input from them can be made to "sense" the environment. It can be also connected to all kinds of actuators, such as lights, motors, and other devices, and can control them to "affect" that same environment. It also comes with a simple development environment for writing software that can interpret received input values from the sensors and produce output instructions that control the operation of the actuators. Since its release, hundreds of thousands of these inexpensive electronics boards have been sold worldwide, enabling enthusiasts to create all sorts of interactive objects and environments. Arduino boards also found their way into the schools of architecture worldwide, sparking the imagination of students and reigniting the vision of dynamic built environments that could change on the fly. Buildings could thus become "alive" by sensing what was happening in and around them and by adjusting their spatial configuration and the environmental conditions immediately. The dynamically changing buildings, imagined in science–fiction novels from the 1960s and 1970s, started to emerge as an attainable not–so–distant technological possibility. For instance, Ruiz–Geli's Media TIC building features a number of control systems, based on over one hundred networked Arduino boards, that can sense various changes in the environment and then produce a corresponding reaction not only in shading but also how the building is lit, and so on.

Fig. 3. Arduino Uno microcontroller board.

TOWARD AN ARCHITECTURE OF CHANGE

Accepting the dynamics of buildings and cities [...] can turn architectural change into an ecologically efficient process as well as a new urban experience.
Ed van Hinte et al., *Smart Architecture*, 2003

In *Flexible: Architecture That Responds to Change*, Robert Kronenburg (2007) argues that for a building to be "flexible," it must be capable of: 1) adaptation, as a way to better respond to various functions, uses, and requirements; 2) transformation, defined as alterations of shape, volume, form, or appearance; 3) movability; and 4) interaction, which applies to both the inside and the outside of a building. Such capacities in buildings will be provided by "intelligent" building systems, which will be driven by many factors, from environmental ones, such as the control of energy use, to changing the appearance of the building through varying images and patterns. The systems could be either automatic or "intuitive," suggesting a capacity of the system to infer from the context an appropriate set of responses without overly explicit inputs.

If we were to accept change as a fundamental contextual condition—and time as an essential design dimension—architecture could then begin to truly mediate between the built environment and the people who occupy it. As Ed van Hinte and his colleagues (2003) note, "instead of being merely the producer of a unique three–dimensional product, architects should see themselves as programmers of a process of spatial change." The principal task for architects is to create "a field of change and modification" that would generate possibilities instead of fixed conditions. The inhabitable space would then become an indeterminate design environment, subject to continuous processes of change, occurring in different realms and at various time scales:

> *"It is the form that is no longer stable, that is ready to accept change. Its temporary state is determined by the circumstances of the moment on the basis*

of an activated process and in–built intelligence and potential for change. Not product architecture then, but a process–based architecture whose form is defined by its users' dynamic behaviour and changing demands and by the changing external and internal conditions; an architecture that itself has the characteristics of an ecological system, that emulates nature instead of protecting it and therefore engages in an enduring fusion of nature and culture."

Ed van Hinte et al., *Smart Architecture*, 2003

As Van Hinte and his colleagues point out, "that would be a truly ground–breaking ecological architecture." But to get there, we need to first answer some fundamental questions pertaining to change as a conceptual dimension and time as a phenomenological dimension in architecture. We need to go beyond the current fascination with mechatronics and explore what change means in architecture and how it is manifested: buildings weather, programs change, envelopes adapt, interiors are reconfigured, systems replaced. We need to explore the kinds of changes that buildings should undergo and the scale and speed at which they occur. We need to examine which changes are necessary, useful, desirable, possible…

LOW–TECH ADAPTIVE ENVIRONMENTS The notion of adaptive environments is not new. In a traditional Japanese house any room could be a living room or a bedroom (or a dining room). What makes this adaptability in use possible are two key features: first, all furniture is lightweight and could be removed into large storage closets; second, the size of a space could be easily changed using sliding partitions (*fusuma*) that separate adjacent rooms. Such spatial porosity is also present in traditional Korean houses.

The modernist "open plan" is based in large part on these East Asian precedents, as were the associated notions of adaptability and flexibility. Gerrit Rietveld's seminal Schröder House, built in 1924, features on the upper floor an adaptive large space that can be left open or subdivided using sliding and revolving partitions into four separate rooms—i.e., three bedrooms and a living room. Similarly, Steven Holl's apartment complex in Fukuoka, Japan, completed in 1991, relied on hinged wall partitions to create adaptive apartment units, in which spaces could change daily or on a larger time scale as family size changes (figure 4). A similar use of hinged panels created an incredibly effective, puzzle–like transformable facade of the Storefront for Art and Architecture in New York (figure 5), which was designed jointly by Steven Holl and Vito Acconci and built in 1993.

Fig. 4. Steven Holl's Hinged Space Housing in Fukuoka, Japan, completed in 1991.

Fig. 5. Transformable facade of the Storefront for Art and Architecture in New York, completed in 1993, designed by Steven Holl and Vito Acconci.

As more and more designers and firms begin to experiment with innovative sensing, control, and actuation technologies to create kinetic, adaptive spaces and systems, it is worth remembering that wheels and hinges—if used imaginatively—could create very potent transformable environments that need not rely on any fancy mechatronic setups. The Naked House in Kawagoe, Japan, designed by Shigeru Ban and completed in 2000, features four movable rooms on wheels inside a large, shed–like space (figure 6). The six–square–meter rooms are open on two sides and can be located anywhere within the large interior space or even moved outside; they could be also joined to form larger spaces if needed. The Sliding House in Suffolk, UK, designed by dRMM and completed in 2009, features an enclosure that can move along recessed tracks to cover or uncover different buildings along its twenty–eight–meter–long linear path (figure 7): the house, garage, or the annex (and a swimming pool that could be added in the future). The four electric motors that move the enclosure are integrated into its wall thickness; each motor is powered by car batteries that are charged by mains or PV solar panels.

Fig. 7. dRMM's Sliding House (2009) in Suffolk, UK, during different stages of its transformation.

Fig. 6. Shigeru Ban's Naked House (2000) features movable rooms on casters.

We should not lose sight of low–tech solutions in our current quest for adaptive systems infused with the latest sensing, control, and activation technologies. Oftentimes, simply adding wheels and tracks (and/or hinges) to elements that are then moved by people is all that is necessary for some adaptive designs to be effective spatially and programmatically. Buildings used to have adaptive facades with hinged and louvered shutters fixed outside the windows that were used to provide security or privacy, or to modulate light. Such simple solutions still have a place in contemporary architecture that seeks to provide user–controlled adaptability in buildings.

There is also a good chance that any mechatronic solution that depends on the current state–of–the–art technologies could become obsolete relatively quickly. One way of addressing this challenge of obsolescence is to rely on solutions that are already seen as "obsolete"; as such they won't become obsolete—they already are. For example, Jan and Tim Edler from realities:united, who took on the challenge of designing the media facade for the Kunsthaus in Graz by Peter Cook and Colin Fournier, considered all sorts of the latest and the greatest contemporary technologies, such as LEDs, plasma screens, projections systems, etc., but were concerned with their potential life span. In the end they settled for the humble but utterly "obsolete" round neon lights that were ubiquitous in kitchens in the 1960s (figure 8). They discovered that the intensity of those lights could be controlled with a simple capacitor that could be connected to a custom–designed controller board with a user–friendly screen interface. Thus, a low–tech, low–resolution monochrome BIX facade (BIX stands for the "building pixel") made from technologically obsolete components was devised to withstand these inevitable challenges of time and technological progress.

on the sky conditions; at night they are illuminated, emanating bright white light like a large lantern. The architects have managed to produce a dynamic building skin that registers and responds to environmental conditions (light, wind) without any sophisticated mechatronics. It represents an excellent example of minimalist, simple tectonics producing complex, subtle spatial and surface effects. Such simplicity (complexity attained through simple means) is perhaps another promising trajectory for dynamic building skins.

Fig. 8. BIX Facade (Kunsthaus Graz), designed by realities:united, was built using round neon lights that became ubiquitous in the 1960s.

Fig. 9. Children's Museum of Pittsburgh (2011) pavilion facade, by Koning Eizenberg Architecture with Ned Kahn, is made from tens of thousands hinged resin flaps.

Any cutting–edge technological system of today becomes an obsolete technology rather quickly. This dimension of time is fairly critical for the designers of adaptive, responsive, interactive building systems of tomorrow.

EMBEDDED LOW–ENERGY RESPONSIVENESS

The new pavilion added to the Children's Museum of Pittsburgh (figure 9) offers a compelling example of a dynamic yet tectonically and technologically simple facade. Koning Eizenberg, architects of the pavilion, developed together with Ned Kahn, a sunscreen called Articulated Cloud that consists of tens of thousands of hinged resin flaps that flutter in the wind. During the day, their color depends

The future of dynamic building skins will likely belong to low–energy systems that can harvest the heat from the sun or the kinetic energy of the wind. Material–based activation systems are being developed and tested by a number of design research teams: Achim Menges and his research group at the University of Stuttgart are exploiting hygroscopic properties of wood fibers to create responsive skins that react to different levels of humidity in the environment (figure 10); Doris Sung at the University of California is working with bimetallic strips that curl when exposed to the sun's heat, creating apertures that can ventilate interior spaces (figure 11); Nick Puckett, when he was at the University of Kentucky, experimented with shape–memory polymers strips that produce similar action—i.e., open and close

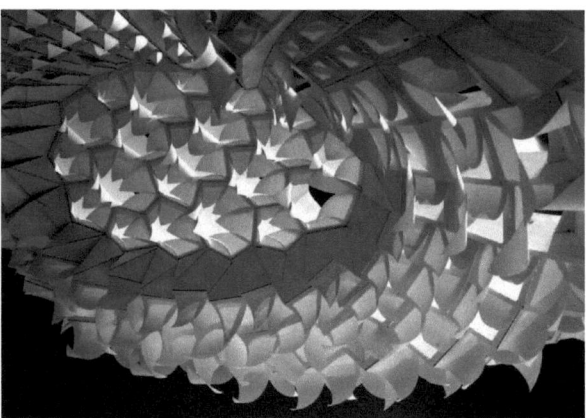

Fig. 10. HygroScope by Achim Menges and his ICD research group at the University of Stuttgart.

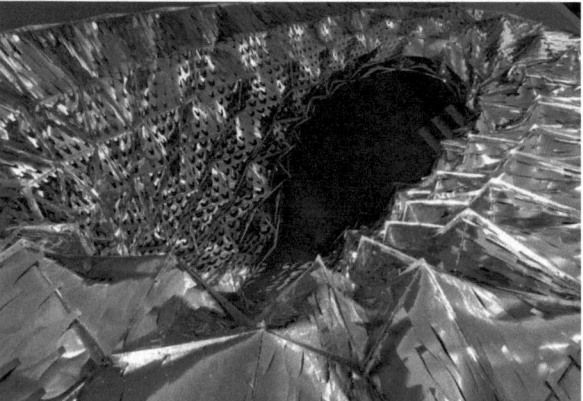

Fig. 11. Doris Sung's Bloom canopy in Los Angeles is made from thousands of bimetallic components.

Fig. 12. Nick Puckett's dynamic skin prototype is made of heat–activated shape–memory polymer.

when exposed to the sun's heat (figure 12). None of these examples required sophisticated sensory, control, or actuation systems to produce a dynamic response to changing environmental conditions; instead, they cleverly exploited the embedded, intrinsic properties of the materials.

TOWARD PASKIAN RESPONSIVE ENVIRONMENTS

Another critical issue in the design of any highly automated adaptive and responsive system is the user override. For example, louvers in an automated, "high performance" facade could automatically come down in bright sunlight to shade the interior spaces, but that action could not only be distracting to people who might be in an important meeting, it could also block a highly desirable and attractive view to a nearby park or lake. If an installed, automated system requires frequent manual overrides by annoyed users, its "life" is not going to be that long; a simple people–activated high–performance and low–tech solution would probably more than suffice in such cases. Social and cultural factors need to be taken into account in setups that rely on automated systems to attain certain technical performance goals. We shouldn't be blinded by technologies of the day and should not lose sight of the qualitative, i.e., non–quantifiable performative, aspects of the project and whether they could be better served by no–tech or low–tech solutions.

There is also the ever–present danger of creating "gimmicky" architecture that becomes boring very quickly. The primary goal of constructing a truly responsive, adaptive architecture is to imbue buildings with the capacity to interact with the environment and their users in an engaging way. Architecture that echoes the work of Nicholas Negroponte could be understood as an adaptive, responsive machine—a sensory, actuated, performative assemblage of spatial and technical systems that creates an environment that stimulates and is, in turn, stimulated by users' interactions and their behavior. Arguably, for any such system to be continually engaging, it has to be designed as inherently indeterminate in order to produce unpredictable outcomes. The user should have an effect on the system's behavior or its outcome and, more importantly, on how that behavior or outcome is computed. That requires that both inputs and outputs of the systems be constructed on the fly. It is this capacity to construct inputs and outputs that distinguishes interactive from merely reactive systems.

The distinction between interactive and reactive is what enables adaptive, responsive architecture to be seen as an enabler of new relations between people and spaces. When Philip Beesley and his colleagues (2006) describe a responsive environment in *Responsive Architectures: Subtle Technologies* as a "networked structure that senses action within a field of attention and responds dynamically with programmed and designed logic," they are referring to what is essentially a reactive system. In contrast, Michael Fox and Miles Kemp (2009) argue that in "interactive" architecture, the interaction is circular—systems "interact" instead of just "react." The distinction between interaction and reaction (i.e., a system's response) is not clear–cut, because a dynamic action of a component, for example, could be seen not simply as a reaction but also as part of the overall scenarios of interactivity. Tristan D'Estree Sterk (2006) distinguishes direct manipulation (deliberate control), automation (reflexive control), and hybridized models as forms of interaction between the users and the technologies behind responsive systems. For Sterk, "the hybridized model can also be used to produce responses that have adjustable response criteria, achieving this by using occupant interactions to build contextual models of the ways in which users occupy and manipulate space."

As Usman Haque (2007) puts it, the goal is "a model of interaction where an individual can directly adjust the way that a machine responds to him or her so that they can converge on a mutually agreeable nature of feedback: an architecture that learns from the inhabitant just as the inhabitant learns from the architecture." Thus, one of the principal challenges is how to construct (Paskian) systems that would provide enough variety to keep users engaged, while avoiding randomness, which could lead to disengagement if the output cannot be understood. The key challenge is to design an architecture that avoids boredom and retains a high degree of novelty. As observed by Haque, "unlike the efficiency–oriented pattern–optimization approach taken by many responsive environmental systems, an architecture built on Pask's system would continually encourage novelty and provoke conversational relationships with human participants."

There are other, more operational–based challenges that have to do with resolution of potential conflicts within systems. For example, Sterk discusses the coordination of responses at coincident—i.e., shared boundaries between spaces, as in a movable partition wall between two spaces—which can have actuators accessible by two independent control processes.

Another issue is that while change is desirable, for most purposes, it would have to occur in predictable and easily anticipated ways. If that is not possible, then there ought to be a way (in certain circumstances) for users to preview changes before they are executed, or to choose among alternatives for one (perhaps suboptimal) that fits the current circumstances, needs, and/or desires. Users may need to be informed of the impact that selected changes would have on the environment or the shape and configuration of the space. The overall issue of control is critical, as was already mentioned. In *Smart Architecture*, Ed van Hinte (2003) warns that "sometimes a simple and hence ostensibly 'dumb' building is smarter than a technology–dominated living–and–working machine over which the user has lost control."

THE WORK AHEAD When it comes to designing adaptive, responsive environments, the "software" side does not seem to present as many challenges as the "hardware" side—the building itself, whose majority of systems is inherently inflexible. That is perhaps where the biggest challenges and opportunities exist, as buildings would have to be conceptually completely rethought in order to enable them to adapt (i.e., to reconfigure themselves). Then there is the "middleware" that sits among the software and hardware and the users as devices that facilitate the feedback loops between the components of the system.

There are also some fundamental questions that have yet to be adequately addressed. For example, while Beesley and his colleagues (2006) predict that "the next generation of architecture will be able to sense, change and transform itself," they fail to say clearly toward what ends. Even though they ask what very well may be the key question—how do responsive systems affect us?—they do not attempt to answer it explicitly. Similarly, Fox and Kemp (2009), in their *Interactive Architecture* book, avoid explaining fully—and admit as much—why interactive systems are necessary, meaningful, or useful, and simply state, "The motivation to make these systems is found in the desire to create spaces and objects that can meet changing needs with respect to evolving individual, social, and environmental demands." Fox and Kemp position interactive architecture "as a transitional phenomenon with respect to a movement from a mechanical paradigm to a biological paradigm," which, as they explain, "requires not just pragmatic and performance–based technological understandings, but awareness of aesthetic, conceptual and philosophical issues relating to humans and the global environment."

In short, much remains to be done: I would argue that change in architecture is far from being adequately addressed or explored theoretically, experimentally, or phenomenologically. As we probe and embed adaptability, interactivity, and responsiveness into buildings and spaces, we must not unconditionally and blindly chase the latest technological advancements. As I have argued in this essay, an effective adaptive, responsive system could be based on simple, low–tech, low–energy solutions. It could be actuated by users, who could push, pull, turn, flip, and move things—and it could be intelligently augmented with sensors and an Arduino board here and there, as needed.

references

- Ballard, James Graham (2001) "The Thousand Dreams of Stellavista." In: Vermilion Sands. London: Vintage. Originally published in 1971.
- Beesley, Philip, S. Hirosue, J. Ruxton, M. Trankle, and C. Turner (2006) Responsive Architectures: Subtle Technologies. Cambridge: Riverside Architectural Press.
- Eastman, Charles (1972) "Adaptive–Conditional Architecture." In: N. Cross, ed., Design Participation, Proceedings of the Design Research Society Conference. London: Academy Editions, pp. 51–57.
- Fox, Michael, and Miles Kemp (2009) Interactive Architecture. New York: Princeton Architectural Press.
- Haque, Usman (2007) "The Architectural Relevance of Gordon Pask." In: Lucy Bullivant, ed., 4dsocial: Interactive Design Environments, Architectural Design, No. 77. London: Wiley Academy.
- Kronenburg, Robert (2007) Flexible: Architecture That Responds to Change. London: Laurence King Publishing.
- Negroponte, Nicholas (1975) Soft Architecture Machines. Cambridge, MA: MIT Press.
- Pask, Gordon (1969) "Architectural Relevance of Cybernetics." In: Architectural Design 39 (September), pp. 494–96.
- Sterk, Tristan d'Estree (2006) "Responsive Architecture: User–Centered Interactions within the Hybridized Model of Control." In: GameSetandMatch II: On Computer Games, Advanced Geometries and Digital Technologies. Rotterdam: Episode Publishers, pp. 494–501.
- Van Hinte, Ed, Marc Neelen, Jacques Vink, and Piet Vollaard (2003) Smart Architecture. Amsterdam: 010 Publishers.

Vera Bühlmann

/ Writer, Editor, and Lecturer in Philosophy on Technics, Media, Computation, and Design.
/ Founder and Head of the theory–lab for applied virtuality, Chair for CAAD, ETH Zurich.

Postscript

₪ "As an example of human achievement," John Orton maintains in his book *Semiconductors and the Information Revolution: Magic Crystals that made IT Happen*, the semiconductor ought to "rank alongside the Beethoven Symphonies, Concord, Impressionism, medieval cathedrals and Burgundy wines and we should be equally proud of it" (Orton 2009, p. 2). Why is it, indeed, that this demand feels odd? Of course this lack of appreciating our current form of technics is owed partially to its abstractness and the degree of expertise it seems to demand from us. But has this not been the case for any of the abovementioned artifacts we all meanwhile hold as precious and dear? An understanding of how semiconductor electronics works, what it is conditioned by, and to which ends we might be able to cultivate it, hold a promise of no lesser enjoyment:

> "I only hope that my attempt to explain something of its appeal will help the layman to obtain the same kind of enjoyment from an understanding of semiconductor electronics that he or she might experience in contemplation of any of these [achievements]"
> John Orton, 2009

₪ *Alive: Advancements in Adaptive Architecture* demonstrates in exemplary manner how architecture currently sets out to explore its own quick and vibrant reality—a reality that is saturated by electronic currents and metabolizes a proper, immanent kind of actual and virtual activity, an activity proper to built environments that can be coded to behave, in principle (if not, at least for the time being, altogether in practice) ad libitum. Especially in this context, I will argue, Orton's question deserves our unbound attention. In addition to issues of abstractness and expertise, there seems to be an obstacle in guiding our ambitions, as laypeople, toward learning to appreciate our most recent expressions of art and technics that seems more profound. There is something inherently uncanny implied in what Orton demands, which I would tentatively characterize as the waking up to a kind of neo–Babylonian confusion:

The Quickness of Matter, doped in its Polyalphabetic Textuality: or, The Articulation of Articles, beyond Prescript and Postscript

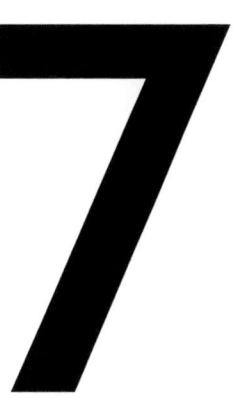

as architects, scientists, economists, engineers, designers, we are learning to speak our common "language," the language of mathematics, information, and code, *in many different tongues.*

¶ Raising the topos of the Tower of Babel, and the confusion we are allegorically said to have inherited from it, would be no news in itself if the situation would concern the many manners of how people speak *about* the things and the realities in which they live, or if architects were speaking *about* the structures and buildings they erect. In language, we are today ready to generously grant that sense can and shall be made in manifold and arbitrary manner. This generosity can be granted, we feel, because the mathematical and formal descriptions of things chemical, physical, or biological are capable of unambiguous representation—if not yet entirely pure and perfect, so at least with an increasingly greater and greater degree of approximation. It is in regard to this, I would like to suggest, that we seem to be caught up in a neo–Babylonian kind of situation: matter, like language formerly, can meanwhile be articulated in manifold manners, and none of their articulations can be regarded as strictly equivalent with all the others. In short, while the former Babylonian confusion meant that we have many names for the same thing, the confusion of our times inverses the situation: we now have many things for the same name. Matter that is informed can be assumed to exist in pure and original form as little or as much as this can be assumed of language.

¶ But still, why this concern with language and text, when our declared interest is in semiconductor electronics? Even in a literal (non–allegorical) manner—and this in a time when everyone is fascinated by the activity and agency proper to objects that are networked, objects that individuate within particular environments. Our interest with this concern is in learning to obtain reflected and critically distanced enjoyment from understanding these "things in their quickness"— an enjoyment like the one we have learned to obtain from appreciating other cultural artifacts aesthetically. We take *aesthetically* thereby to mean, without being subjected to the spells a cathedral (for example) casts on its visitors, as long as it is "alive" in all its not–explicitly mediated symbolic corporeality. However, since the eighteenth century, aesthetics has been much preoccupied with registers of form—formal (irr)regularity and expressions of aesthetical content in various gestalts and styles. With regard to our interest in these quickened pieces of matter, the emphasis comes to lie somewhere different: aesthetics, applied to the metabolism of things through their electronic circuit, must relate to the contractual discreetness of symbolized quantity much more than the regular continuity of form. It is with this emphasis on discreetness and distributedness that the "originality" of these electronically quick things we are interested in can be said to be more straightforwardly "textual." Because what makes any of them possible is that the symbolic notations of algebra *are* the "textual" substrate of our computational procedures: without algebra, no domestication of electricity; without electricity, no synthetic chemistry; without Boolean algebra, no coding of electrical current. In short, without algebra, no programming that comes anywhere close to the sophistication we have grown capable of. Without programming, no informing of materials in their chemical and subatomic consistency. It is within algebraic formulation that the mathematical quantity of "information" complements and specifies the physical quantities of generic "matter" and "energy" (let us recall Norbert Wiener's famous dictum that "information is information, not matter or energy" [1948, p. 55]). It is within algebraic formulations that light can be energized and turned into specified matter in physics that operates on a quantum level (Feynman 1985). To put it drastically: the manner in which we formulate all things, today, is algebraic (formulaic and equational) *before* we can think of it as formal (functional, a specification of direction within a formula). And for this reason, algebraic text is very different from aligning words into sentences and developing paragraphs to build upon each other to manifest an argument. Algebraic text essentially means *to develop an equation*: to spell out a space of reciprocal transformability between two sides that we want to consider as equivalent. Algebraic text is like the constitution that makes it possible to formulate reasonable sentences in discourse. In this, we can see the structure of our new Tower of Babel, where one and the same word relates to many things (as opposed to many words referring to the same thing).

¶ In its literal meaning, algebra signifies the reunion of broken parts. Thus we might hold against the point this text tries to make: are we not then living in an era in which the legendary Babylonian confusion can finally be fixed and undone, rather than waking up to a neo–Babylonian confusion?

¶ Indeed, we must not look far to find all sorts of spiritualistic phantasms that nourish and prosper from the fact that we are "communicating" today "mathematically." In such communications, it appears, we can devote ourselves to our intellectual appetites without worrying about hubris and the illegitimate acclamation of divine power, because those intellectual appetites are the appetites of *reason–in–general*. In the beginning was not the word, we can read in the positions of many atheist stances today, but information; not an evocation on the basis of subjectivity, but an objective quantity. Some people go as far as claiming that the physical laws of conservation ought to be subjected to the Laws of Information, which are claimed to be more comprehensively *natural*.

¶ But in all this enthusiasm, at work is a blind spot to which Jacques Derrida has, to a certain degree, attempted to draw our consideration. *General reason* reasons about *life in general*, he claims. And life–in–general cannot possibly be *alive*. The problem at stake is the very nature of the units with which such reasoning proceeds; that is, the nature of information. Information, as a unit for mathematical communication, cannot have a *positive* identity—it is what it is precisely because its nature is sheer determinability without essential content. Thus, what does it mean to live intellectually, he asks, in the scene of *archi*–writing rather than in the legacy of an *original* text? With information, communicating—literally *fitting–together what is essentially disparate*—spreads through and characterizes all things on the level of their energetic makeup.

¶ Text that is produced, in Derrida's scene of archi–writing, is not anymore text that is meant to passively preserve, for times to come, a present moment that is already and forever past: rather, it is completely unbiased and open for realizing any kind of sense that may be made. This is because, he maintains, in the beginning we do not find self–evident presence, but "original prints": we must learn to think, somewhat paradoxically, that everything begins with "re–production" (Derrida 1972, pp. 84ff). Rather than capturing something that is not meant to remain—a sound, a word—writing ought to be liberated from its obligations as merely representing speech and attend mostly to reproduce from the stock that has already been written, and to concentrate on self–preserving as much of it as possible through repetition. Repetition proceeds in a circuitous path, and in proceeding like this, it alone is capable of instituting a postponement, a deferral, which—and this is the nucleus of Derrida's argument—is capable of giving the space a thing takes, according to whatever gestalt it might adopt throughout each of the numerous acts of intellection in which its differential identity is being considered and appreciated. What we do in writing, Derrida argues, is not articulating a thing's identity by voicing it, but inscribing a thing's locus in a time and in a space that is only "there" and "actual" in remembering. Hence, we are literally in–scripting the possibility for a thing to remain present—intellectually. This is what he calls *spacing*.

¶ In a strikingly straightforward manner, this view seems to find its positive concretization in the technical substrates on which our real infrastructures run today: printed electronics as a truly generic materiality that might be inscribed (coded) to perform in any manner imaginable. In an almost literal sense, printed electronics presents us a textual kind of materiality where each produced piece spaces out a possibility.

¶ But Derrida's spacing—and this is crucial for his post–structuralist thinking—is symbolic in a non–physical, non–corporeal, non–positive sense. The spacing of course inscribes itself into a kind of "materiality"—yet it is not that of a sound or a phoneme. Derrida imagines *the alphabet* decoupled from its relation to the vivid bodies of actual sounds, and instead raised into an infinite and combinatorial mode. In other words, the alphabet is turned into a form that generalizes all the spellings and articulations possible within it: the alphabet is considered as *the alphabetical*. To keep speed—movement—and hence allow for (combinatorially) new inscriptions and (combinatorially) new things, we ought to treat all things actually physically manifest *as dead*. In order to keep intellectual originality alive and quick, we must defend its liveliness by building stocks of the original memory–force. Derrida's argument is a complicated one, and it would be far too ambitious to attempt to discuss it here with any appropriate amount of care. But what I would like to take from it is its elevation of the phonetic alphabet into a more abstract and symbolical level; however, if these considerations are meant to help find a way of appreciating algebra *as* language, things as technical as its articulations, and its articulations (e.g., semiconductor electronics) as ranking alongside Beethoven's symphonies, then we have to depart from Derrida's position at the point where he considers this more abstract level in reified and apparatus–like form, as *the alphabetical*. Instead, we can consider it as the *template of a plurality of alphabets of coding*, and like this we can connect his line of reasoning with our interest in the generic materiality of semiconductors.

¶ In electronics, I would like to suggest, it is Derrida's alphabetical that is multiplied and raised into an infinitary mode. Derrida's interest is to mark out that the letters in an alphabet apparatus are not characters properly, but ciphers that depend upon deciphering. Yet the limit of his point of view is that he relates the deciphering to the preservation of the alphabetical order that articulates units of sound, not units of energetic electrical current—his writing seeks to trace sense in its absence, as *grammé*. Yet electrical current circulates *in* symbolic inscriptions, and exchanges *quantums of potentiality*. Here, the means of expression is not the letters of the phonetic alphabet, but an open number of *alphabets of coding*.

¶ Thus, how might we learn to make sense of such a notion of algebraic text? How might we learn to make sense of it in a manner that can be captured neither in terms of *prescripts* (formula as laws) or *postscripts* (tracing a text's sense in the absence of its originality)? If we are to learn to appreciate aesthetically and critically the impressive and fascinating quickness of matter today, we ought to shift registers from representation to saturation in how we think about text, form, and quantity.

references

- Derrida, Jacques (1972) "Freud and the Scene of Writing." Yale French Studies, "French Freud: Structural Studies in Psychoanalysis," no. 48, pp. 74–117.
- Feynman, Richard (1985) QED: The Strange Theory of Light and Matter. Princeton, NJ: Princeton University Press.
- Orton, John (2009) Semiconductors and the Information Revolution: Magic Crystals That Made IT Happen. Elsevier: Academic Press.
- Wiener, Norbert (1948) Cybernetics, or Control and Communication in the Animal and the Machine. Cambridge, MA: MIT Press.

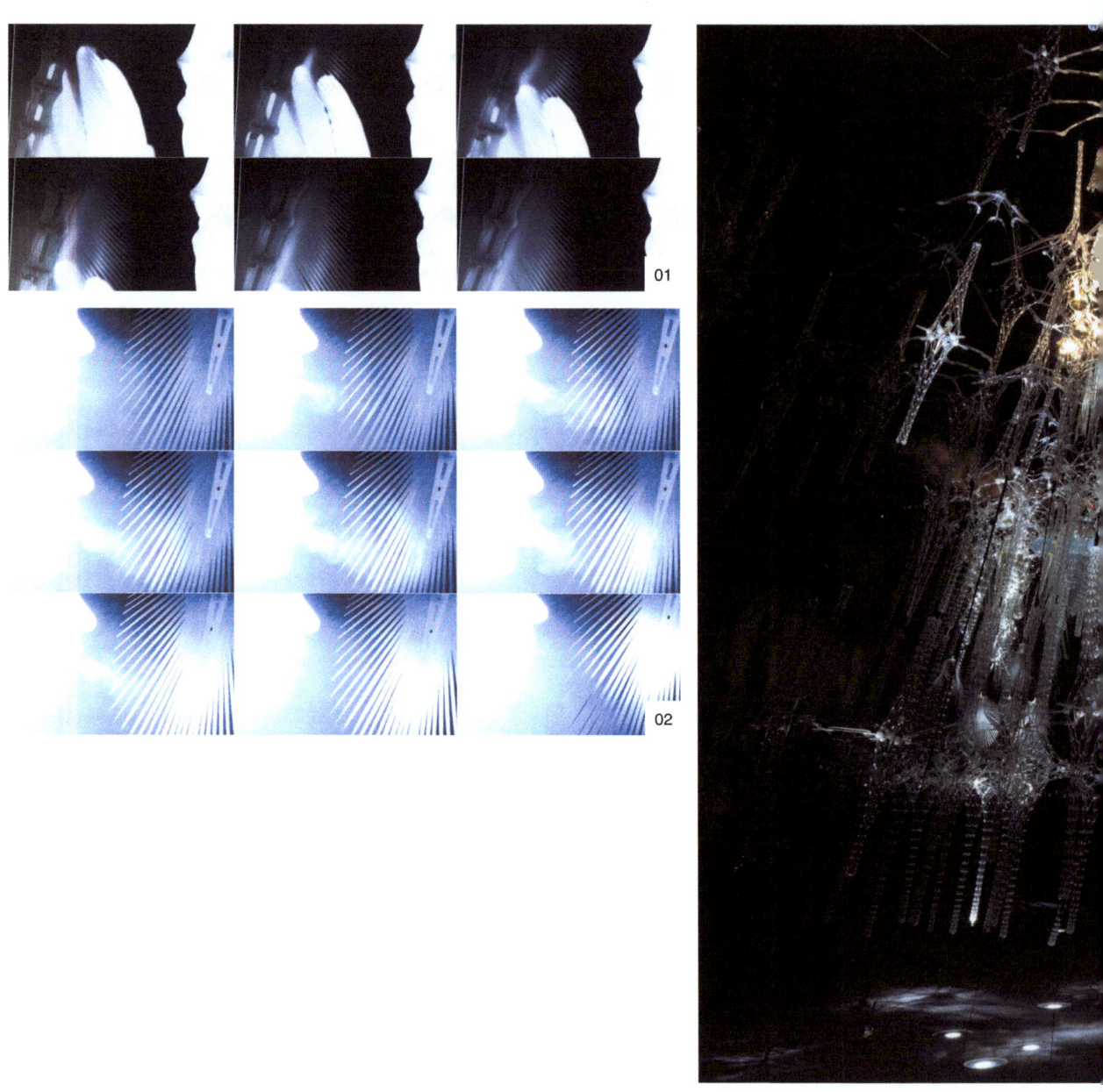

01 Cyclical exchanges of heat between a human figure and a polymer frond are recorded through thermal imaging.
02 Revealing subtle dynamics within an ambient environment, an "ingestion" of heat–energy occurs as temperatures within polymer tine details travel inward, implied by the darker tones of its outer edges.

03　　Elevation view of *Epiphyte Chamber*, Aleph Project, MMCA, Seoul, 2014: Layered systems line a public chamber, including shape–memory actuated tentacle clusters, thermoformed acrylic free–form diagrid spars, organic power–cell triggered sound, and protocell inorganic chemical metabolisms.

04 Shape–memory alloy mechanisms respond to touch, rippling and resonating together in near–synchronized movements. *Hylozoic Ground*, Venice Biennale, Italy (2010).
05 Complex assemblies of intricate kinetic components, arrays of microprocessors, and synthetic biology work in concert, pursuing tribal beginnings for public emplacement. *Epiphyte Chamber*, Museum of Modern and Contemporary Art, Soul, Korea (2013).

06 Recent textile–like forms imply intimate, diffusive boundaries within enclosing space. *Epiphyte Spring*, Hangzhou Triennial of Fiber Art, Hangzhou, China (2013).

07 *METAfolly* FRAC Collection / Detail of the fibrous structure, Orleans (2013).
08 *METAfolly* FRAC Collection / Detail of the sensing system, Orleans (2013).

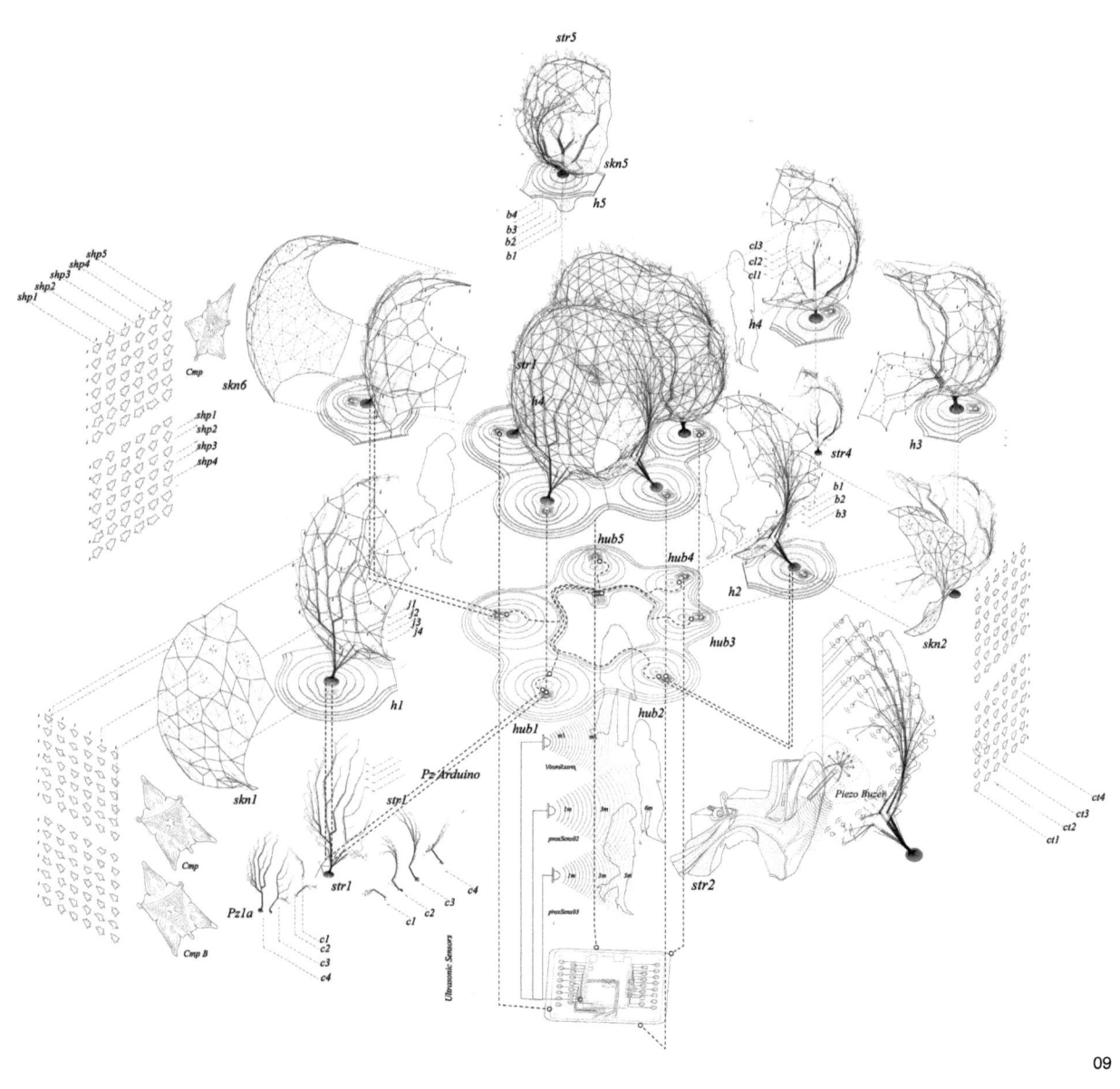

09 *METAfolly* FRAC Collection / Exploded Axonometric, Orleans (2013).

10 *METAfolly* for the Metropolitan Landscape for ArchiLab9, FRAC Collection Orleans (2013).
11 *HORTUS* Urban Algae Farm at the Architectural Association, London (2012).

12 *HygroScope – Meteorosensitive Morphology* / Responsive structure suspended in climate controlled glass case.
13 *HygroScope – Meteorosensitive Morphology* / Open at 85% relative humidity.
14 *HygroScope – Meteorosensitive Morphology* / Closed at 50% relative humidity.

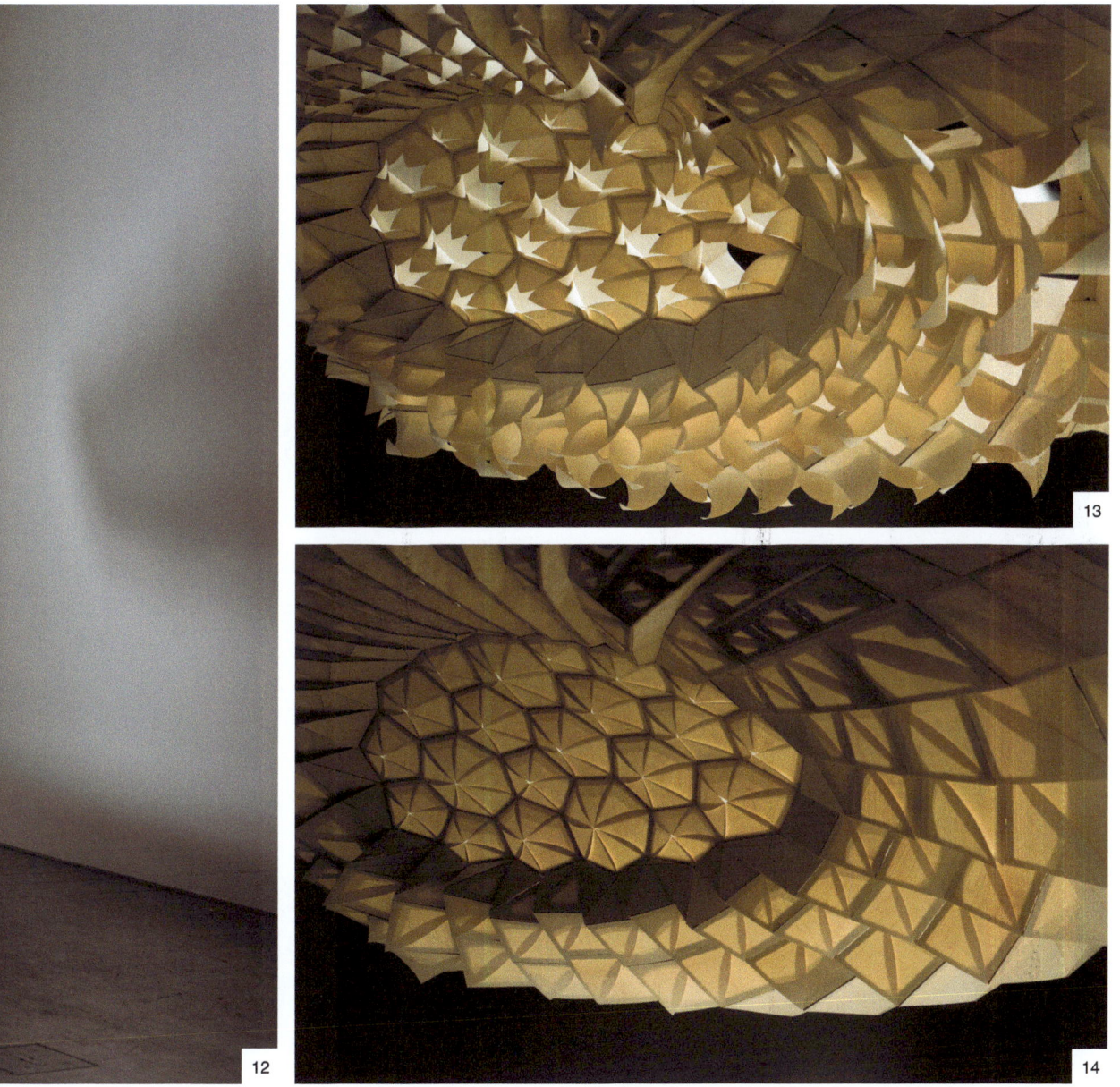

15 *HygroSkin – Meteorosensitive Pavilion* / Exterior view in Stadtgarten Stuttgart.
16 *HygroSkin – Meteorosensitive Pavilion* / Closed at 85% relative humidity.
17 *HygroSkin – Meteorosensitive Pavilion* / Open at 50% relative humidity.

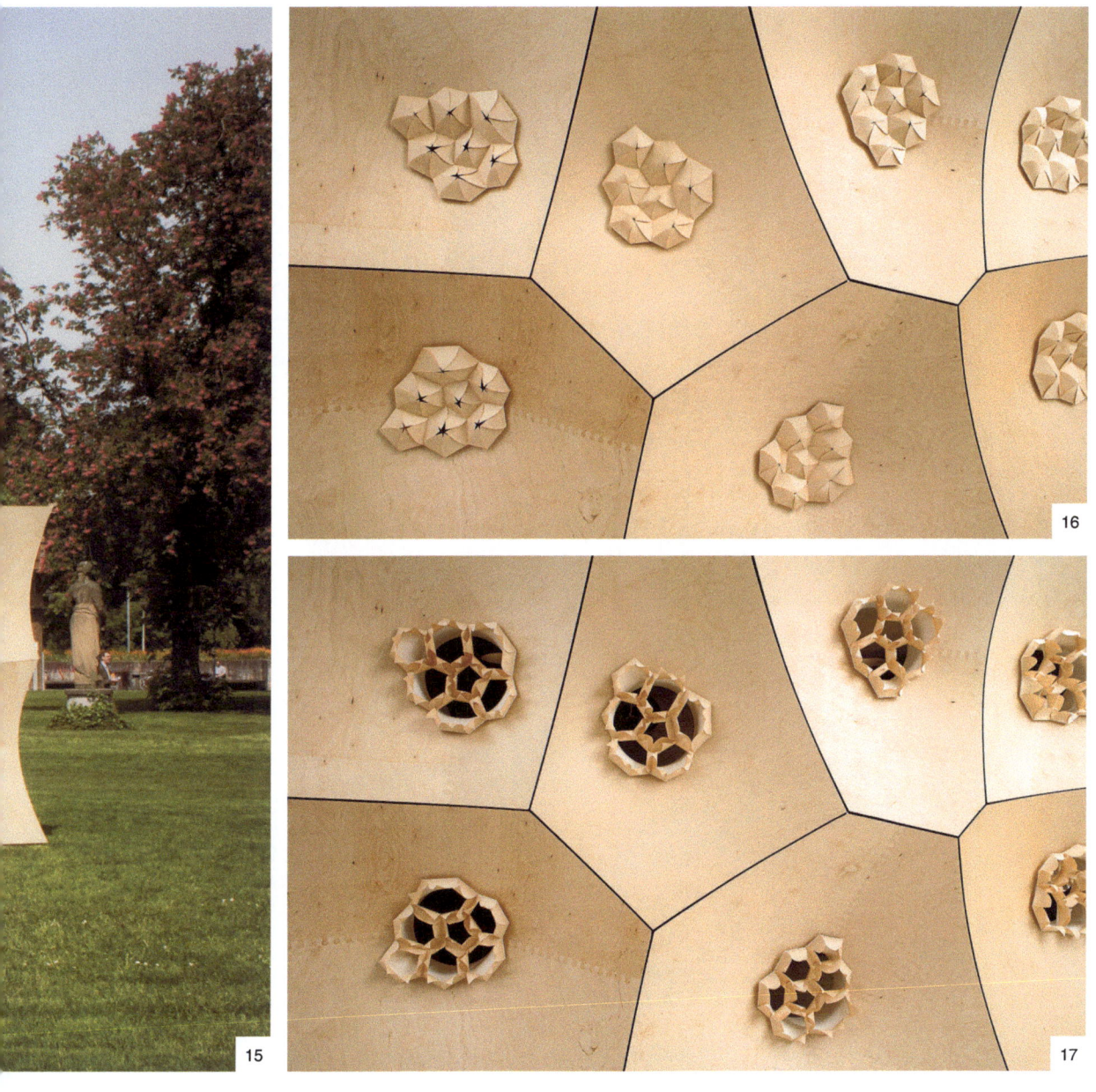

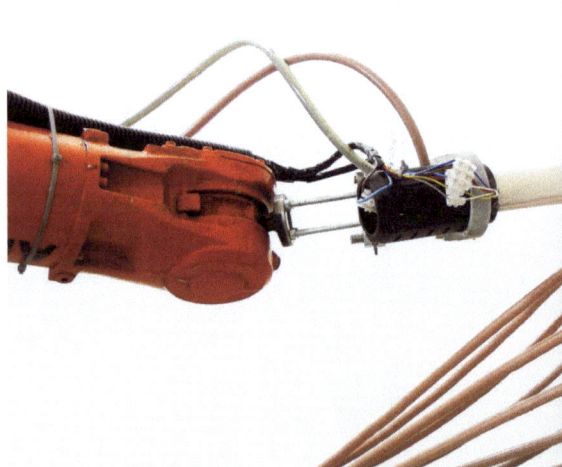

18   *Smart Concrete Tiles* (2013).
19   *Bio–Ceramics* (2013).
20   IAAC Solar Buildings / *Endesa Pavilion* (2012).

20
21 IAAC Solar Buildings / *Fab Lab House* (2010).
22 *Mataerial* (2012).

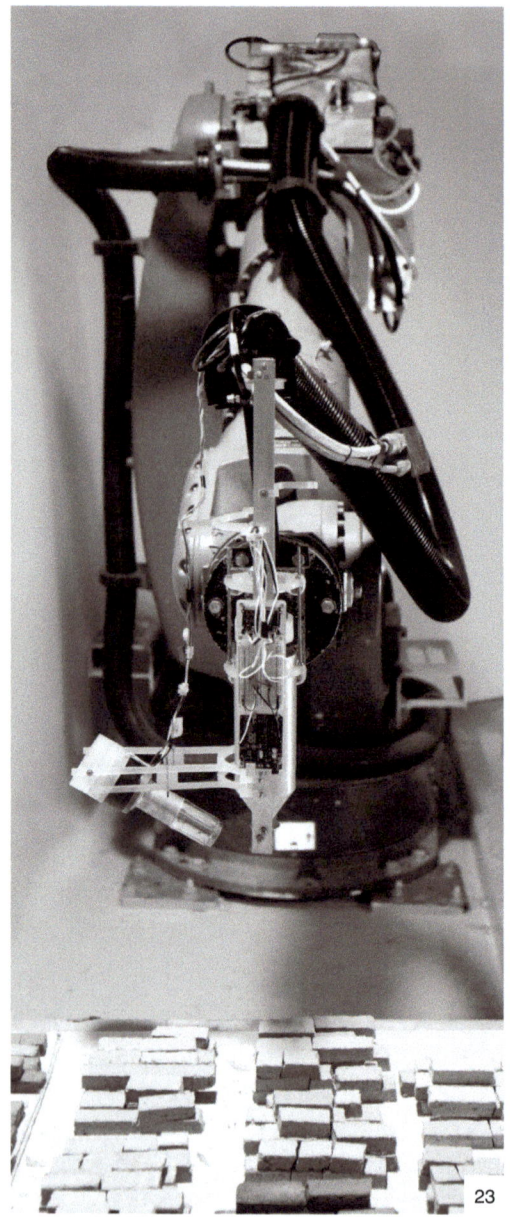
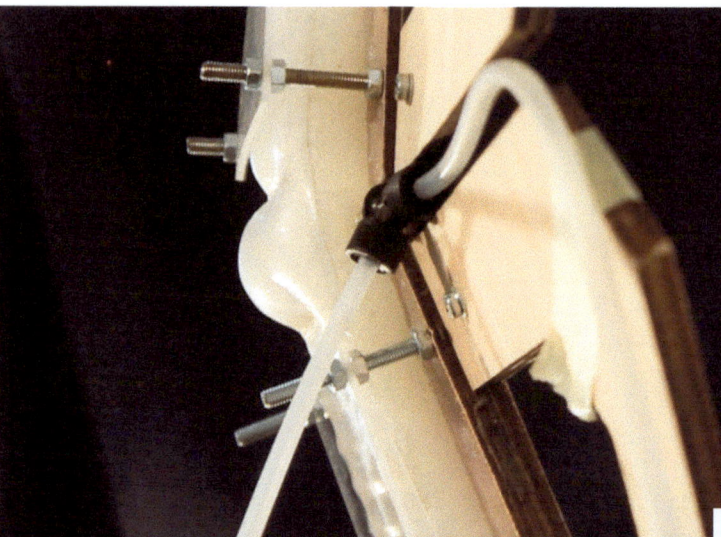
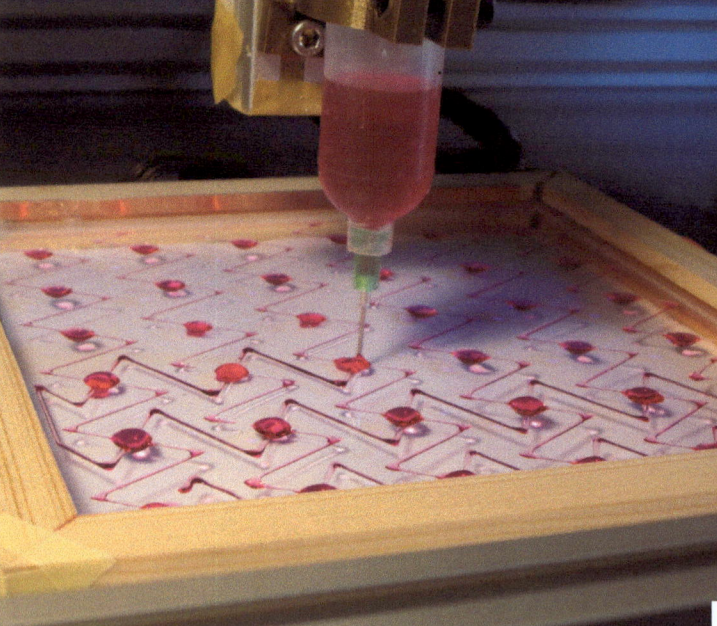

23 *Pylos* (2013).
24 *Ground Floor* (2013).
25 *Kaleidoscope* (2013).

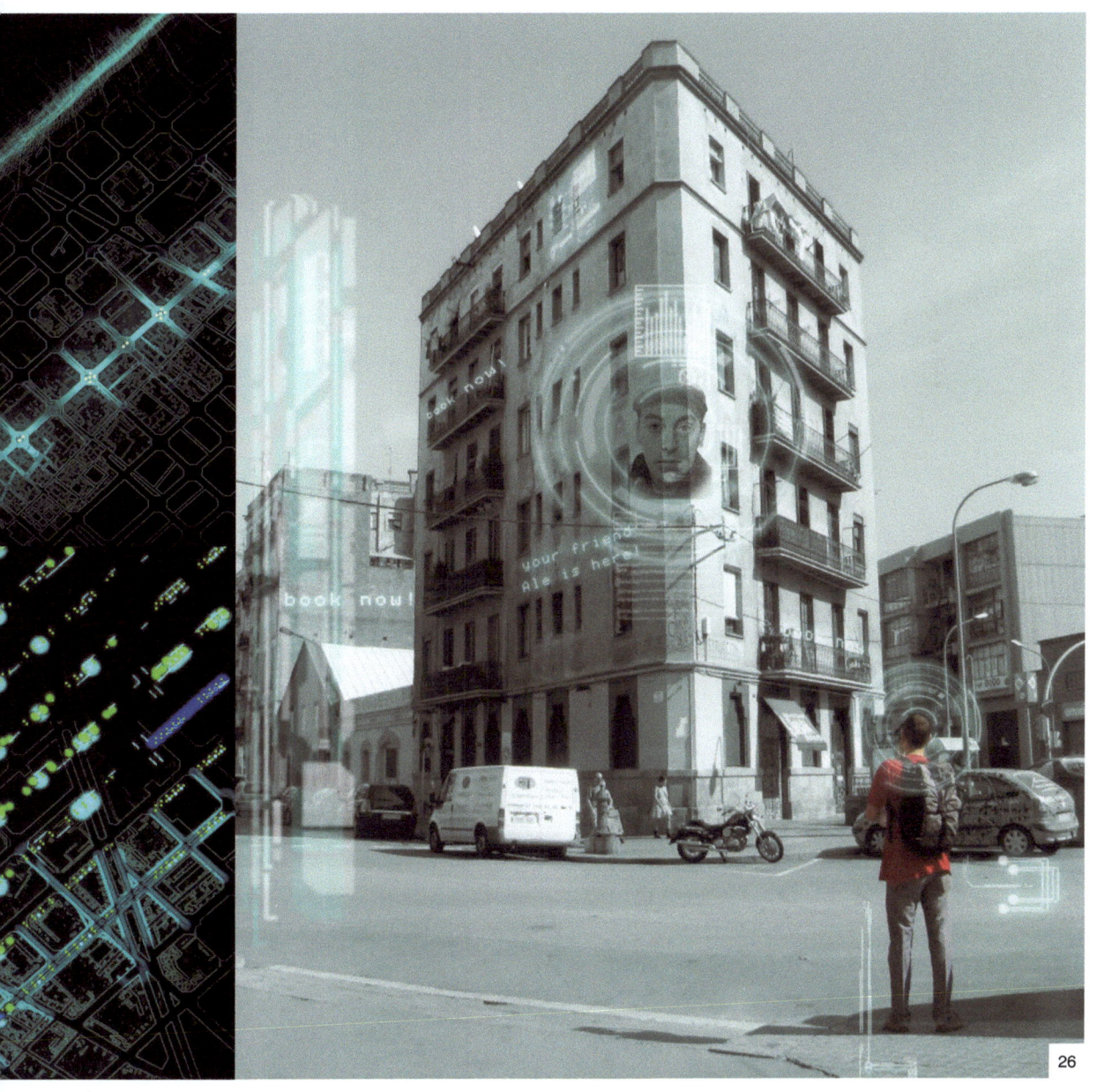

26 *Smart Public Space* (2012).

27 *Sensualscaping* / The dance of architecture and nature.
28 *The Floating Forest* / Motorised nomadic parkland.

29 30 *Lighthive* / Luminous architectural surveillance.

31   *Worldscape* / Inhabiting and eating the world.

32 33   *Mobile Orchard* / Inhabitable urban fruit trees.

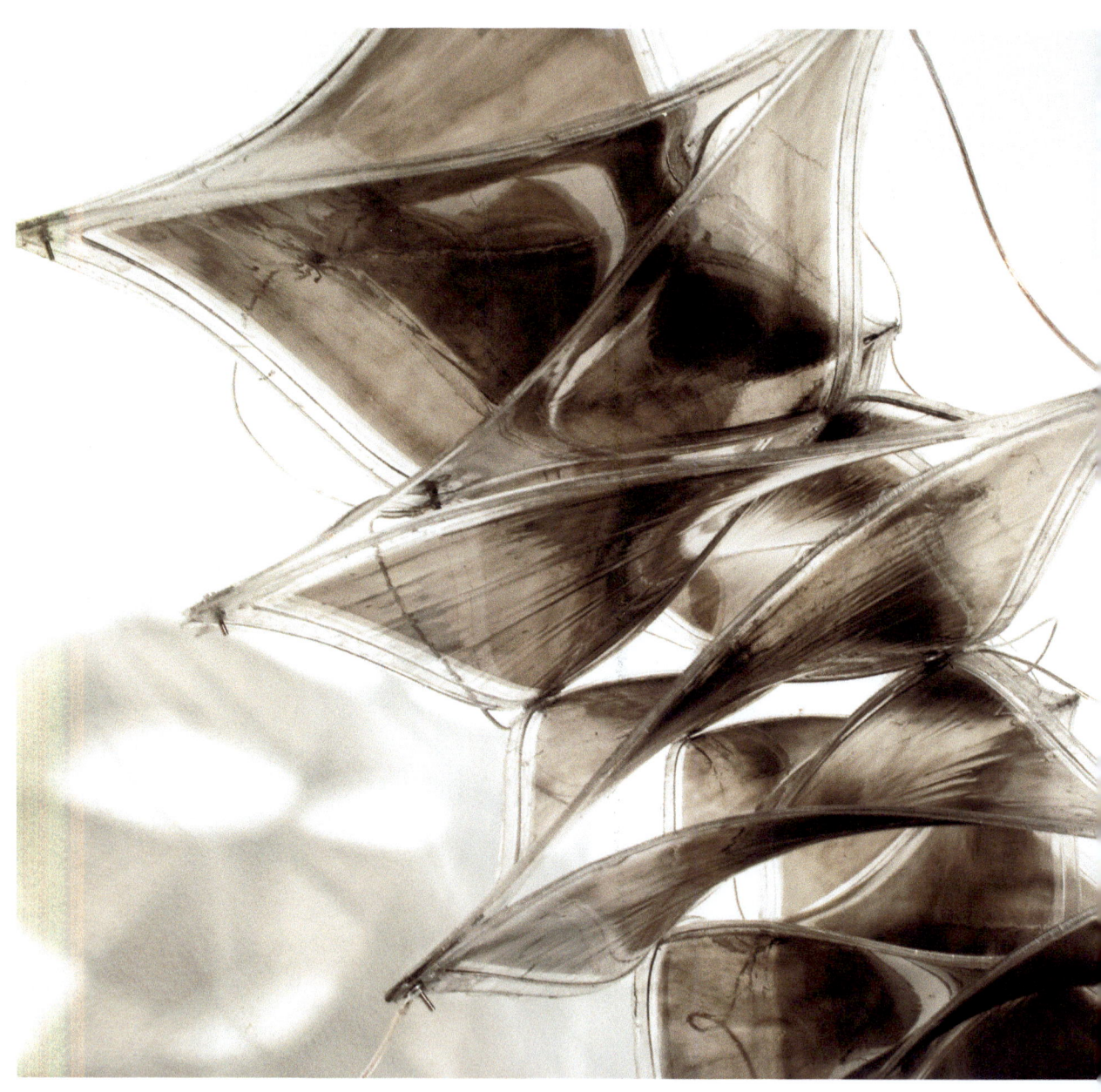

34 The kinetic minimum–energy structure *ShapeShift* as exhibited at Gallery Starkart, Zurich (2010).

35 36   *Phototropia* proposed an autonomous installation consisting of self–made solar cells, electroluminescent displays, electroactive polymers in a bioplastic structure (2012).

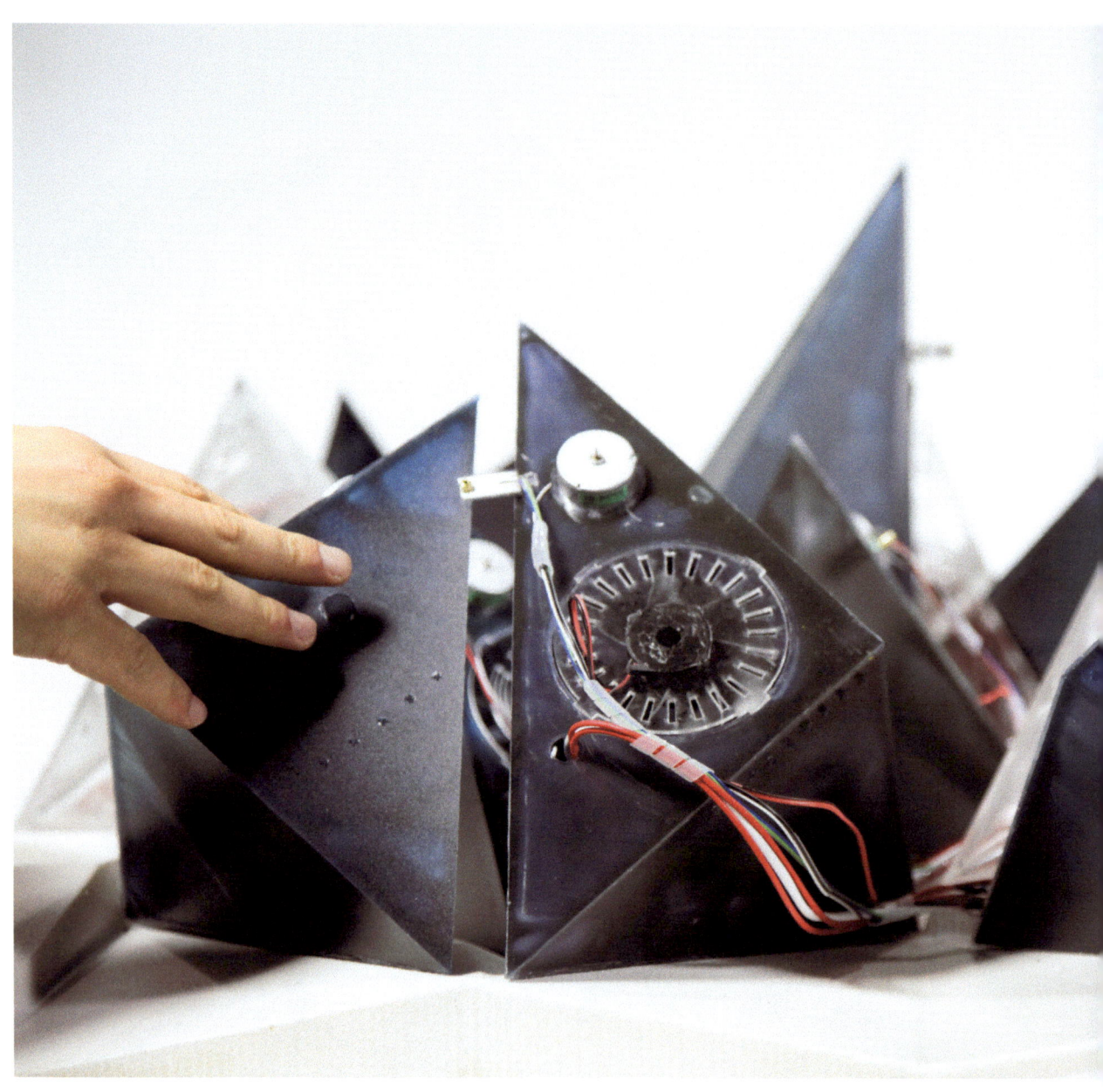

37 *Resinance* was an installation made from forty thermoreactive components that responded to each other's behavior in a swarm–like manner (2013).

38 39   *Resinance 2.0* built upon the *Resinance* installation and was exhibited during the Acadia Conference in Waterloo, Canada (2013).

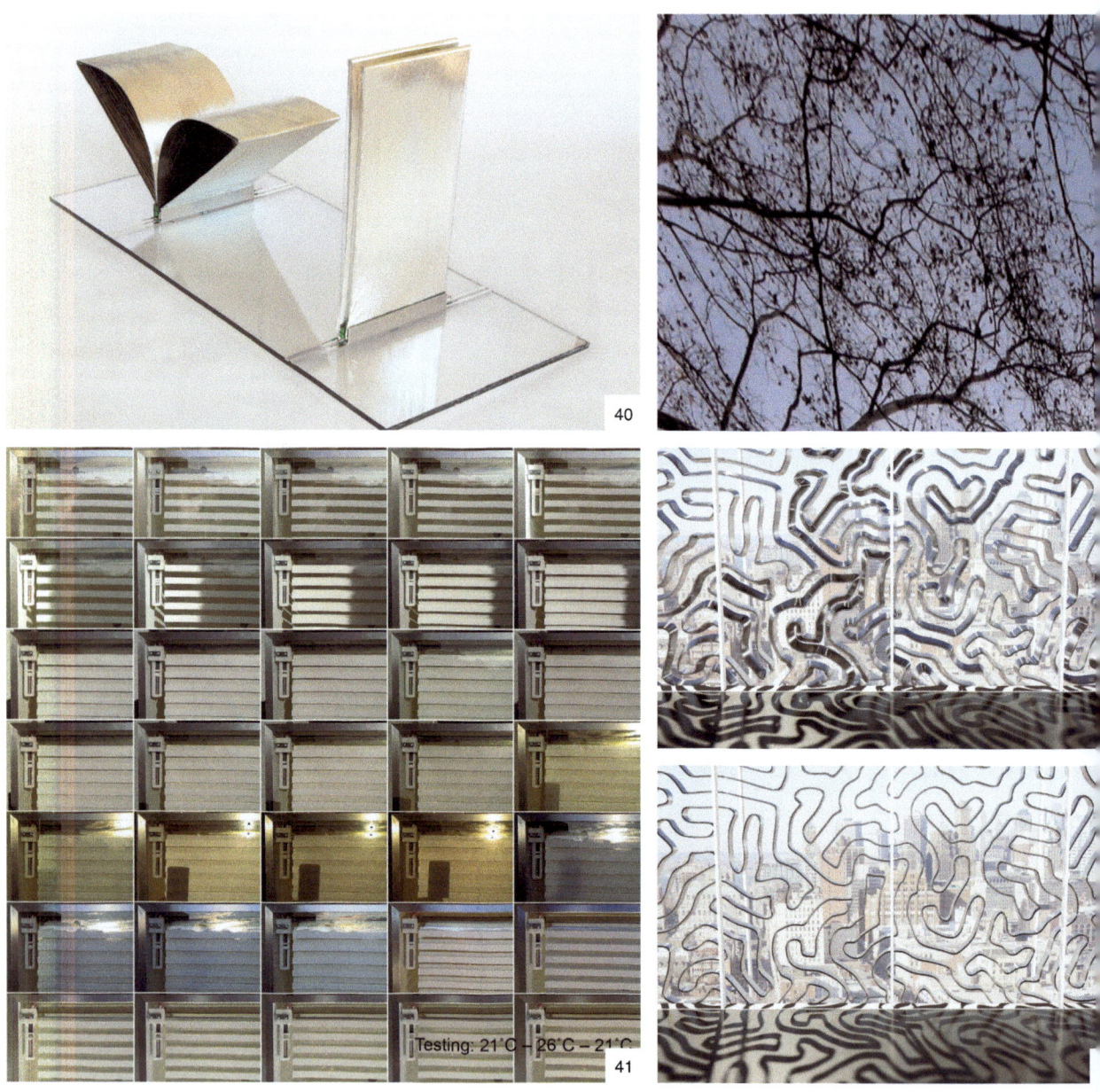

40 *Homeostatic Facade System* / Sectional Model of DEAP muscle wrapped over a flexible polymer core. The DEAP includes a silver coating on both faces that serves as electrodes and assist the system by reflecting and diffusing light.
41 Testing of the *SmartScreen III* prototype over the course of a day, at temperatures ranging from 21 to 26 degrees Celsius.

42 Interior Perspective of the *Homeostatic Facade System* / Ribbons of DEAP muscles open and close to control solar heat gain through a building's double–skin glass façade.
43 Exterior Perspective of the *Homeostatic Facade System*.

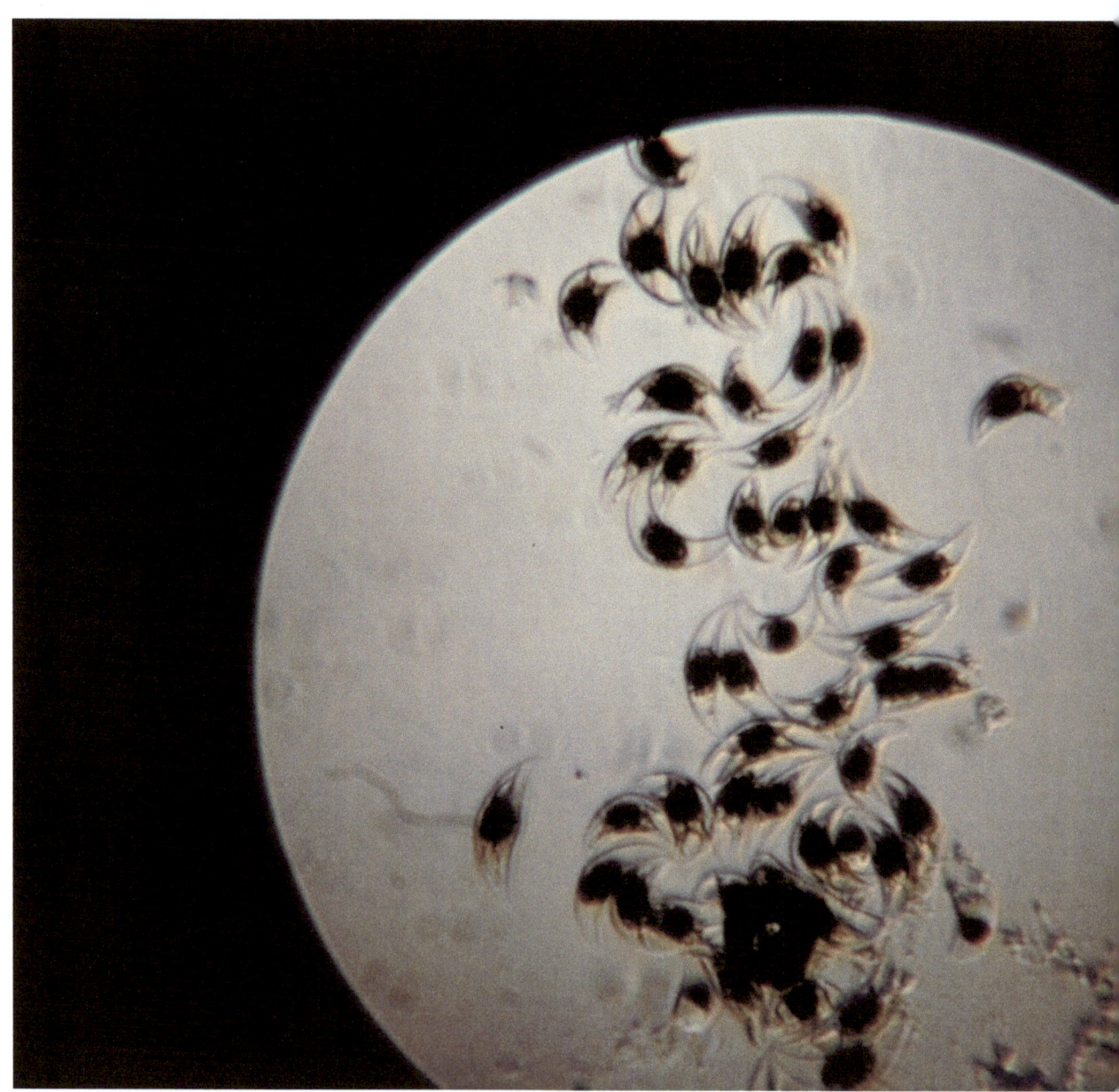

44 Microscopic image of Pyrocystis lunula taken at 100–fold magnification.

45 *Bioluminescent Field* (2009), dinoflagellates emitting flashes of blue light as a response to disturbance caused by visitors.

46 *Interference* (2012), installation set-up.

47 *Interference* (2012), visual outcome of dinoflagellate bioluminescence triggered by acoustic waves.

48 49   *Reef*, a self-actuated ceiling changing with the wind.

50　Details from *Reef*, cloud of electroactives polymers underpinned by dielectric elastomer structures.
51　Details on dielectric elastomer structures opening and closing according to wind speed.

52 *NOpolder*, concept for a distributed agricultural metropolis.
53 Capturing Wi–Fi signals for crowd management.

54 *ProtoCELL* Hyperbody MSc2 project, full-scale prototype of iWEB v4 built by Hyperbody students and staff (2009).

55

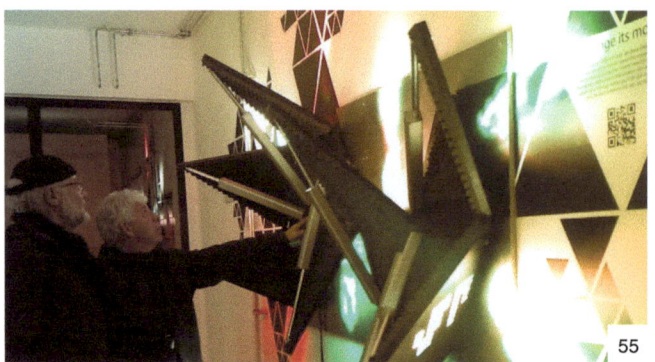

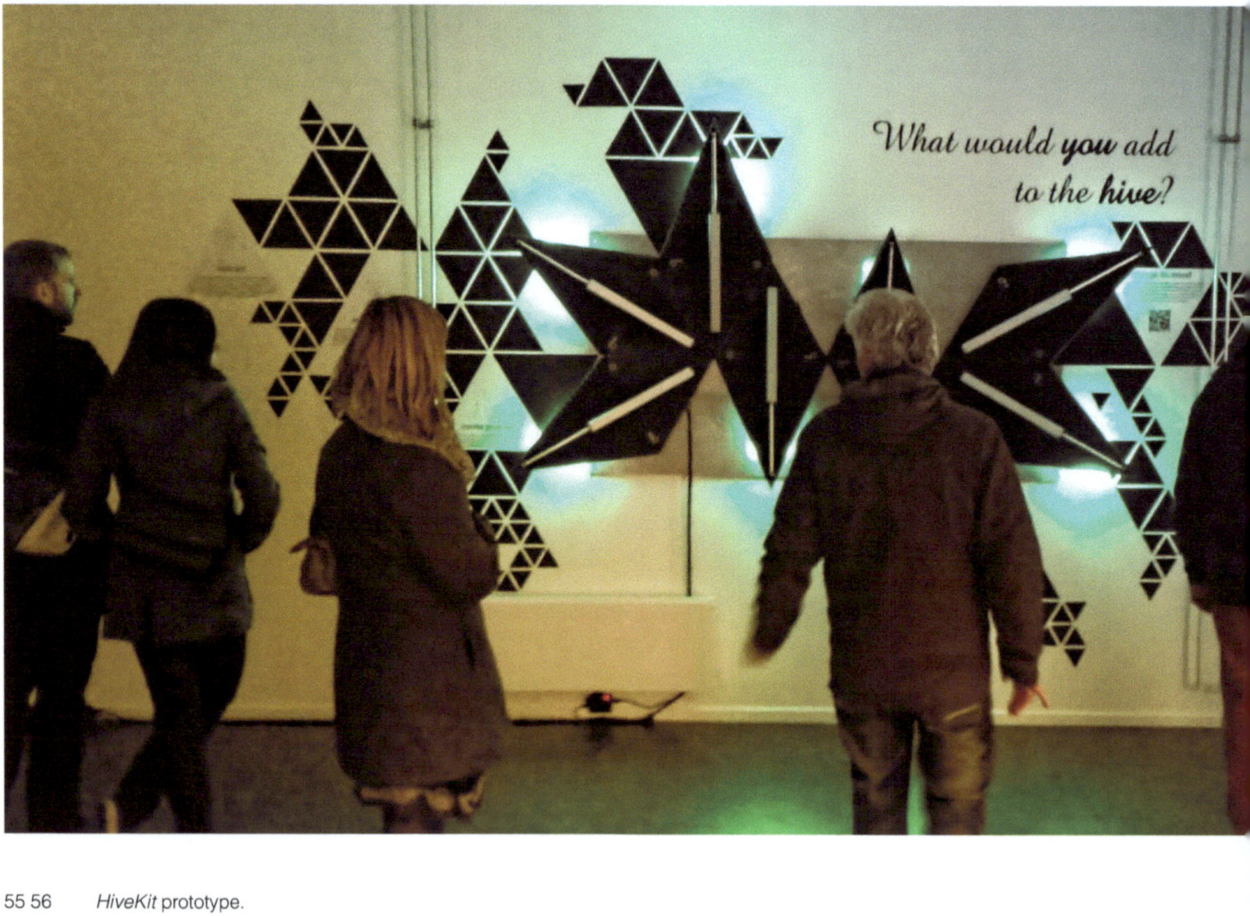

55 56 *HiveKit* prototype.

57 *Seina* installation at Interaction_14 conference exhibition.

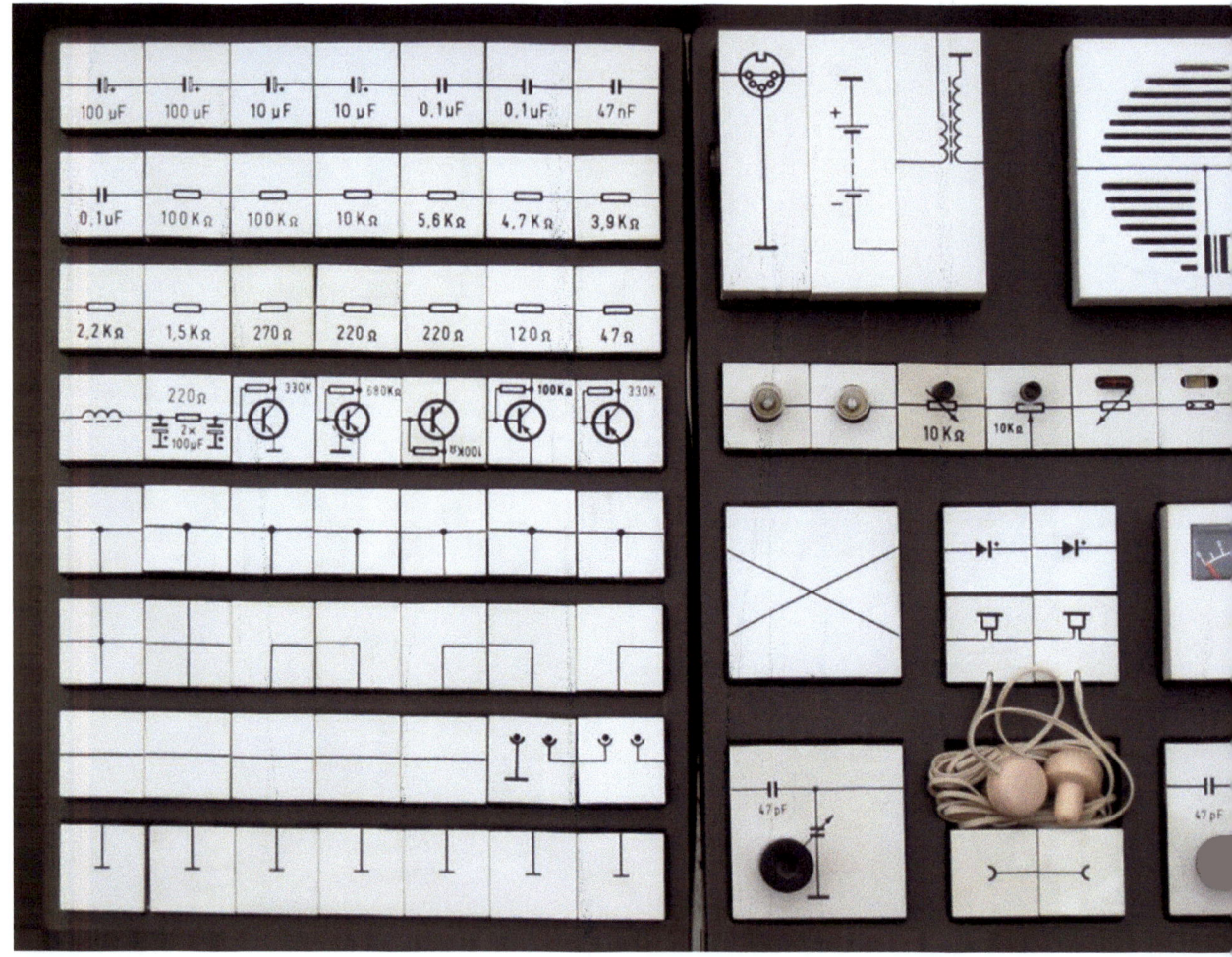

58   Braun Lectron tile set.
59   Braun Lectron circuit.
60   Paper voxel of truncated octahedrons. Dotes denote topological constrains.

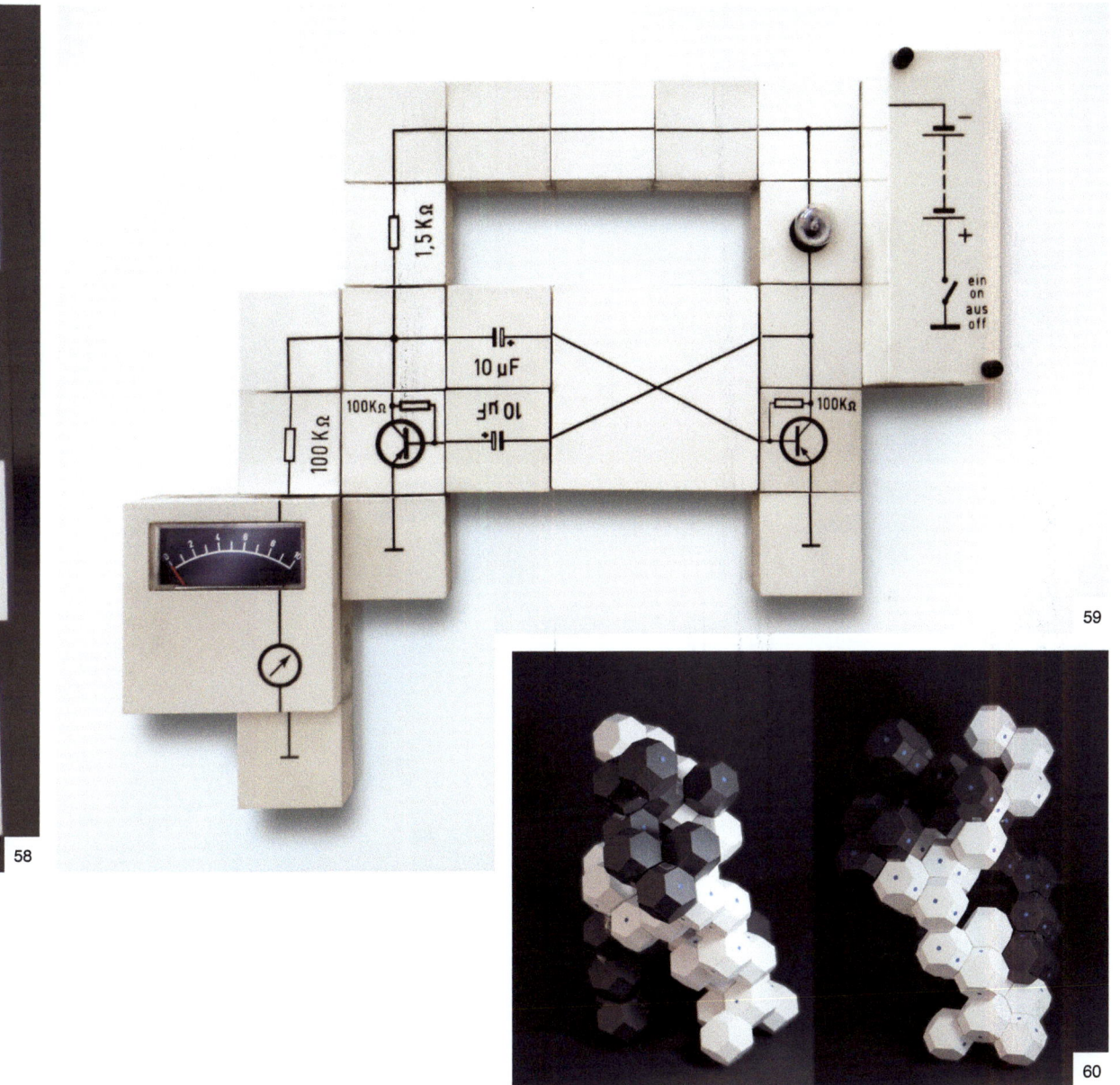

61 *Polyomino* individual tiles.
62 3D printed *Polyomino* assembly.
63 3D printed *Polyomino* assembly.

61

62

63

64 *Panda Eyes*, WWF, private collection, UK.
65 *Showtime*, W Hotel, Leicester Square, London, UK.

66 *Nature Trail*, Great Ormond Street Hospital for Children, London, UK.

67　"Living" bridges made out of growing tree roots in the Indian province Meghalaya.
68　D|E|Form panels and assembly generation visualization.

69   Interactive lighting design enabled by *HiveKit*.
70   *Seina* installation at Interaction_14 conference exhibition.

PHILIP BEESLEY MRAIC OAA RCA (Professor at Architecture School, University of Waterloo; Director of Integrated Group for Visualization, Design and Manufacturing; Director of Riverside Architectural Press) is a practicing architect, designing responsive kinetic environments that approach near – alive systems. He is cited as a pioneer in the rapidly expanding technology of responsive architecture with wide press including WIRED, TEDx, Discovery Channel features.He has authored and edited eight books, three international proceedings and a number of catalogues, and appears on the cover of Artificial Life (MIT), LEONARDO and AD journals. Current projects are in Paris, Edmonton, Hangzhou and Seoul. He was selected to represent Canada for the 2010 Venice Biennale for Architecture and the 2012 Biennale of Sydney. A series of dresses with Iris Van Herpen were recently launched at Paris Fashion Week Distinctions include Prix de Rome in Architecture (Canada), VIDA 11.0, FEIDAD, RAIC Allied Arts, ACADIA Emerging Digital Practice, Dora Mavor Moore awards. He is chair for the ACADIA 2013 Adaptive Architecture international conference.
http://www.philipbeesleyarchitect.com/

JASON BRUGES, trained as an architect at Oxford Brookes University and the Bartlett School of Architecture (UCL), he brings environmental awareness and technical skill to his creative projects. He worked with Foster +Partners for three years before moving to Imagination to become a Senior Interactive Design Consultant. Jason set up his own practice is 2002 and now works with a talented team of people to develop and deliver interactive projects worldwide. The studio comprises an experienced team of architects, lighting designers, interaction designers, and visualisers as well as specialists in electronics, programming and project management. Jason Bruges Studio has become internationally renowned for producing innovative installations, interventions and ground breaking works. This practice involves creating interactive spaces and surfaces that sit between the world of architecture, site specific installation art and interaction design. Considered a pioneer of this hybrid in-between space, Jason has subsequently paved the way for a new genre of design studios, artists and designer-makers. They are currently working on a number of global projects, including interactive resources for Tate Modern art gallery; a public artwork for a new development in Toronto, Canada; and a New Media Lounge at San Diego International Airport. Jason Bruges Studio recently completed a distraction piece for Great Ormond Street Hospital in London for children on their route to surgery and a number of artworks for the London 2012 Olympics.
http://www.jasonbruges.com/

NICOLA BURGGRAF is a product designer. She has graduated with Distinction from the University of Art and Design (HfG) Offenbach am Main. Her work has been published widely and distinguished with several awards (e.g. Bayerischer Staatspreis für das Handwerk, Materialica Design and Technology Award, DesignPlus). Since her graduation project, she has been working on the topic of bioluminescence from a design and research perspective.
http://www.nicolaburggraf.com/

VERA BÜHLMANN is founder and head of the theory–lab for applied virtuality at CAAD ETHZ. She studied English Language and Literature and Philosophy at the University of Zürich, and holds a PHD from the Institute for Media Sciences, University of Basel. She seeks to understand better how a semiotics of mathematics, code and programming languages fit within a general literacy of generic objects as architectonic articulations. Key references for her work are Louis Hjelmslev's glossematics, Gilles Deleuze's atomism of the power to imagine and an algebra of what it means to think, and Michel Serres' notion of how to sign a natural contract. She is author of the forthcoming book Die Nachricht, ein Medium, Annäherungen an Herkünfte und Topoi städtischer Architektonik (Vienna: ambra, 2014) and co–editor with Martin Wiedmer of pre–specifics, Investigations on Research in Art and Design (jrp ringier: Zurich 2008), with Ludger Hovestadt of Printed Physics, Metalithicum I (Vienna: ambra, 2012), EigenArchitecture, Compubility as Literacy (Vienna: ambra, 2013), Sheaves, When Things Are Whatever Can Be the Case (Vienna: ambra, 2013), and of Domesticating Symbols, Metalithicum II (Vienna, ambra, 2014 (forthcoming)).
http://www.monasandnomos.org/

CAROLE COLLET is a researcher, designer and curator whose interest lies in exploring emerging and disruptive technologies through design to create a more sustainable future. After pioneering and directing the MA Textile Futures course at Central Saint Martins College for 10 years, Carole is now a full time Professor and Deputy Director of the Textile Futures Research Centre at Central Saint Martins, University of the Arts London and Head of the Design with Living Systems Research Lab. She has been contributing worldwide on the subject of sustainable design practices, future materials, climate change and the role of science in design. Carole recently curated 'Alive, New Design Frontiers' at the Espace EDF Foundation in Paris which showcases how emerging sciences such as synthetic biology could impact on the design of our everyday horizon 2050.
http://www.csm.arts.ac.uk/

MARTINA DECKER is an assistant professor at the New Jersey Institute of Technology (NJIT) in the College of Architecture and Design. She is originally from Munich, Germany, where she received her professional architecture degree from the University of Applied Sciences. Martina Decker has worked on a wide range of award-winning projects that represent a penchant for interdisciplinary work, including: art installations, consumer

products, and buildings. She and her firm Decker Yeadon LLC are known for their pursuit of design innovation through emergent materials, and work directly with various types of smart materials and nanomaterials. They investigate their properties, discover their capabilities, devise applications for them, and fabricate prototypes that demonstrate their potential. In the context of NJIT, Ms. Decker continues her interdisciplinary endeavors and her investigation of emergent materials and technologies in her Material Dynamics Lab.
http://www.deckeryeadon.com/

STEFAN DULMAN received the PhD degree in Computer Science with the thesis "Data-centric architecture for wireless sensor networks" (2005, University of Twente, The Netherlands). During the period 2009–2013 he held the Assistant Professor position at the Embedded Software Chair at the Delft University of Technology and is at the moment a researcher at CWI (Amsterdam, The Netherlands). His research interests include the design and control of large-scale embedded networks (wireless sensor networks, robotic swarms, mobile ad-hoc networks) using self-adaptive mechanisms and spatial computing techniques. He pays a particular interest to the real-world applicability of his research, collaborating extensively with industry and being actively involved in start-ups. He co-founded Ambient Systems BV, a Dutch SME specialized in providing wireless embedded solutions for transport and logistics and Hive Systems, a startup specialized in providing software solutions for designing interactive systems. He was involved in several large research projects, both at European level and Dutch national level. He has coauthored more than sixty research papers in peer-reviewed publications.
http://www.hive-systems.net/

ALEX HAW is director of the award-winning UK art/ architecture practice atmos. His work, which spans the scales from buildings to installations, masterplans to furniture, seeks a synthesis of mind & body – creating meaningful, pleasurable, immersive and enduring experiences. Much of his work involves sculptural ergonomics, innovative fabrication technologies and digital mapping, exploring the connectivity of people to their place in the world.
http://www.atmosstudio.com/

LUDGER HOVESTADT is Professor for Computer Aided Architectural Design (CAAD) at the Swiss Federal Institute of Technology (ETH) in Zurich since the year 2000. His approach, broadly speaking, is to look for a new relationship between architecture and information technology. He aims at developing a global perspective that relates to and integrates with developments in different fields such as politics and demographics, as well as technology, in a post-industrial era. He is the inventor of the digitalSTROM® chip and founder of several spin-off companies in the fields of Smart Building Technology and Digital Design and Fabrication. A showcase of his recent work can be found in Beyond the Grid – Architecture and Information Technology. Applications of a Digital Architectonic (Birkhäuser, Basel / Boston 2009).
http://www.caad.arch.ethz.ch/

TOMASZ JASKIEWICZ is an architect, interaction designer, academic researcher and educator. Since 2005 he holds master degrees of architecture and urban design from the Gdansk Univesity of Technology and TU Delft. He has practiced as architect and project manager, among others in the architecture firm ONL [Oosterhuis_Lénárd]. In 2013 he finished his PhD research at TU Delft, Architecture, Hyperbody section, where he developed an integrated design framework for development of evolving interactive architectural ecosystems. Since 2011 until 2013 he had been the manager of TU Delft's Architecture design laboratory "protoSPACE," an innovative prototyping facility and think-tank where numerous research, commercial and educational projects on out-of-the-box applications of technology to architectural design have been developed. In 2013 he co-founded the company Hive Systems developing software solutions for design and deployment of interactive systems, Since February 2014 he is assistant professor of interactive design prototyping at the Industrial Design Engineering faculty of TU Delft. In all his work, Tomasz transgresses the boundaries between conventionally established disciplines and practices. He explores new paths leading towards creation of architecture approached as a complex adaptive system. In this way, he aspires to produce artificial spatial ecologies operating in a proactive symbiosis with their human inhabitants and with the natural environment.
http://www.studiolab.ide.tudelft.nl/

BRANKO KOLAREVIC holds a Chair in Integrated Design and is a Professor in the Architecture Program at the University of Calgary Faculty of Environmental Design. He has taught architecture at several universities in North America and Asia and has lectured worldwide on the use of digital technologies in design and production. He has authored, edited or co-edited several books, including "Manufacturing Material Effects" (with Kevin Klinger), "Performative Architecture" (with Ali Malkawi) and "Architecture in the Digital Age." He holds doctoral and master's degrees in design from Harvard University and a diploma engineer in architecture degree from the University of Belgrade.
http://www.evds.ucalgary.ca/

MANUEL KRETZER is an architect, researcher and educator, currently working at the Chair for Computer Aided Architectural Design (CAAD), ETH Zurich. His research aims at the notion of a soft and dynamic architecture with a specific focus on advanced material performance. In late 2012 he initiated the materiability research network, a free educational community platform that attempts to

familiarize architects and designers with cutting edge new materials. The website forms a continuously growing database on a wide range of (Smart) Materials, provides in depth instructions and tutorials to self-produce these and promotes their assembly in temporary and speculative experimental projects. He is also founding partner at responsive design studio, based in Zurich and Cologne, an architecture and design practice that explores opportunities in creating responsive and adaptive solutions for vivid architectural geometries that interact with their user in the process of creation but also in the built shape, materialization, surface and visual behaviour.
http://www.materiability.com/

OLIVER DAVID KRIEG is a doctoral candidate at the Institute for Computational Design at the University of Stuttgart. With the completion of his Diploma degree in 2012 he also received the faculty's Diploma Price. Prior to that, he was working as a Graduate Assistant at the institute's robotic prototype laboratory "RoboLab" since the beginning of 2010. With a profound interest in computational design processes and digital fabrication in architecture, he participated in several award winning and internationally published projects. In the context of computational design, his research aims to investigate the architectural potentials of robotic fabrication in wood construction.
http://www.oliverdavidkrieg.com/

ARETI MARKOPOULOU is a Greek architect and professor at IaaC, Barcelona. Her research and practice design explores new architectural models investigating applications of ICT, Energy and Fabrication allowing built and public space to dynamically adapt to behavioral and environmental changes over time. She is currently the Director of the Masters in Advanced Architecture and the R+D department at IaaC in Barcelona as well as the initiator and partner of Fab Lab Athens in Greece. She holds a Bachelor in Architecture & Engineering from DUTH, Greece, an MArch from IaaC and a Fab Academy diploma on Digital Fabrication offered by the MIT CBA and the Fab Lab Network. She is a Phd candidate in the UPC, Barcelona and has published several articles internationally. Co-founder of the Mycity-me non profit organization,her practice includes collaborations with multidisciplinary offices and has collaborated in R+D projects ranging from Intelligent Cities (such as "Smart BCN") at Barcelona City Council, 2013), Self Sufficient Buildings (such as "Fab Lab House" at Solar Decathlon Europe, 2010), Digital Fabrication (such as "Fabrication Laboratory" at DHUB, 2010) and the Internet of Things (such as "Hyperhabitat" at the XI Venice Biennale, 2008).
http://www.iaac.net/

ACHIM MENGES is a registered architect and professor at the University of Stuttgart where he is the founding director of the Institute for Computational Design. Currently he also is Visiting Professor in Architecture at Harvard University's Graduate School of Design. Achim Menges has published several books on computational design research, and he is the author/coauthor of numerous articles and scientific papers. His projects and design research has received many international awards, has been published and exhibited worldwide, and form parts of several renowned museum collections, among others, the permanent collection of the Centre Pompidou in Paris.
http://icd.uni-stuttgart.de/

AURÉLIE MOSSÉ is a textile designer and researcher working at the intersection of textile, architecture and smart technologies. Based across CITA (Center for IT & Architecture) Royal Danish Academy of Fines Arts, School of Architecture, Copenhagen and TFRC (Textile Futures Research Centre), Central Saint Martins, University of the Arts, London, she has developed a practice-based and design-led PhD exploring how the design of three-dimensional dynamic textiles can contribute to a domestic culture in which technology cultivates a relationship of interconnectivity with nature. Since October 2012, Aurélie is also sharing her expertise as a part-time lecturer in Ecole Nationale Supérieure des Arts Décoratifs (Paris) while pursuing her investigations on photokinetic textiles at CITA.
http://aureliemosse.com/

KAS OOSTERHUIS is since 2000 appointed professor of digital design methods at the Delft Technical University and is currently leading a staff of twelve researchers at Hyperbody, the knowledge center for Nonstandard and Interactive Architecture at the TU Delft, Netherlands. He studied architecture at Delft Technical University. From 1987–1988 he taught at the AA (London) and worked/lived one year in the studio of Theo van Doesburg (Paris) together with visual artist Ilona Lénárd. Their corporate design studio was in 2004 renamed into ONL [Oosterhuis_Lénárd]. As from 2007 Kas Oosterhuis is a registered architect in Hungary, executing as General Designer the CET project. In his most recent book "Towards a New Kind of Building, a Designers Guide to Nonstandard Architecture" [NAi Publishers 2011] Oosterhuis reveals the fundaments of his personal design universe, which embraces the paradigm shift from standard to nonstandard structures and from static to dynamic buildings as the initial condition. He has lectured worldwide at numerous universities, academies and international conferences since 1990. Kas Oosterhuis has initiated two GSM conferences at the TU in Delft on the subjects multiplayer game design, file to factory design and build methods and open source communication in the evolutionary development of the 3d reference model. In 2008 ONL received the Autodesk BIM Experience Award for the CET Project in Budapest.
http://www.oosterhuis.nl/

CLAUDIA PASQUERO is an architect, engineer, author and educator. She has worked in London as an architect for international offices such as Ushida Findlay Partnership and Erick van Egeraat Architects before co-founding the ecoLogicStudio in 2006 together with Marco Poletto. Claudia has completed a public library in Cirie' (Turin) among other projects and she has been exhibiting ecoLogicStudio work at the Venice Architectural Biennale in 2006, in 2008 and 2010, where she has been presenting three different interacting prototypes, investigating the boundaries between architecture, science and tradition. Claudia has lectured and taught internationally; Claudia has been Unit Master at the AA in London from September 2007 to September 2012; Visiting Lecturer at the IAAC, Barcelona since 2006; Hans and Roger Strauch Visiting Critic in Cornell University, Ithaca, NY in 2011/2012; director of CyberGardening the City AAMilan from September 2010; Director of Digital Fabrication: Fabrication Ecologies at the IAAC in Barcelona since October 2012 and Unit Master for the Graduate School in Urban Design at the Bartlett, UCL London since October 2012.
http://www.ecologicstudio.com/

MARCO POLETTO is an architect, author and educator. He now leads the BIO Urban Design Research Cluster at the Bartlett School of Architecture, focussed on development of bio-inspired urban design strategies and bottom-up energetic infrastructures. Over these past few years Marco have been Unit Master at the Architectural Association in London, Senior Tutor at the IAAC in Barcelona and Visiting critic at Cornell University. His projects have been published and exhibited internationally, in particular in Orleans (9th Archilab – FRAC Collection, 2014), in Paris (EDF Foundation, 2013), in Venice Biennale (STEMv3.0 the lagoon experiment, 2008; The Ecological Fotrprint Grotto, 2010), in Seville Biennale (STEMcloud, 2008), Istanbul (Fibrous Room, 2008) and Milan (Aqua Garden, 2007). He is author of "Systemic Architecture – Operating manual for the self-organizing city" published by Routledge in 2012. In 2005 Marco co-founded ecoLogicStudio that has built an international reputation for its innovative work on 'systemic' design, a method defined by the combination and integration of ecologic thinking, computational and interaction design and digital prototyping. This "broadened" approach to design – ranging from the micro to the macro and from nanotechnologies to urban networks – is embodied into an experimental practice, where projects and installations become laboratories of "interactions." Locally activated design protocols synthesize a form of expanded "hyper-reality" hacking larger organizational systems. For ecoLogicStudio this form of "artificial ecology" is a quest for new hybrids promoting the end of the mechanistic paradigm in architecture in favour of a new "bio-technological" one.
http://www.ecologicstudio.com/

STEFFEN REICHERT is a research associate and doctoral candidate at the Institute for Computational Design at University of Stuttgart. Steffen Reichert received the degree of Diplom Designer Produktgestaltung from the Academy of Art and Design Offenbach as well as the degree of Master of Science in Architecture Studies in the field of Design and Computation from the Massachusetts Institute of Technology. He has authored and contributed to several articles and scientific publications. His work is exhibited and included in several renowned museum collections like e.g. the permament collection of the Centre Pompidou in Paris. Steffen Reichert received several awards and scholarships.
http://www.steffenreichert.net

JOSE SANCHEZ is an Architect / Programmer / Game Designer based in Los Angeles, California. He is partner at Bloom Games, start-up built upon the BLOOM project, winner of the WONDER SERIES hosted by the City of London for the London 2012 Olympics. He is the director of the Plethora Project (www.plethora-project.com), a research and learning project investing in the future of on-line open-source knowledge. The project has over 180 videos and an open-source library of code with over 700.000 completed video session since 2011. His background in computational design and digital manufacturing is linked to Biothing with Alisa Andrasek, were he was one of the principal designers in numerous projects and exhibitions since 2009. Today, he is an Assistant Professor at USC School of Architecture in Los Angeles. His research 'Gamescapes', explores generative interfaces in the form of video games, speculating in modes of intelligence augmentation, combinatorics and open systems as a design medium.
http://www.plethora-project.com/

JOHN SARIK earned his Ph.D. at Columbia University in April 2013. For his dissertation "Systems for Pervasive Electronics and Interfaces" he prototyped energy harvesting wireless sensor nodes and developed lab exercises to teach the fundamentals of display science and technology. During his studies he has worked in the Microdevices Division at IBM Tokyo Research Lab on modeling vertical cavity surface emitting laser (VCSEL) structures and in the Sensor and Devices Group at Microsoft Research Cambridge on integrating 3D printing and printable electronics. He is currently the Co-Founder and Vice President of Engineering of Lumiode, Inc. Lumiode is developing a new microdisplay platform that is 30 times brighter and 10 times more efficient than other technologies. This platform can be applied to visible light applications (head-mounted displays, projection displays, augmented reality) and non-visible light applications (depth mapping, 3D printing).
http://www.johnsarik.com

PROJECT CREDITS

BIO–CERAMICS | IAAC 2013, Iker Luna with Ceramica Cumella.

FLOATING FOREST | Design: atmos (Alex Haw, Fred Vitzthum, Pablo Milara, Mayssa Jallad) Construction Team :Pablo Milara, Mayssa Jallad, Friedrich Vitzthum, Alex Haw, Imogen Wall, Jen McLennan, Aidan Geboers, Elaine Chan, Seif Alhasani, Simon Warren, U–Sun Hu, Zach Gomperts-Mitchelson, Jonny Chapman, Abbas Nokhasteh, Marek Wasniewski, Iskra Tsaneva, Thomas Lindner (A huge thank you to those generous friends who lent a hand)
CNC fabrication: Jim Haste, PMP Ltd

GROUND FLOOR | IAAC 2013, Moritz Begle

HYGROSCOPE – METEOROSENSITIVE MORPHOLOGY | Permanent Collection, Centre Pompidou, Paris
Achim Menges Architect, Frankfurt
Achim Menges, Steffen Reichert, Boyan Mihaylov (Project Development, Design Development) Institute for Computational Design, University of Stuttgart Prof. Achim Menges, Steffen Reichert, Nicola Burggraf, Tobias Schwinn with Claudio Fabrizio Calandri, Nicola Haberbosch, Oliver Krieg, Marielle Neuser, Viktoriya Nikolova, Paul Schmidt (Scientific Development, Design Development, Robotic Fabrication, Assembly) Transsolar Climate Engineering, Stuttgart Thomas Auer, Daniel Pianka (Climate Engineering)

HYGROSKIN – METEOROSENSITIVE PAVILION | Permanent Collection, FRAC Centre, Orleans Achim Menges Architect, Frankfurt
Achim Menges, Steffen Reichert, Boyan Mihaylov (Project Development, Design Development) Institute for Computational Design, University of Stuttgart Prof. Achim Menges, Oliver David Krieg, Steffen Reichert, Nicola Burggraf, Zachary Christian, David Correa, Katja Rinderspacher, Tobias Schwinn with Yordan Domuzov, Tobias Finkh, Gergana Hadzhimladenova, Michael Herrick, Vanessa Mayer, Henning Otte, Ivaylo Perianov, Sara Petrova, Philipp Siedler, Xenia Tiefensee, Sascha Vallon, Leyla Yunis (Scientific Development, Detail Development, Robotic Fabrication, Assembly)

KALEIDOSCOPE | IAAC 2013, Dulce Luna.

MATAERIAL | IAAC 2012, Petr Novikov, Saša Jokic with Joris Laarman Lab.

MOBILE ORCHARD | Design: atmos (Alex Haw, Jeg Dudley, Natalie Chelliah, Xiaolin Gu, Maite Parisot, Juan Carlos Bueno, Adamantia (Mando) Keki, Miriam Fernandez)
Structural Engineering: Blue Engineering (James Nevin)
Lighting Design: Arup Lighting (Arfon Davies, Dwayene Shillingford)
Lighting all sponsored by: LED Linear / Wibre / Architectural FX (Stuart Knox)
Plywood sponsored by: DHH Timber
Microsite Web Design: Eightfold (Sinead Mac Manus)
Fabrication: Nicholas Alexander (Jak Drinnan, Nicholas Runeckles, Anna Baker)
+ a ton of amazing volunteers, including:
Nicola Agresta, Malick Ainy, Hussain Ali, Samra Ali, Olga Amitousa, Eleonora Angeli, Pietro Belli, Chrysanthi Illyriana Bekta, Richard Bobs, Juan Carlos Bueno, Fernando Cano, Eunice Cardoso, Rachel Carmody, Neftali Carreira, Vera Cerbone, Natalie Chelliah, Jessica Chiu, Yvette Cox, Max Crichton, Laura Crosby, Milan Dankhara, Kate Dornan, Jeg Dudley, Elisabeth Fargues, Miriam Fernandez, Edith Fung, Kahli Gaskin, Irina Ghiuzan, Amarilnto Gkiosa, John Griffin, Xiaolin Gu, Ashik Gurung, Holly Gwazdacz, Jochem Ermboud Hamoen, Alex Haw, Raidah Hayat, Charlie Hill, Hafid Houari, Ricardo Ibusquiza, Fionnuala Jackson, Liz Kalinauckas, Monika Kanicki, Mando Keki, Mehreen Uneeb Khalid, Kulsoom Khimjee, Louise King, Maha Komber, Mina Koov, David Koroma, Mina Kouvara, Lina Laraki, Anthony Lazarus, Mike Lopez, Ellis Lui, Flora Malpas, Sofia Marin, Elissaveta Marinova, Chris Marriott, Maria Matesanz, Tina McArdle, Sarah McKendry, Ross Melbourne, Juliana Mejia, Olahut Mircea,Elham Moazami, Francesco Modica, Marjorie Mohler, David Monney, Luke Murphy, David Munoz, Gary Nash, Wendy Natera, Beth Niroomand–Rad, Amitousa Olga, Leidy Ossa, Paniz Pakshir, Nicola Pasquini, Marco Pantaleoni, Maite Parisot, Nicola Pasquini, Emma Payne,Ergys Peka, Hannah Pells, Samantha Perry, Miguello Pez Romero, Eunice Pinto, Sylvia–Sofia Plumridge, Malick Quratulain, Aarti Popat, Judith Pye, Lisa Quinn, Fatima Raza, Matza Rozz, Ali Samra, Kirstin Sands, Mattia Santi, Laura Seiver, Barbara Serraglini, Leah Shand, Max Shubber, Misbah Siddique, Beant Singh, Miguel Silva, Francasca Silvi, Ergy Speka, Iulia Ioana Stefan, Zak Stratfold, Marios Styliani, Elena Tamosiunaite, Winshen Teh, Sonia Theodosia, Ellen Thomas, Sonia Theodosiadi, Myrtle Tzortzi, Kostas Voukelatos, Hannah Wallace, Barry Walsh, Megan Wan, S Wang, Michele Williams, Feng Yang, Joanne Woffinden, Antonia Zabala, Alex Zoupa
Client: City of London Festival (Emma McGovern) Festival Tree Sponsor: Bloomberg
Real orchard trees donated by: YouGarden (Peter McDermott) & The Worshipful Company of Fruiterers
Hosts: Broadgate Estates, Devonshire Square Management, Land Securities, 30 St Mary Axe Management Company Ltd
Logistics: Tellings Transport
Special Thanks: Sinead Mac Manus; Professor John Price (WCoF); Ed Gillespie; Olivia Sibony; Corporation of London.

PHOTOTROPIA | supervision: Manuel Kretzer Team: Katia Ageeva, Diana Alvarez, Orestis Argyropoulos, Stella Azariadi, Tianyi Chen, Yun–Ying Chiu, Ivana Damjanovic, García Pepo Martínez, Melina Mezari, Bojana Miskeljin, Evangelos Pantazis, Stanislava Predojevic, Stylianos Psaltis, Meda Radovanovic, Daniel Rohlek, Miro Roman, Castro Mauricio Rodríguez, Teemu Seppänen, Grete Soosalu
special thanks to: Luke Franzke, Florian Wille / ZHdK IAD, Paul Liska / EPFL LPI, Andrei Pruteanu, Agostino di Figlia / TU Delft ES group Jorge Ellert / ULANO Corp. Beat Karrer / Studio Beat Karrer, John Meschter / G24 Innovations

PYLOS | IAAC 2013, Sofoklis Giannakopoulos with Monolite/D–Shape.

REEF | The development of Reef was supported by the Danish Government via a PhD position undertaken at CITA, Centre for IT & Architecture, Copenhagen, in collaboration with TFRC, Textile Futures Research Centre, Central Saint Martins, University of the Arts, London. The research was supervised by Carole Collet and Mette Ramsgaard Thomsen. The project was subsequently supported by cross–disciplinary collaborations with Anne Ladegaard Skov, Anca Gabriela Bejenariu, Danish Technical University, Copenhagen and David Gauthier, Copenhagen Institute for Interaction Design and the sponsoring of MetOne.

RESINANCE | supervision: Manuel Kretzer co–supervision: Benjamin Dillenburger and Hironori Yoshida, CAAD, Weixin Huang and Lei Yu, Tsinghua University, China
Tomasz Jaskiewicz and Mariana Popescu, Hyperbody, TU Delft, Netherlands
Andrei Pruteanu and Stefan Dulman, Embedded Software Group, TU Delft, Netherlands
Team: Baldwin Mark, In Jessica, Janjusevic Tihomir, Jiang Nan, Letkemann Joel, Miranda Turu Nicolás, Prieler Irene, Schildberger David, Shammas Demetris, Smigielska Maria, Tanigaito Aki, Xexaki Evi, Xydis Achilleas, Yuko Ishizu

RESINANCE 2.0 | supervision: Manuel Kretzer Design and Material Research: Achilleas Xydis Electronics and Interaction Design: Joel Letkemann
Collaborators: Demetris Shammas, Evi Xexaki, Maria Smigielska, Mariana Popescu, Nan Jiang, Yuko Ishizu
ACADIA support: Farzin Asad, Zak Fish, Connor O'Grady

SEINA | Minor Interactive Environments, IDStudioLab, Delft University of Technology, Fall Semester 2013. Instructors: A.v.d. Helm, M. Rozendaal, and C. Kievid. Students: T. Hemmes, A. El Coudi Amrani, T. Giele, J. Dudok, T.M. Martin de la Sierra Baena, D. Politin, T. Langbroek, J. Beem, and D. Stam.

CREDITS

SHAPESHIFT | supervision: Manuel Kretzer
Team: Edyta Augustynowicz, Sofia Georgakopoulou, Dino Rossi, Stefanie Sixt
special thanks to: Christa Jordi, Gabor Kovaks, EMPA

SMART CONCRETE TILES | IAAC 2013, Pedro Moraes with Breinco.

SMART PUBLIC SPACE | IAAC 2012, Díaz de León, Luna, Carson, Narula, Nejad, Gungor, Choi, Sharma, Rashda, Birgönül.

WORLDSCAPE | Concept & Design: atmos (Alex Haw, Pablo Milara, Friedrich Vitzthum)
Development: Alex Haw, Pablo Milara, Friedrich Vitzthum, Dom Rago–Verdi, Xiaolin Gu, Melissa Reynaud, Ana Maria Diaz, Ana Sidorova, Nick O'Neill, Dan Mahoney, Chris Green, Jeg Dudley, Rowan Taylor
Construction: above + Anibal Puron, Martin, Sinead Mac Manus, Stefan Simanowitz, Marcus Keohane, Jonathan Taylor, Leo, William Hardie, Andrew Atkins, Anke Weber
Fabrication: kindly sponsored by The Cutting Room (very special thanks to Mark Durey)
Plywood: kindly sponsored by DHH Timber
With very special thanks to Thomas Ugo Ermacora (Lime Wharf), Alison Davenport (Stratford Old Town Hall), and Sinead Mac Manus – the very centre of this world.

POLYOMINO | (USC Post Professional MArch students) Research Director: Jose Sanchez
Students: Can Jiang, Yanping Chen, Jingjing Li, Tingting Xu, Yuchen Cai, Setareh Ordoobadi.

QUOTATIONS

p.2 Kiesler, Frederick, Bogner, Dieter, and Noever, Peter (2001) Frederick J. Kiesler: Endless Space. Ostfildern–Ruit: Hatje Cantz, p. 54.
p.24 Richard Feynman, "Simulating Physics with Computers," International Journal of Theoretical Physics, volume 21, 1982, pages 467–488, at page 486 (final words)
p.60 David Greene, Amazing Archigram Vol. 1, 1961
p.112 Bruce Sterling, "The computer revolution is running out of steam," Heise Online, Interview with Stefan Krempl, 06.05.1998 http://www.heise.de/tp/artikel/2/2344/1.html

IMAGE CREDITS

COVER
Photo by Evangelos Pantazis and Miro Roman.

INTRODUCTION
p.16 fig.1 Whole Earth Catalog / Courtesy of Department of Special Collections and University Archives, Stanford University Libraries and Stewart Brand. http://2.bp.blogspot.com/–7Ye9gqrbxo/UiT8vSb8dLI/AAAAAAAAPFE/2Uqn1guuA5s/s1600/4–01.jpg
p.16 fig.2 Ant Farm, Inflatocookbook / Self published, 1973. http://web.media.mit.edu/~bcroy/inflato-splitpages-small.pdf
p.16 fig.3 Amazing Archigram 4 / Zoom Issue. Cover by Warren Chalk, May 1964. http://www.luxsure.fr/wp-content/uploads/2010/08/135–01–ARCHIGRAM.jpg
p.17 fig.4 Photo by Manuel Kretzer.
p.19 fig.5 The Fountain of Youth, Lucas Cranach der Elder, 1546, oil on panel. The Yorck Project: 10.000 Meisterwerke der Malerei. DVD-ROM, 2002. ISBN 3936122202. Distributed by DIRECTMEDIA Publishing GmbH. Via Wikimedia Commons. http://en.wikipedia.org/wiki/File:Lucas_Cranach_d._%C3%84._007.jpg
p.20 fig.6 – fig.7 All photos by Manuel Kretzer.
p.20 fig.8 Image courtesy of Michael Hansmeyer.

BIOINSPIRATION
p.29 fig.1 Image courtesy of Donald Winnicott.

MATERIABILITY
p.63 fig.2 – p.64 fig.3 All images courtesy of Ludger Hovestadt.
p.64 fig.4 left: Flexible Solar Cells, Brückner Technology Center http://www.brueckner.com/en/brueckner-maschinenbau/technology-center/news-room/latest-news/successful-stretching-of-fluoro-thermoplastics/; right: Flexible OLED, Holst Centre http://www.holstcentre.com/en/NewsPress/PressList/Agfa_ITOfree_OLED.aspx.
p.65 fig.5 Image courtesy of Ludger Hovestadt.
p.66 fig.6 left: 88W8686–Chip of the 90 nm WLAN–Single Chip Solution by Marvell, 2007. www.amkor.com/services/test/Test_datasheet.pdf; right: Chipworks 2007.
p.66 fig.7 left: Intel 4004, Intel, Schematics drawn by: Lajos Kintli and Fred Huettig; right: Olivetti Valentine (1969), Design: Ettore Sottsass, Perry A. King Licenza: by–sa 2.5 (IT). Foto: Davide Casali, Alessandro Gabbiadini, Marcello Mainardi. http://commons.wikimedia.org/wiki/File:Olivetti-Valentine.jpg.
p.68 fig.8 left: Image courtesy of Ludger Hovestadt; right: Familie Holzinger in Regau, Oberösterreich, 2008 http://atholzis.blogspot.ch/2008_10_01_archive.html
p.69 fig.9 Image courtesy of Ludger Hovestadt.
p.69 fig.10 left: Java, Indonesia. Author Gunkarta Gunawan Kartapranata. Licensed under the Creative Commons Attribution-Share Alike; right: Rural Solar Installations, Suncertain http://suncertain.com/farming.html.
p.93 fig.1 – p.94 fig.2 All images courtesy of John Sarik.

CONVERSATIONS
p.54 – p.59, p.98 – p.111, p.140 – p.147 All photos by Demetris Shammas.

OUTLOOK
p.149 fig.1 Photo by Branko Kolarevic.
p.149 fig.2 Image courtesy of Enric Ruiz Geli / Cloud 9 Architecture.
p.150 fig.3 Image courtesy of Arduino.
p.151 fig.4 Image courtesy of Paul Warchol / Steven Holl Architects.
p.151 fig.5 Image courtesy of Storefront for Art and Architecture, 2011.
p.152 fig.6 Photo by Hiroyuki Hirai.
p.152 fig.7 Sliding House, Location: Suffolk, UK, Architect: dRMM (www.drmm.co.uk), Client: Ross Russell, Photo by Alex de Rijke.
p.153 fig.8 Image courtesy of Realities–United.
p.153 fig.9 Image courtesy of Ned Kahn Studios, Sebastopol, CA.
p.154 fig.10 Image courtesy of ICD, University of Stuttgart.
p.154 fig.11 Image courtesy of Doris Kim Sung / DOSU studio architecture.
p.154 fig.12 Image courtesy of Nick Puckett.

\#
01 – 06 All images courtesy of Philip Beesley Architect Inc.
07 – 11 All images courtesy of ecoLogicStudio.
12 – 17 All images courtesy of ICD, University of Stuttgart.
18 – 26 All images courtesy of IAAC, Barcelona.
27 – 28 All photos by Alex Haw.
29 – 30 All photos by David Thrower.
31 – 33 All photos by Alex Haw.
34 Photo by Manuel Kretzer.
35 – 36 All photos by Evangelos Pantazis and Miro Roman.
37 Photo by Demetris Shammas.
38 – 39 All photos by Achilleas Xydis.
40 – 43 All images courtesy of Decker Yeadon LLC.
44 – 47 All photos by Nicola Burggraf.
48 – 51 All photos by Anders Ingvartsen.
52 Image courtesy of Wikipedia.
53 NOS news 24 Jan 2014.
54 Image courtesy of Hyperbody.
55 – 56 All images courtesy of Hive Systems.
57 Photo by Ciara Taylor, Core77.
58 Image courtesy of Jose Sanchez.
59 Image courtesy of Wikipedia.
60 – 63 All images courtesy of Jose Sanchez.
64 – 65 All images courtesy of Jason Bruges Studio.
66 Photo by James Medcraft.
67 Photo by Satish Krishnamurthy.
68 – 70 All images courtesy of Hive Systems.

2001: A Space Odyssey 133

Abelson, Harold 121, 124
abundance 21, 64, 65, 77, 94, 109
Acconci, Vito 151
actuator 32, 44, 66, 72, 73, 78, 79, 123, 137, 145, 149, 150, 155
Adam, Barbara 87, 89, 91
Adam, Douglas 19
Addington, Michelle 87, 88, 91
additive manufacturing 45, 100
aerogel 75
aesthetics 36, 43, 72, 73, 87, 109, 156, 160
age
   digital 51
   industrial 51
   machine 43
aggregation 32, 124, 127
agriculture 50, 115, 118, 196
Akyildiz, Ian F. 121, 124
algae 84
   bioluminescent 84
   growth 38
   photobioreactor 75
algebra 160, 162, 208
algorithm 20, 38, 43, 55, 106, 128, 137, 138, 140, 141, 149
Angelico, Fra 28
anisotropy 39
Ant Farm 17, 213
Anthropocene 35
Archigram 16, 17, 134, 139, 213
Archilab 117, 211
ArchiLab 36, 41
Architectural Association 23, 38, 52, 170, 211
Arduino 95, 96, 123, 136, 150, 156, 213
Articulated Cloud 153
artificial 19, 36, 37
   ecosystem 138
   heartbeat 53
   intelligence 10, 44, 124, 133, 148
   learning 137
   life 50, 208
   light 82
   muscle 76, 78
audience 22, 63, 75, 84, 113, 123, 129, 130, 131, 132
augmentation 117, 148, 156, 211. See also reality
automation 22, 41, 62, 154, 155
   system 134, 149
automaton 50, 51, 53, 144
   cellular 20, 51, 121
autonomy 18, 20, 21, 22, 67, 76, 85, 92, 128, 130, 137, 185

Baba Yaga 133
Babylon 17
Babylonian 22, 158, 159, 160
bacterium 58, 82, 83
Baird, George 26
Ballard, James Graham 148, 157
Ban, Shigeru 151, 152
Bateson, Gregory 36
Beal, Jacob 122, 124
Beesley, Philip 5, 21, 25, 26, 27, 29, 31, 33, 58, 79, 88, 91, 136, 155, 156, 157, 208, 213
Beethoven, Ludwig van 158, 162
beetle 13, 14
Bicci, Neri di 28
Biennale 31, 84, 166, 208, 210, 211
Big Brother 116, 117
bimetal 153, 154
bio
   –cybernetics 35
   –diversity 38, 50
   –hacking 35
   –logy 8, 9, 18, 20, 21, 23, 35, 38, 39, 43, 50, 51, 57, 58, 72, 82, 84, 85, 112, 156, 159, 166, 208
   –luminescence 22, 61, 75, 82, 83, 84, 85, 191, 193, 208
   –mimicry 9, 20, 23, 35, 39, 44, 56, 57, 58
   –plastic 75, 76, 185
   –sphere 18, 20, 35, 37, 116
   –technology 35, 37
Block, Ben 50, 53
blueprint 51, 80
bluetooth 92, 93
BMW 105
body 18, 19, 29, 31, 33, 40, 53, 56, 79, 80, 117, 118, 162
Bogost, Ian 128
Bonnemaison, Sara 88, 91
bottom–up 33, 43, 53, 122, 135, 136, 143, 211. See also top–down
Braun Lectron 125, 126, 200
bridge
   root 133, 206
Bruges, Jason 5, 22, 113, 129, 131, 132, 208, 213
budget 103, 140
BugLabs 95
Bühlmann, Vera 5, 22, 62, 158, 208
building industry. See industry
Bullivant, Lucy 88, 91, 157
Burggraf, Nicola 5, 22, 61, 82, 83, 84, 85, 208, 212, 213

camouflage 45, 83

capacitor 153
capitalism 110
carbon
   dioxide 30, 80
   footprint 12, 13
Carlo Ratti Associati 52
Castells, Manuel 11, 67
ceiling 89, 134
   self–actuated 86, 89, 194
cell 8, 39, 49, 51, 82, 83, 84. See also solar cell
   connectivity 114
   density 83, 84
   power– 165
   senso– 148
   wood 40
cellular. See also automaton
   colony 76
   process 83
   reaction 83
Centre Pompidou 40, 210, 211, 212
chemical 8, 78, 94, 95, 159
   consistency 160
   interaction 72
   reaction 82
   system 20, 35
chemistry
   organic 70
   protocell 31
   synthetic 160
Children's Museum of Pittsburgh 153
Chris Kievid Design 138
circuit 54, 90, 92, 125, 126, 160, 200
Cisco 135
city 13, 18, 20, 43, 46, 47, 49, 50, 52, 80, 115, 118, 134, 143, 150
   intelligent 45
   mega– 46
   smart 48, 120
CityEngine 67
City Protocol 46
Clement, Gilles 37, 38
climate 27, 34, 80
   change 79, 81, 87, 208
   –conditioning 55
   –controlled 172
   designer 119
   dynamics 40
   micro– 20, 41
   –responsive 39, 41
   world 12
   zone 40, 134
cloud, the 52, 98, 135
CNC 44, 52, 100, 116, 137, 212
Collet, Carole 5, 8, 208, 212
color 13, 76, 153
   change 45, 76, 78, 86
   –coded 127
comedy 68

complexity 38, 42, 72, 75, 76, 92, 98, 126, 129, 141, 146, 153
computing 10, 18, 62, 78, 106, 114, 148
   amorphous 121, 124
   distributed 120, 121, 123
   embedded 87, 88
   spatial 22, 113, 120, 121, 124, 137, 138, 209
   ubiquitous 124
   wearable 120, 124
connectivity 18, 67, 77, 114, 117, 118, 119, 121, 127, 209
   hyper– 135
   inter– 22, 35, 47, 61, 86, 89, 90, 91, 136, 210
consciousness 29, 31, 84
consumption 20, 33, 47, 57, 63, 64, 88, 92, 94, 107
Conway, John 51
Cook, Peter 134, 139, 152
Corbusier, Le 17, 43, 73, 77
craft 26, 31, 37, 54, 56, 57
craftsman 105
crowd 36, 120, 121, 122
   –funding 136
   management 196
   –sourcing 53, 116, 117, 125
Cubelets 126
culture 14, 44, 50, 51, 57, 58, 70, 90, 107, 134, 151, 210
cybernetics 12, 13, 17, 34, 87, 102, 148, 157, 163
   bio– 35

database 45, 75, 119, 210
decadence 67
decay 19, 21, 73, 107
Decker, Martina 5, 22, 61, 78, 79, 81, 208, 209, 213
Decker Yeadon LLC 78, 209, 213
dECOi 126
D|E|Form 136, 137, 138, 139, 206
deformation 45, 79
Delvoye, Wim 50
Derrida, Jacques 12, 161, 162, 163
Devall, Bill 88, 91
Diamandis, Peter 18
digital
   fabrication 44, 45, 138, 210
   manufacturing 45, 211
digitalSTROM 98
Dillenburger, Benjamin 20, 212
dinoflagellate 83, 84, 85, 191, 193
disciplinary
   cross– 21, 212
   inter– 22, 75, 77, 80, 85, 99, 124, 208, 209
   multi– 47, 210
disease 18, 107

diversity 18, 38, 83, 121
    bio– 38, 50
Dixons 116, 117
DIY 52, 75
DNA 8, 18, 103
domestication 14, 15, 21, 61, 62, 70, 160, 208
Dorigo, Marco 121, 124
dRMM 152, 213
Dulman, Stefan 5, 22, 113, 120, 121, 123, 124, 138, 209, 212
durability 73, 74, 76, 106, 143, 144, 145
dystopia 13, 19

Eastman, Charles 148, 149, 157
E.A.T. 17
ecoLogicStudio 21, 34, 36, 38, 211, 213
ecology 21, 26, 34, 35, 42, 43, 55, 57, 58, 89, 106, 151, 211
economy 14, 18, 19, 70, 80, 101, 110, 114
ecosystem 8, 20, 35, 47, 95, 133, 134, 135, 136, 138, 209
Edison 92
Edler, Jan and Tim 152
education 16, 18, 70, 72, 77, 146
    self– 75
Einstein, Albert 22, 23
Eizenberg, Koning 153
electricity 13, 14, 62, 63, 64, 65, 69, 70, 71, 78, 86, 160
electroactive polymer 75, 76, 78, 79, 89, 90, 185
electroluminescence 74, 75, 76, 185
emplacement 27, 32, 107, 166
Endesa Pavilion 44, 176
EnHANT 93, 94
entropy 128
envelope 27, 41, 55, 149, 151
equilibrium 34, 39
Erlandson, Wilma 133, 139
evolution 10, 16, 18, 20, 21, 22, 47, 51, 80, 120, 136

Fab Lab House 44, 102, 136, 177
facade 17, 140, 141, 142
    adaptive 149
    automated 154
    BIX 153
    interactive 138
    media 131, 152
    smart 78
    transformable 151
fashion 32
feedback 21, 41, 85, 106, 123, 149, 155

loop 12, 135, 156
    system 51
ferrofluid 75
fertility 26, 28, 31, 32, 33, 50, 57, 68
Feynman, Richard 13, 24, 160, 163, 213
fiction 19, 69
    science– 133, 148, 150
firefly 82
    synchronization 138
Flectofin 55
Floating Forest 52, 180
Fournier, Colin 152
Fox, Michael 72, 77, 88, 91, 155, 156, 157
FRAC 36, 41, 168, 169, 170, 211, 212
Frazer, John 17, 23
frequency 84, 85, 131
Friedman, Yona 17, 134, 135, 139
fruit 53, 183
Fuller, Buckminster 13, 20, 23
Fun Palace 135, 148

game 67, 70, 110, 116, 125, 126, 127, 128, 210, 211
    of life 51
Gamescapes 125, 128, 211
gardening 37, 38, 52
    cyber– 38
Generator 148
generic
    city 12, 67
    materiality 160, 161, 162
    network 67
    , the 14, 108
geometry 13, 14, 27, 28, 31, 37, 41, 62, 127
    non–Euclidean 13
Gershenfeld, Neil 125, 128
globalization 14, 15, 18, 66, 102, 108
Gore, Al 67
Gorlatova, Maria 93, 94, 96
GPS 66
Grasshopper 123, 138
Grey, Aubrey de 18
growth 19, 20, 28, 29, 38, 44, 51, 53, 80, 119, 137
Gruber, David F. 21, 23, 82, 83, 85
Guéneau, Catherine 88, 91

habitat 43, 47, 133, 134, 135, 136
Hadid, Zaha 12
Hansmeyer, Michael 20, 213
Haque, Usman 155, 157
Hardt, Michael 67
Hariri, Robert 18

Hatch, Mark 136, 139
Haus Rucker Co 17
Haw, Alex 5, 21, 25, 49, 209, 212, 213
Heijne, Bas 116
Herron, Ron 16
Himmelb(l)au, Coop 17
Hive
    –Kit 123, 124, 138, 139, 141, 198, 207
    Panels 138
    Systems 22, 120, 133, 138, 209, 213
Hoffman, Eva 89, 91
Holl, Steven 151, 213
homeostasis 51
Homeostatic Facade System 78, 104, 107, 188, 189
Homer 50
Hortus 37, 38, 170
Hovestadt, Ludger 5, 10, 11, 13, 15, 21, 61, 62, 63, 65, 67, 69, 71, 208, 209, 213
Human Genome Project 26, 80
humanity 10, 19, 21, 26, 51, 107, 118
humidity 32, 39, 40, 41, 42, 153, 172, 174
HygroScope 40, 42, 154, 172, 212
hygroscopicity 39
HygroSkin 40, 41, 42, 174, 212
Hylozoic Ground 31, 136, 166
Hyperbody 22, 114, 116, 142, 197, 209, 210, 212, 213
HypoSurface 126

IAAC 43, 44, 45, 46, 48, 102, 176, 177, 211, 212, 213
IBM 124, 135, 211
iconography 28
identity 15, 18, 29, 59, 68, 70, 115, 118, 128, 145, 161
illusion 29, 30
Incel 52
Indiegogo 136
industrialization 110, 125
Industrial Revolution 43, 89, 100, 125
industry 8, 34, 76, 105, 140, 209
    building 74, 104, 105, 106, 108, 109
    car 105
    construction 80, 104
    design 87
    electronics 92
infancy 28, 29, 30, 121
information 38, 62, 66, 93, 116, 117, 135, 160, 161
    age 11
    network 45, 47
    society 11, 43, 143

superhighway 47
technology 10, 11, 21, 22, 43, 46, 71, 148, 209
infrastructure 13, 18, 35, 43, 46, 47, 67, 68, 80, 110, 135, 144, 161, 211
Institut du Monde Arabe 149
Intel 92, 213
Interference 84, 192, 193
internet 92, 120, 122
    2.0 102
    of architecture 135
    of cities 46, 47
    of people 114, 116
    of things 22, 46, 61, 92, 93, 94, 95, 96, 98, 114, 116, 120, 135, 136, 210
    platform 75
I, Robot 133

Japan 151
Jaskiewicz, Tomasz 5, 22, 113, 133, 135, 137, 139, 209, 212
Jeska, Simone 73, 77
junkspace 12, 67

Kelly, Kevin 58
Kemp, Miles 72, 77, 88, 91, 155, 156, 157
Kickstarter 136
Kiesler, Frederick J. 2, 213
Kinect 52, 114, 130
kit–of–parts 125, 126, 144
know–how 36, 87, 136
Kolarevic, Branko 5, 22, 148, 149, 209, 213
Koolhaas, Rem 12, 67
Kretzer, Manuel 5, 16, 61, 72, 209, 212, 213
Krieg, Oliver David 5, 21, 25, 210, 212
Kronenburg, Robert 150, 157
Kubrick, Stanley 133
Kunsthaus 152, 153
Kurzweil, Ray 18, 23
Kymissis, Ioannis 92, 96

Lakenbrink, Hubert 73, 77
language 12, 13, 58, 80, 101, 102, 108, 109, 118, 159, 162
    eco– 36
    form– 27, 33
    generative 28
    meta– 37
    programming 122
Latour, Bruno 12
Latz, Michael 83, 85
Laughlin, Robert 122, 124

LED 52, 65, 66, 82, 114, 137, 152, 212
Lego 125
light 38, 53, 64, 65, 69, 82, 86, 94, 95, 137, 150, 153
 biological 83, 84, 85
 blue 84
 cold 82
 design 82
 emission 65, 74, 82, 83, 84, 92
 pattern 122
 Philips Hue 136
 photon 78
 source 82, 84
 spectrum 82
 speed of 65
 sun– 76, 78, 154
Lightfall 52
Lighthive 52, 181
literacy 71, 101, 208
littlebits 95
Little Bits 126
living system 8, 16, 26, 27, 37, 72
Llachinski, Andrew 51, 53
Lochmatter, Patrick 72, 77
logistics 45, 65, 67, 110, 209
London 8, 21, 22, 23, 34, 38, 49, 50, 52, 53, 77, 91, 129, 130, 131, 140, 143, 157, 170, 204, 205, 208, 210, 211, 212
 Olympics 52
longevity 17, 18, 23, 74, 77, 105, 140
loom 51
Lucas Cranach the Elder 19, 213
Lucretius 56
Luhmann, Niklas 12
Luminale 84
Luminato festival 32
Lumiskin 52
Lynn, Greg 117, 118

machine 10, 11, 12, 13, 14, 66, 67, 88, 118, 144, 155
 adaptive, responsive 154
 age 43
 architecture– 148
 for living 43
 of nature 35
 of precision 125
 of war 50
Macy, Christine 88, 91
maintenance 140, 143
manifold 13, 159
Margolies, Robert 93, 96
marine
 bioluminescence 82, 83
 organism 83
Markopoulou, Areti 5, 21, 25, 43, 210
Maslow, Abraham 28, 29

materiability research network 16, 21, 72, 75, 136, 209
material. See also matter
 composite 44, 45
 intelligence 44
 polymorphic 78
 printed 66
 science 86
 self–healing 51
 smart 21, 22, 44, 45, 61, 72, 73, 74, 75, 77, 78, 80, 86, 87, 88, 89, 91, 92, 100, 103, 108, 120, 209
 toxic 88
Materials Genome Initiative 80, 81
matrix 28, 31, 131
matter 21, 38, 79, 125, 135, 159, 160
 adapting 78
 digital 43, 44, 125
 neural 31
media 70, 79, 131, 213
 content 36
 digital 101
 facade 152
Media TIC 149, 150
mega
 –city 66
Meghalaya 133, 206
Menges, Achim 5, 21, 25, 153, 154, 210, 212
metabolism 27, 31, 33, 34, 39, 47, 51, 160, 165
METAfolly 36, 37, 168, 169, 170
micro
 –chip 34, 65
 –controller 76, 90, 137, 150
 –management 134
 –processor 66, 93, 166
Microsoft Gadgeteer 95
Middle Ages 101
Minecraft 126
Minsky, Marvin 114, 118
Mitchell, William J. 47, 48
Mobile Orchard 53, 183
modernity 14, 15, 63, 70, 101, 145
Moholy–Nagy, Lázló 130
moisture 38, 39, 40, 42
money 140. See also economy
Moore, Gordon E. 92, 208
Moore's Law 92
Morgan, Richard K. 19, 23
Morley, David 88, 91
morphogenesis 121, 128
morphology 27, 40
mortality 18, 33, 56, 107, 108
Mossé, Aurélie 5, 22, 86, 87, 89, 91, 210
movability 134, 150, 152, 155
myth 14, 15, 19, 70

Nagpal, Radhika 122, 124

Naked House 151, 152
nano
 –flake 36
 –scale 21, 43, 44, 100
 –technology 79, 100
 –world 9
narcissism 19, 131
Nature Trail 132, 205
Negri, Antonio 67
Negroponte, Nicholas 148, 154, 157
network
 multi–hop 93, 94
newspaper 63, 66, 116
New York 23, 50, 77, 78, 91, 92, 124, 139, 151, 157
Nouvel, Jean 149

object–oriented
 design 128
octahedron 126, 127
Oosterhuis, Kas 5, 22, 113, 114, 115, 117, 119, 209, 210
open
 access 16, 75
 exchange 77
 innovation 47
 plan 151
 –source 92, 95, 108, 128, 150, 211
optimization 10, 12, 28, 34, 35, 44, 54, 55, 67, 80, 94, 98, 121, 155
Origami Shape Language 122
Orton, John 158, 163
Outreach 52
ownership 115, 134
Oxman, Neri 44, 48, 73

Palladio, Andrea 13
Panda Eyes 130, 141, 204
Pask, Gordon 17, 148, 155, 157
Pasquero, Claudia 5, 21, 25, 34, 35, 37, 211
pavilion 20, 31, 36, 37, 41, 102, 153
performance 12, 13, 21, 55, 74, 75, 76, 77, 79, 96, 98, 103, 107, 119, 134, 154, 156
permeability 41, 88, 143
phone
 cell 109
 mobile 66, 135
 smart– 13, 38, 66, 98, 114, 116, 121, 122, 133, 142
photobioreactor 38, 75
photosynthesis 69, 83
Phototropia 76, 185
photovoltaic 63, 64, 65, 66, 70, 92, 94. See also solar cell

physics 9, 64. See also quantum
 printed 21, 61, 62, 71, 208
physiology 27, 28, 30, 32
phytoplankton 83
Pieribone, Vincent 82, 83, 85
piezo
 –buzzer 37
 –crystal 75
 –electric 36, 44, 66, 92
pixel 13, 52, 85, 153
planet 8, 19, 65, 66, 67
plastic 16, 72, 101
 bio– 75, 76, 185
 polymorph 75
Plato 27, 31, 33
plug–and–play 95
plug–in 123, 138
Poletto, Marco 5, 21, 25, 34, 35, 37, 211
politics 11, 14, 16, 18, 67, 70, 101, 102, 110, 115, 128, 209
Polyomino 22, 113, 125, 126, 128, 202
population 18, 46, 84, 115
potentiality 128, 162
precision 30, 36, 68, 98, 100
 control 22, 125
pre–specific 14
Price, Cedric 17, 108, 134, 135, 139, 148
printing 63, 65, 66, 99
 3D 45, 96, 114, 136, 202. See also additive manufacturing
 ink–jet 79, 100
 press 63, 70, 101
 quantum 64, 67
privacy 92, 117, 120, 152
probability 13, 70, 71, 128
product 66, 74, 109, 110, 114, 116, 117, 126, 136
 design 75, 81, 82
Prometheus 50
protocell 31, 32, 165
Protodeck 142
prototype 36, 43, 47, 74, 87, 94, 129, 154, 188, 197, 198
prototyping 22, 36, 44, 48, 96, 124, 133, 136, 209, 211
Puckett, Nick 153, 154, 213
Pyrocystis lunula 83, 190

quantum
 physics 13, 14, 160
 printing 63, 64, 67
 space 70
 thinking 67, 68, 71
 writing 67

raindrop 27, 28, 33
randomness 20, 32, 51, 155
reaction 32, 73, 155

INDEX

bioluminescent 82
cellular 83
chemical 82
–diffusion 20
light 83, 84
realities:united 152, 153
reality 30, 87, 89, 158
  augmented 53, 132
  corpo– 160
  virtual 10, 18, 117
recycling 36, 37, 67, 88, 137, 140
Reef 86, 89, 90, 91, 194, 195, 212
Reichert, Steffen 5, 21, 25, 211, 212
religion 28, 30, 36, 56, 107
representation 86, 87, 159, 162
resin 76, 153
Resinance 76, 186, 187
resonance 21, 28, 31, 32, 33
RFID 93, 116
Rhino 123, 138
Riemann, Bernhard 13
Rietveld, Gerrit 151
Riley, Terence 88, 91
Roaf, Sue 79, 81
robot 34, 133, 134
robotic
  arm 41, 45, 50
  biosphere 116
  fabrication 22, 41, 100, 210
  manufacturing 41, 125
  prefabrication 41
  proto– 51
robotics 50, 75, 114
  soft 75
  swarm 121
Rohr, Jim 83, 85
Roosegaarde, Daan 136
Ruiz–Geli, Enric 149, 150

Sanchez, Jose 5, 22, 113, 125, 127, 211, 213
Sarik, John 5, 22, 61, 92, 93, 95, 96, 97, 211, 213
satellite 14, 35, 52
Schodek, Daniel 87, 88, 91
Schofield, Richard 73, 77
Schröder House 151
Sculpture City 117
sea 82, 83
SeeedStudio Grove 95
Seina 123, 138, 199, 207
self
  –actualization 28
  –education 75
  –expression 16, 18
  –organization 20, 38, 47
  –portrayal 19
  –projection 15
  –sufficiency 38, 44
semiconductor 158, 159, 162
sensor 32, 35, 40, 44, 46, 47, 52, 66, 78, 84, 85, 93, 106, 119, 121, 130, 133, 137, 145, 149, 150, 156, 209, 211
Sensualscaping 51, 180
Serres, Michel 12, 14, 15, 208
shape–memory
  alloy 32, 78, 79, 166
  material 44
  polymer 153, 154
ShapeShift 76, 184
shelter 20, 49, 51, 107, 115
Showtime 131, 204
singularity 18, 23
skin 28, 32, 33, 45, 146
  architectural 42
  building 149, 153
  double– 78, 189
  material 31
  responsive 41, 153
Sliding House 152, 213
Smart Geometry 57
smart material. See material
smartphone. See phone
Smart Public Space 46, 179, 213
SmartWrap 100
Snowden, Edward 13
snowflake 28, 33, 118
Society of Mind 114
soil 28, 31, 32, 38, 57, 58
solar 104, 106. See also solar cell
  building 176, 177
  energy 44, 78
  foil 65, 70, 103
  heat gain 78, 189
  illumination 94
  panel 103, 152
  path 44
solar cell 44, 63, 64, 65, 74, 100, 185. See also photovoltaic
  dye–sensitized 75, 76
  thin–film 93, 94
Solar Decathlon 102, 210
sound 37, 84, 86, 88, 150, 161, 162
space
  public 43, 46, 47, 79, 142, 143, 210
SpaceChem 126
sphere 11, 27, 31, 33
standardization 17, 73, 89, 95, 125
Starner, Thad 120, 124
STEM 79, 80, 99, 105
Sterk, Tristan d'Estree 149, 155, 157
Storefront for Art and Architecture 151, 213
storm 107
  lightning 52
  thunder 80
Stützle, Thomas 121, 124

substrate 18, 72, 79, 82, 92, 99, 100, 160, 161
Sung, Doris 153, 154, 213
Sunlands 52
Superstudio 17
sustainability 8, 21, 23, 35, 37, 38, 43, 47, 54, 65, 67, 86, 87, 88, 89, 91, 105, 107, 208
swarm 37, 114, 115
  behavior 20, 22, 120
  expert 119
  intelligence 9
  of devices 142
  of sensors 52
  robotics 121
Sydney 52, 208
symbiosis 9, 34, 138, 209
symbolism 15, 26, 109

tech
  high– 22, 39, 149
  low– 22, 52, 149, 151, 152, 153, 154, 156
  no– 39, 154
temperature 20, 31, 40, 42, 76, 77, 78, 79, 80, 129, 137, 144, 150, 164, 188
temporality 14, 15, 21, 86, 87, 88, 89, 90, 91, 107, 143
Tesla, Nikola 62, 63
textile 8, 31, 75, 86, 91, 167, 208, 210, 212
theatre 53, 68, 129, 130
thermochromics 75, 76
thermodynamics 30
thermostat 135, 146, 149
  Nest 136
Timberlake, Kieran 100
timescape 22, 61, 86, 87, 89, 90
top–down 33, 53, 122, 123, 135, 136, 143. See also bottom–up
Tower of Babel 159, 160
tragedy 14, 68
transformation 18, 36, 46, 73, 78, 121, 130, 134, 135, 137, 150, 152
transistor 92
translucency 30, 44
Trans–Ports 117
tree 52, 53, 103, 133, 134, 183, 206, 212
  fantasy 53
trend 72, 79, 87, 114, 121, 134, 135, 136
turbulence 27, 33, 57, 83, 84

unpredictability 38, 72, 89, 90, 117, 118, 129, 155

utopia 101

Van Herpen, Iris 32
Van Hinte, Ed 150, 151, 155, 157
Vaucanson, Jacques de 50, 51
Venter, J. Craig 18, 23
Venturi, Robert 50, 53
Virtools 116
virtual 38, 40, 51, 137, 138, 158. See also reality
  space 47, 135
Vita–More, Natasha 18
Vitruvius, Marcus 50, 77, 143, 144, 145
vocabulary 11, 80, 102
Voltaire 50
voxel 126, 127, 200

Wallerstein, Immanuel 12, 67
Waterpavilion 117
wave
  acoustic 83, 84, 193
  –length 82
wealth 11, 19, 109
wearable 114, 120
Weather Projection 52
Weiser, Mark 124
Wiener, Norbert 160, 163
wi–fi 92, 116, 117, 196
WikiHouse 136
wind 86, 89, 153, 194
  speed 80, 90, 195
Winnicott, Donald Woods 29, 30, 33, 213
wireless
  communication 77, 120
  device 93
  networking protocol 94
  sensor network 93, 121, 209
wood 39, 40, 41, 45, 72, 101, 144, 153, 210
Worldscape 52, 182
world wide web 92. See also internet
Wright, Frank Lloyd 19, 20, 23

Zarzycki, Andrzej 79, 81
Zeitgeist 58, 59
Zigbee 94
Žižek, Slavoj 36
Zumthor, Peter 12

ALIVE: Advancements in Adaptive Architecture
Applied Virtuality Book Series, Vol. 8

Editors
Dipl.-Ing. (arch) Manuel Kretzer: materiability research network, Chair for Computer Aided Architectural Design (CAAD), Institute of Technology in Architecture ITA, Swiss Federal Institute of Technology ETH, Zurich, Switzerland / www.materiability.com

Prof. Dr. Ludger Hovestadt: Chair for Computer Aided Architectural Design (CAAD), Institute of Technology in Architecture ITA, Swiss Federal Institute of Technology ETH, Zurich, Switzerland / www.caad.arch.ethz.ch

Layout and Cover Design
Demetris Shammas

Copyediting
Max Bach

Typeface
Adobe Garamond Pro, GT Walsheim, Helvetica.

Library of Congress Cataloging-in-Publication data.
A CIP catalog record for this book has been applied for at the Library of Congress.

Bibliographic information published by the German National Library.
The German National Library lists this publication in the Deutsche Nationalbibliografie; detailed bibliographic data are available on the Internet at http://dnb.dnb.de.

This work is subject to copyright. All rights are reserved, whether the whole or part of the material is concerned, specifically the rights of translation, reprinting, re-use of illustrations, recitation, broadcasting, reproduction on microfilms or in other ways, and storage in databases. For any kind of use, permission of the copyright owner must be obtained.

This publication is also available as an e-book
(ISBN 978-3-99043-668-4).

© 2014 Birkhäuser Verlag GmbH, Basel
P.O. Box 44, 4009 Basel, Switzerland
Part of Walter de Gruyter GmbH, Berlin/Boston

Printed on acid-free paper produced from chlorine-free pulp. TCF ∞

Printed in Germany

ISBN 978-3-99043-667-7

9 8 7 6 5 4 3 2 1   www.birkhauser.com

We hereby want to thank all contributing authors for their continuous support and the variety and quality of the content presented here which truly make this book *alive*. In alphabetical order, Philip Beesley, Jason Bruges, Nicola Burggraf, Vera Bühlmann, Carole Collet, Martina Decker, Stefan Dulman, Alex Haw, Tomasz Jaskiewicz, Branko Kolarevic, Oliver David Krieg, Areti Markopoulou, Achim Menges, Aurélie Mossé, Kas Oosterhuis, Claudia Pasquero, Marco Poletto, Steffen Reichert, Jose Sanchez, and John Sarik. Additionally we would like to thank Ruairi Glynn, Dino Rossi, and Simon Schleicher, who spoke at the *Alive 2013* symposium, but who unfortunately weren't able to prepare articles for this volume. Thanks go also to Max Bach for copyediting the articles and to Morgan Alexander Ip for his great feedback on the introduction. Moreover we are very thankful to David Marold and Angelika Heller from Birkhäuser Verlag for their constant availability and encouragement and to Rochus Urban Hinkel from Spurbuch Verlag, who had the initial idea of turning the conference into a printed publication. For the conference we are very grateful for the financial support from the Swiss National Science Foundation and the Departement of Architecture, ETH Zurich. The initial funding application was co–written together with Stefan Dulman, Tomasz Jaskiewicz, and Andrei Pruteanu from TU Delft. The conference would not have been possible without the great help of Mario Guala and our MAS students at the Chair for Computer Aided Architectural Design: Tihomir Janjusevic, Nicolas Miranda, Evi Xexaki, and in particular Achilleas Xydis and Demetris Shammas for the photo and video documentation of all the lectures (http://alive2013.wordpress.com/videos). We want to thank our colleagues at the Chair for CAAD, our friends, and family for their help in making decisions and their endless encouragement. Finally we want to express our deepest gratitude to Demetris Shammas not only for designing the booklet, flyer, and poster of the conference but for his amazing job in designing and preparing the present publication.

Manuel Kretzer, Ludger Hovestadt, 2014

Bei Fragen zur Produktsicherheit wenden Sie sich bitte an:
If you have any questions regarding product safety,
please contact:

Birkhäuser Verlag GmbH
Im Westfeld 8
4055 Basel, Schweiz
productsafety@degruyterbrill.com